WRITING
EN

Taking Ovid's *Metamorphoses* as its starting point, this book analyses fantastic creatures including werewolves, bear-children and dragons in English literature from the Reformation to the late seventeenth century. Susan Wiseman tracks the idea of transformation through classical, literary, sacred, physiological, folkloric and ethnographic texts. Under modern disciplinary protocols these areas of writing are kept apart, but this study shows that in the Renaissance they were woven together by shared resources, frames of knowledge and readers. Drawing on a rich collection of critical and historical studies and key philosophical texts including Descartes' *Meditations*, Wiseman outlines the importance of metamorphosis as a significant literary mode. Her examples range from canonical literature, including Shakespeare's *A Midsummer Night's Dream* and *The Tempest*, to Thomas Browne on dragons, together with popular material, arguing that the seventeenth century is marked by concentration on the potential of the human, and the world, to change or be changed.

SUSAN WISEMAN is Professor of Seventeenth-Century Literature at Birkbeck College, University of London. She is the author of *Conspiracy and Virtue: Women, Writing, and Politics in Seventeenth-Century England* (2006), *Politics and Drama in the English Civil War* (1998) and *Aphra Behn* (1996; second edition 2007). She has co-edited *The Nice Valour* for *Thomas Middleton: The Collected Works* (2007).

WRITING METAMORPHOSIS IN THE ENGLISH RENAISSANCE

1550–1700

SUSAN WISEMAN

CAMBRIDGE
UNIVERSITY PRESS

CAMBRIDGE
UNIVERSITY PRESS

University Printing House, Cambridge CB2 8BS, United Kingdom

Cambridge University Press is part of the University of Cambridge.

It furthers the University's mission by disseminating knowledge in the pursuit of education, learning and research at the highest international levels of excellence.

www.cambridge.org
Information on this title: www.cambridge.org/9781316507629

© Susan Wiseman 2014

This publication is in copyright. Subject to statutory exception and to the provisions of relevant collective licensing agreements, no reproduction of any part may take place without the written permission of Cambridge University Press.

First published 2014
First paperback edition 2015

A catalogue record for this publication is available from the British Library

Library of Congress Cataloguing in Publication data
Wiseman, Susan.
Writing Metamorphosis in the English Renaissance : 1550–1700 / Susan Wiseman.
pages   cm
Includes index.
ISBN 978-1-107-04165-3 (hardback)
1. English literature – History and criticism.   2. Animals, Mythical, in literature.
3. Metamorphosis in literature.   4. Monsters in literature.   I. Title.
PR149.A7W58   2013
820.9´3620903 – dc23   2013039526

ISBN 978-1-107-04165-3 Hardback
ISBN 978-1-316-50762-9 Paperback

Cambridge University Press has no responsibility for the persistence or accuracy of URLs for external or third-party internet websites referred to in this publication, and does not guarantee that any content on such websites is, or will remain, accurate or appropriate.

Contents

Illustrations		*page* vi
Acknowledgements		vii
A note on texts		ix
Abbreviations		x
	Introduction: writing metamorphosis	1
1	Classical transformation: turning *Metamorphoses*	14
2	Sacred transformations: animal events	58
3	Transforming nature: strange fish and monsters	86
4	Metamorphosis and civility: werewolves in politics, print and parish	137
5	Transformation rewritten? Extreme nurture, wild children	161
	Coda: Descartes and the disciplines	196
Notes		208
Index		236

Illustrations

1. Asse, Edward Topsell, *Historie of Foure-Footed Beasts* (1607)   page 14
2. Title page of *Blacke Dogge of Newgate* (1596). Copyright British Library.   33
3. Title page of *The Discovery of a London Monster* (London, 1638). Copyright British Library.   43
4. Plaster relief, Orpheus taming the beasts, Haddon Hall, Derbyshire. Copyright Tim Armstrong.   57
5. Cat, Edward Topsell, *Historie of Foure-Footed Beasts* (1607) 103. Copyright British Library.   58
6. Cockatrice, Edward Topsell, *Historie of Serpents* (1608) 119. Copyright British Library.   86
7. Jacob Rueff, *The Expert Midwife* (1637) 12. Copyright British Library.   97
8. Ambroise Paré, *Works* (1634) 966. Copyright British Library.   100
9. Dragon, St Mary's Church, Wiston, Suffolk. Copyright Tim Armstrong.   104
10. Dragon made from ray, Ulisse Aldrovandi, *De piscibus* (Bologna, 1613). Copyright British Library.   108
11. Wolf, Edward Topsell, *Historie of Foure-Footed Beasts* (1607) 734. Copyright British Library.   137
12. Frontispiece, *A True Discourse Declaring the Damnable Life and Death of One Stubbe Peeter* (1590). Copyright British Library.   142
13. Bear, Edward Topsell, *Historie of Foure-Footed Beasts* (1607) 435. Copyright British Library.   161
14. *Valentine and Orson: The Two Sonnes of the Emperour of Greece* (1637) np. Copyright British Library.   181
15. Bear suckling humans, Bernard Connor, *History of Poland* (1698) vol. 1, 342. Copyright British Library.   182

Acknowledgements

For reading drafts, discussing, sharing ideas, giving me references, and having fun I am very grateful to Erica Fudge, Paul Salzman and above all Tim Armstrong. I am grateful to Tom Healy for reading related materials published in *Renaissance Transformations*. I am very grateful to the two anonymous readers who read the materials for Cambridge University Press and who gave constructive and engaged suggestions which changed the shape of the book. Remaining errors are my own.

For references, sharing work and advice I am grateful to Anthony Bale, Anke Bernau, Luisa Calè, Daniel Carey, Stephen Clucas, Isabel Davis, Patrizia diBello, John Drakakis, Jessica Dyson, Catherine Edwards, Anne Goldgar, Linda Grant, Margaret Healy, Tom Healy, Judith Hudson, the late Ann Jennison, Kevin Killeen, Esther Leslie, Gordon MacMullan, the late Kirsty Milne, Michelle O'Callaghan, Louise Owen, Edward Paleit, Emily Senior, Erica Sheen, Adam Smyth, John Stokes and Colin Teevan. For support at key moments Anthony Bale, Luisa Calè, Hilary Fraser, Anne Janowitz. At Birkbeck, thanks to Catherine Catrix, Shabna Begum, Mandy-Shay Riggins and Anne-Marie Taylor. Thanks too to the School of Arts Research Fund for financial support for illustrations. For further support for illustrations I am very grateful to the Marc Fitch Fund.

I have given talks derived from this work at many places, starting with the Outsiders conference in Stirling, and, to name but two more, University College Galway and the SEDERI conference in Huelva, at the invitation of Zenon Martinez. I am grateful for these opportunities and for the conversations that ensued.

I am grateful to the staff at the British Library, particularly to staff in Rare Books; London Metropolitan Archives; National Archives, Kew.

At Cambridge University Press Sarah Stanton's willingness to consider the topic and her precise and constructive critical engagement made this monograph possible. Rebecca Taylor, Sarah Roberts and Samantha Richter (in sequence) and Penny Wheeler have been patient and helpful.

Above all, Nicholas Wiseman and Tim Armstrong, who have lived with this and, worse, with me, deserve better. Thank you both.

A note on texts

The text follows the spelling and punctuation of pre-modern texts and editions used. Where editions using modernised spelling have substantial advantages those have been used. Golding's use of Roman numerals is followed but other Roman numerals are usually changed.

Abbreviations

AHR	*American Historical Review*
CSPD	*Calendar of State Papers*
EHR	*English Historical Review*
ELH	*English Literary History*
ELR	*English Literary Renaissance*
HLQ	*Huntington Library Quarterly*
HMC	Historical Manuscripts Commission
JHI	*Journal of the History of Ideas*
MLR	*Modern Language Review*
NQ	*Notes and Queries*
OED	*Oxford English Dictionary*
RES	*Review of English Studies*
SEL	*Studies in English Literature*
SP	State Papers
SQ	*Shakespeare Quarterly*

Introduction: writing metamorphosis

This is a study of the English writing of metamorphosis from the Reformation to the late seventeenth century. It asks what work is done by the imagining of transformation in this period and explores events and creatures which may seem to us fantastic: animated stones, werewolves, wild children. Looking at a range of writing in English from literary texts to court records, *Writing Metamorphosis* argues that the seventeenth century is marked by concentration on the potential of the human, and indeed the very matter of the world, to change or be changed. Versions of the idea of metamorphosis were widely available and therefore the writing of metamorphosis discloses vernacular epistemologies as well as elite modes of knowledge.

The project began as a study of how the animal–human border was understood and written about in the English Renaissance. However, as I began to research the movement between beasts and humans the question of metamorphosis rapidly emerged as a possibility which fascinated and troubled the writers I was looking at.[1] As I read texts not usually placed together within disciplines, metamorphosis emerged increasingly clearly as a topic of cultural significance for Protestants, poultry-keepers, physicians, philosophers. It became evident that the idea of metamorphosis was pervasive in sixteenth- and seventeenth-century England and that it did significant cultural work in a range of texts which, under modern disciplinary dispensation, are rarely considered together. In using the concept or concepts, writers' unease was balanced by a sense that metamorphic stories expressed things that needed to be articulated – they were 'good to think with'.

The term 'metamorphosis' entered English very early, being among the earliest fifteen per cent of words in the *Oxford English Dictionary* with a citation as a noun by Geoffrey Chaucer in 1390. Coming from Greek and registered in France and Italy too, the term apparently derived simply from the name of Ovid's *Metamorphoses*. The basic meaning that readers put to work was 'the action or process of changing in form, shape, or substance' and especially doing so through supernatural agency.² Other senses exist within the word, such as the gospels' resonant use of a wider Greek sense which embraces ideas of transfiguration, and there are many related concepts or versions which cluster around the central term – metempsychosis (involving transformation after death) is one example. Moreover, once 'metamorphosis' is in the vernacular, meanings proliferate and migrate. One crucial characteristic suggested by the word's trajectory through the dictionary is that it is used to describe emergent fields of culture, such as a significant application to plant and animal development, dated by the dictionary to 1665. Because at the same time few meanings fell into desuetude, it seems that it was used increasingly widely and often during the period investigated here.

The context of shifting and sometimes accumulating meanings of metamorphosis in sixteenth- and seventeenth-century writing has suggested the flexible rather than restricted definition of metamorphosis adopted here. Evidently, the idea of change of state was longstanding in English but, for all the apparent simplicity of the concept, it had a complex life in the understandings of readers and writers. Thus, when we find the substitution of an animal for an infant at the font addressing the question of the infant's transformation by baptism, the question of metamorphosis is present both in terms of the change of state in the infant and in the questioning of that change, using the substitution of animal for human. As Caroline Walker Bynum puts it, metamorphosis can indicate 'the substituting of one thing for another – sneakers for high heels – or it can mean that one thing alters its appearance or qualities or modes of being'.³ Walker Bynum's description of the twin aspects of metamorphosis as blending and substitution is helpful to keep in mind when approaching the often very specific concerns of post-Reformation texts using metamorphosis. Both the changing, or blending, of states and substitutions feature in the stories that follow and, as this demands, the actual term metamorphosis is used in this study alongside change, transformation and other terms, but all used in relation to the possibility and actuality of a change of state.

Seventeenth-century ideas of change can seem unruly, even exotic to a late modern investigator; they were diverse and spread across a range of writings that are not readily mapped within modern taxonomies of knowledge. Ovid's *Metamorphoses* was both a literary resource and a history of the natural world, and the view that such dual purposes are discordant or surprising is produced not in the seventeenth century but by the disciplinary expectations of our own scholarship. Unavoidably, and as a literary study this undertaking is no exception, pre-modern metamorphosis is at present mainly interpreted through disciplinary protocols. The critical field of the study of metamorphosis includes, both in history of art and literary criticism, some strictly disciplinarily located studies that explore the relationship between Ovidian metamorphosis and mythography and allegory. In literary study such critical work focuses substantially on the poetic traditions usually tracked through the texts of Edmund Spenser and John Milton, particularly in relation to *The Faerie Queene* and *Paradise Lost*. Thus, for example, Louise Gilbert-Freeman writes incisively about Edmund Spenser's *Mutabilitie Cantos* in terms of the image of the divine and the perception of the viewer; she does so with consistent reference to the question of the nature and uses of allegory to accommodate and displace the elements of metamorphosis most troubling to Christian values.[4] Although such approaches can lead to substantial claims (such as Paul Barolsky's assertion that Ovid's bequest to the Renaissance was 'the very play of the imagination as it gave birth to the protean forms of art', and thus he was 'fundamental to the Renaissance idea of art, and to the very idea of art as metamorphosis'), they do so using a tightly defined corpus of material and a frame of reference that largely excludes the social world.[5]

Although allegory and mythography touch the project, the approach taken here is distinct from studies of the influence of Ovid on allegory and the focus is on the very diversity of the kinds of writing that feature metamorphosis and in shaping an understanding of metamorphosis which might take rise with Ovid but finds many textual and cultural manifestations. As it engages with Ovid's *Metamorphoses* what follows draws on the wider understanding of reception found in the work of Charles Martindale and, with regard to the Renaissance, Raphael Lyne.[6] From the point of view of this project's study of textual metamorphosis in a wider view, by far the most productive critical intervention with regard to classical metamorphoses is reception theory which takes a step back from studies of a single genre or tradition to examine the different forms of evidence about reception, most specifically changes in the thinking on the 'reception' of classical texts of transformation in sixteenth- and seventeenth-century English thought and writing. As Jean Seznec and Malcolm Bull have argued, the reception of classical antiquity in the Renaissance is local, contingent and far from the sudden rediscovery claimed by some of its contemporary publicists, both drawing on medieval traditions and embracing commercial as well as philosophical imperatives. Thus, as the work of Charles Martindale and Philip Hardie suggests, classical texts are strongly mediated in culture, not only by being appropriated by writers and readers with distinct purposes but through less clear processes of cultural absorption. This study takes up Martindale's invitation to study the potentially mixed and 'unclassical' reception of classical texts – particularly widely used texts such as the *Metamorphoses*.[7] A further critical development enables us to sharpen our understanding of these materials. Some scholarship within reception studies has begun to press 'reception' towards what might be called, by some measures, 'distant' reception; precisely the kind of use of classical material that may involve uncertain provenance of source. This kind of reception is discussed by Martindale in terms of Velásquez's painting known as *The Spinners*; he notes that not only is what is represented a puzzle (is it a genre painting, history painting, or a mythological painting? Can it be two or more? What is its relationship to Ovid?) but, also, there is no certainty that Velasquez turned to Ovid's texts as opposed to other sources for the image.[8]

Other disciplines, too, analyse change and transformation in the early modern period and this study is bordered by two bodies of such scholarship: the history of science, on the one hand, and, on the other, the multidisciplinary scholarship on animals in seventeenth-century writing. In discussion of generation and monstrosity, for example, this study is underpinned by the scholarship of those reconsidering the question of the discourses of 'science' or 'natural history' in the seventeenth century – as in the essays on animal generation collected by Justin Smith.[9] In thinking about the transformation of the human, and considering the nature of the animal–human border, this study, though not centrally located in the field of 'animal studies,' draws on the literary, historical and to a lesser extent philosophical work of scholars, such as Erica Fudge and Joyce Salisbury, who imagine what it might involve to write a history, or histories, of animals and of animal–human relations.[10]

Finally, some critical writing explores the concept of metamorphosis and the way it has been used in the world. Outside reception study, literary study of metamorphosis as a concept has often taken the concept far beyond a single period. The idea of transformation is analysed transhistorically in two such studies, by Caroline Walker Bynum and Marina Warner. Each takes the concept of change far beyond a single epoch, with Walker Bynum tracing transformation from Ovid, through Dante, to Angela Carter; and Warner canvassing material from the Renaissance to late modernity and ranging into modern science, on the one hand, and the Taino myths of South America on the other.[11] In the service of a study of metamorphosis and identity, Walker Bynum investigates the question of what might change and what endure as the human changes, blends with another, or is displaced. In exploring the tension between complete transformation and an 'unfolding kernal or essence' which endures through change Walker Bynum is drawn to the way in which 'the stories of the past – great stories like those of Dante... and Ovid... explore and comment on, elaborate and explode themselves'.[12] That Warner and Walker Bynum both ground their arguments in the world by exploring how metamorphosis challenges a sense of self or of place suggests the significance of metamorphosis as a cultural figure that troubles, or shows the troubledness of, the human and its others.

Warner's study of metamorphosis and the world it creates an effervescent exploration of where the cultural power of metamorphosis is to be found. Starting with Ovid, Warner explores metamorphosis as 'ways of telling the self' through the processes of metamorphosis that she defines as mutating, hatching, splitting and doubling.[13] For Warner, metamorphosis begins with Ovid where nothing interrupts 'the vital continuum of all phenomena', and in this spirit metamorphosis for her can have the political inflection of a struggle to be free, from Ovid's ancient tales to the stories of the double so characteristic of modernity.[14] The Renaissance, for Warner, is represented by the lost golden age of Hieronymous Bosch and, for all that the metamorphoses that happen between the Reformation and the Royal Society are inflected by serious, even punitive, consequences, in the texts that follow we can see, with Warner, that the idea of a changed state is an imaginative resource at times pressed into service by those who most need change.

The conceptual insights of Walker Bynum and Warner concerning the ability of metamorphosis to trouble the human self's claim to centrality inform this study. Yet, at the same time, the sheer range of material covered in transhistorical studies inevitably over-rides local contexts in favour of a bigger picture and tends to be drawn back to the great (and powerful) texts of metamorphosis at the heart of the European cannon – Ovid, Dante, Bosch, Leonardo da Vinci. *Writing Metamorphosis*, contrastingly, works with a relatively small timescale and geographical range to examine texts in context and even in close, sometimes symbiotic, relationships to one another in their use of change. Where Bynum and Warner illuminate Europe and beyond and work from the medieval to the modern, this study takes as evidence a wider range of kinds of texts from the English vernacular and a specific time-frame. Its central time-frame is bookended by the confirmation of the vernacular as an official language of liturgy and worship at the Reformation and the late seventeenth-century responses to Descartes' changing of the terms on which human and animal exist. Thus, this study seeks to illuminate the place of metamorphosis in a shorter temporal sweep but across a wider, but defined, set of kinds of writing. In distinction to both reception studies and transhistorical discussions, it is the study of the writing of metamorphosis in something which can, roughly and raggedly, be seen as an epoch.

Turning to an example of the uses of metamorphosis, we find an inventory of 1601 gives an example of the place of metamorphosis in the world. It tells us that Bess of Hardwick filled her new dwelling with embroidery and needlework including tapestries of Ulysses in the High Great Chamber and long cushions using the *Metamorphoses* stories include Actaeon and Diana and a version of Europa and the Bull modelled on a woodcut from a Latin edition of the *Metamorphoses*.[15] If the elite used the cushions to slump upon after hunting a beast, then not only they, but their servants, handled and arranged them. The very process of making them involved the acquisition of the book, making of patterns from the illustrations, movement from one to the other. The making of a metamorphic cushion is emblematic, perhaps, of a space being made for transformation in the intellectual, political and wooded location of the estate house, but that reception involves thinking of an intellectual, aesthetic and practical nature. These cushions and hangings are deliberately classical and the cushions were probably designed for Hardwick. In 1551 Bess of Hardwick had ordered several yards of fine linen damask for a 'table clothe with the story of Abraham' and Isaac.[16] This story of substitution and transformation marked typologically for Christians the potential transition to Christianity in foretelling Christ's sacrifice on the cross. The coexistence of Christian sacrifice at dinner and Ovidian ladies squashed under head and elbow after dinner suggests a familiarity with stories of transformation as part of the furniture.[17] About 100 years later, unable to be at her husband's bedside when he died in Sandown prison in 1664 Lucy Hutchinson wrote that 'God had removed me that I might not tempt him to look back upon this world as a flaming Sodom.' Hutchinson is thinking of Genesis 15–19 but also recalling Orpheus and Eurydice in Book 10 of the *Metamorphoses*, which in Arthur Golding's translation reads 'when Orphey did begin / To doubt him lest she followed not; and through an eager love, / Desirous to see her, he his eyes did backward move'.[18] Hutchinson's sad final experience calls up both Biblical and Ovidian metamorphosis and has suggestions of the sense of transfiguration. As these uses imply, metamorphosis was amongst the seventeenth-century resources available for thinking and use by elites but also, potentially, by others of low status. Natalie Zemon Davis has written of 'beliefs, literary and visual works, practices and festivities widely dispersed in society and in their appeal often . . . jumping barriers of birth' and status; examples of metamorphosis are often such phenomena.[19]

Sacred and secular transformation

The 1601 inventory makes it clear that stories of metamorphosis were lodged deeply in English society. However, for all their equalising presence as furnishing, it is hard to imagine that the story of Actaeon and Diana and Abraham and Isaac were similarly understood as metamorphoses. Liturgical and classical discourses both engaged with the concept of transformation, but in distinct ways that underpin the material discussed. The advent of the vernacular *Book of Common Prayer* (1549) and Arthur Golding's verse Englishing of Ovid's *Metamorphoses* (1565, 1567 and in eight editions to 1612) are significant moments in shaping English vernacular understanding of metamorphosis.[20] Let us turn first to change in the reformed liturgy and thought.

'Metamorphosis' is not a property readily claimed by the church in the English Reformation, but versions of change were present in scripture, had long played a crucial role in church thinking and were reactivated by the vernacular texts of the Reformation. Transubstantiation had been the established doctrine of the Roman church since 1215; the idea of transformation of substances was deeply rooted in church practices.[21] A reader might very readily find transformation in her English Bible, or, made up of words from that Bible, the 'revolutionary' *Book of Common Prayer* in English from 1549. *The Book of Common Prayer*'s controversial path is indicated at once by its Englishings and revisions – in 1552 and 1559, with alterations in 1604, replacement by the *Directory of Worship* in 1645 and reissue, revised, in 1662.[22] Obviously, Christ's miracles were one form of transformation about which the simple read and heard, but other instances lacked the explanatory framework of the life of Christ. How, for example, was a reader to understand what had happened to Nebuchadnezzar in all those years as a beast? This story was a topic of controversy for medieval and Renaissance writers from Gervase of Tilbury to James VI and I.[23] More familiar, perhaps, was the Reformation person's encounter with the claim in I Corinthians that '[a]ll flesh is not the same flesh; but, one is the flesh of men, another of beasts', a text hard to square with Nebuchadnezzar's experience, unless, and this became a key point, that experience was illusory. Indeed, I Corinthians seems to imply a definitive separation between beast and human not only at the level of soul but also in terms of the very composition of their being – such a sentence seemed to make the human not only the noblest amongst God's creation and so the one chosen to be endowed with reason and the soul which allowed promise of the hereafter, but also to separate the human from the rest of creation in physical makeup. More elaborately, I Corinthians also promised the faithful 'a mystery' whereby, 'in the twinkling of an eye, at the last trumpet; for the trumpet shall sound and the dead shall again rise incorruptible; and we shall be changed'.[24] The promise of the resurrection, strange enough in itself, was God's alone to give and keep and although it was felt to require that the baptism service indicate clearly that it did not challenge that the authority to change substances was God's alone, this fantastic promise was housed safely in Christian orthodoxy. Perhaps the most profound concern about transformation was experienced in relation to the liturgy, especially with regard to the two English sacraments that remained from seven. Most obviously controversial was the status of the communion bread and wine, but in terms of social impact the issue of what changed, or what was changed, in the infant by the service of baptism was a visible and live social issue.

The situation from 1549 onwards, when parishioners gained ever-increasing access to controversy, was underpinned by an explicit statement of the church on transformation. A formal ruling, the *Canon Episcopi*, stated:

> Whoever therefore believes that anything can be made, or that any creature can be changed to better or to worse or transformed into another species or similitude, except by the Creator himself who made everything and through whom all things were made, is beyond doubt an infidel.[25]

This ruling impacted on understandings of metamorphosis most significantly in the debates on witchcraft. It is heretical to believe, for instance, that the devil can take witches from their bodies and return them, or that he can turn a man into a wolf.[26] Accordingly, in one important strand of thought, such experiences were to be understood as dreams and belief in them was to be condemned as heresy. However, at the same time as condemning beliefs in transformation as heretical (and therefore to be rooted out) the canon explicitly acknowledged, as Robert Bartlett and Hans Peter Broedel note, that the women who imagined themselves transported were indeed perverted by a devil.[27] Denial of actual transformation was far from a denial of witchcraft belief or activity. However, by the fifteenth century theological writers had begun to assert positions that implied literal transformation.[28] Thus, by the Reformation, the situation was confused. Luther, for example, seems to have believed in transformation.[29]

The Latin endorsement of shape-changing, *Malleus Maleficarum*, had to be weighed against Reginald Scot's rare voice of scepticism in his *Discoverie of Witchcraft*, in which he used Ovid to question the power of witches to change shape.[30] Thus, the English interest in witchcraft kept shape-changing on the national agenda. At the same time the vernacular sacraments, liturgy and Bible made available an apparently contradictory literature of metamorphosis on which people expected, or were expected, to base their everyday and eternal lives.

In 1567 the 'single work' which is chronologically 'the clear point of entrance' into written metamorphosis and whose title seems to have established the word in England, was translated into the English vernacular and made known to those who could read or be read to in English.[31] As we have seen, the text had long had a presence in English culture. However, the Englishing of the *Metamorphoses* was undoubtedly a significant event in the extension and shaping of transformation in English texts, and following Arthur Golding's translation of Ovid we can begin to track the integration into English post-Reformation culture of these unruly stories which are, as Marina Warner notes, so deeply different from Judaeo-Christian modes of thought.[32]

The full text of the *Metamorphoses* was translated in 1567. Famously, Golding considers his reader to need guidance in approaching Ovid, and the 1567 version has an epistle addressed to the Earl of Leicester as well as a practical address to the reader, aimed at the 'simple sort'. Golding works hard to frame Ovid's 'philosophy of turnèd shapes' as potentially beneficial, if not benign, in offering 'the praise of virtues and the shame / Of vices'.[33] The epistles aim to offer a path between diverse kinds of readers and Ovid's potentially explosive material. Golding is concerned to emphasise the value of his source text; he acknowledges that Ovid's *Metamorphoses* is inevitably problematic, because the 'true and everlasting God the paynims did not know' and explains to audiences that they are reading about a time when man's sin had led God to 'give him over to his lust to sink or swim therein'.[34]

Golding introduces the book by clarifying the status of the human and thereby sets the terms on which transformation amongst states takes place:

> ... Three sorts of life or soul (for so they termèd be)
> Are found in things. The first gives power to thrive, increase and grow;
> And this in senseless herbs and trees and shrubs itself doth show.
> The second giveth power to move and use of senses five;
> And this remains in brutish beasts, and keepeth them alive.
> Both these are mortal, as the which, receivèd of the air

> By force of Phoebus, after death do thither eft repair.
> The third gives understanding, wit and reason; and the same
> Is it alonely which with us of soul doth bear the name.
> And as the second doth contain the first, even so the third
> Containeth both the other twain. And neither beast, nor bird,
> Nor fish, nor herb, nor tree, nor shrub, nor any earthly wight
> Save onely man can of the same partake the heavenly might.
>
> (32–44)[35]

Here we can see the Aristotelian three-soul model of the natural world unambiguously stated at the start of the period under consideration and in one of the study's key texts. This model was influential and widely considered as true.[36] Golding's comment that 'nothing under heaven doth aye in steadfast state remain' is aligned with both an Aristotelian understanding of a vital universe and with a Christian understanding of the mutability of God's creation. The startling Pythagorean migration of souls represents an extension and changing of this concept to express souls 'removing out of beasts to men, and out of men / To birds and beasts both wild and tame'.[37]

The English life of the *Metamorphoses* is traced throughout the chapters that follow. It was not, however, the only way in which metamorphosis was received in seventeenth-century secular thought but, in 1605, was joined by Francis Bacon's *Advancement of Learning. De Sapientia Verterum* followed, in Latin in 1609, Englished in 1619.[38] Bacon's use of classical texts is a study in itself and his texts are not central in the diet of most of the writers and readers analysed here. However, the fact that he used classical myth to discuss the world and the way in which he did so, are both significant. Bacon secured the place of classical metamorphic fable at the heart of learning about the natural world, putting stories of Proteus, Primavera and others to work in imaginative language and similitudes that expressed his desire to intervene in the natural processes at their origin. Writing about the relationship between nature and art, Bacon insisted that, rather than being nature's 'liberators and champions' because they produce order in nature, the arts aim to bend nature to their ends. 'I do not much care for such fancy ideas and pretty words' he wrote, 'I intend and mean only that nature, like *Proteus*, is forced by art to do what would not have been done without it; and it does not matter whether you call this forcing and enchaining, or assisting and perfecting.'[39]

Bacon's discussion of the power of man to change nature was centrally concerned with metamorphosis, in terms of the ability of matter to change or be changed, and expressed the possibility of change using the classical vocabulary of transformation. As Charles W. Lemmi has noted, Bacon rejected Aristotle's understanding of prime matter and of form, but the associated concept of transmutation or transformation was central in his thinking.[40] The question of the ability to change or be changed drives Bacon's interest in matter. He starts from the understanding of matter as protean and so found either free or in the shapes of Protean energy (bound). Bacon asks whether – given that within that scheme marvels can occur – human intervention could not simply mix or combine elements of nature, and could achieve the transformation of matter at the deepest level.[41]

To express the ability of man to force nature to obey, Bacon turns to the fourth book of the *Odyssey* where Menelaos wrestles with Proteus and forces him to prophesy. Bacon writes of Proteus as the spirit of matter. He is 'Messenger and Interpreter of all Antiquities and hidden Mysteries' – knowing past, present and future, a messenger, and interpreter of all. Wisdom can be extracted from him by:

> catching him in Manacles, and holding him fast therewith; who nevertheless to be at liberty would turn himself into all manner of Forms and Wonders of Nature, sometimes into Fire, sometimes into Water, sometimes into the shape of Beasts, and the like; till at length he were restored to his own form again.
>
> This Fable may seem to unfold the secrets of Nature and the properties of *Matter*. For under the person of *Proteus*, the first Matter (which next to God is the Ancientest thing may be represented: For Matter dwells in the concavity of Heaven, as in a Cave.[42]

Crucially, Bacon wonders whether humans might be able to alter the very atoms of nature. Given nature occurs unbound and bound, and that monsters and marvels (in his opinion) bear witness to extraordinary and apparently unique changes to the very atoms that are nature's building blocks, men might be able to make Protean, struggling, nature take wholly new shapes in the same way nature itself does. Such would indeed be an effective capture of Proteus, wrestled back into his own shape yet under human power.

The vernacular *Book of Common Prayer*, Golding's translation of the *Metamorphoses*, Bacon's English uses of myth can stand as key texts in the shaping of metamorphosis in England and in English. But as important as that they were read is how that reading took place. Each had a relationship with elite and learned culture, but they also existed in a world of debate and comparison where writers and readers drew on many different kinds of experience. At the same time as literary and theological texts canvassed transformation, readers put the stories to work and combined them with others that they knew. The presence of debate and discussion is implicit in the life of most texts on metamorphosis. Adam Fox's discussion of the transition to written records during the Norman period and his statistics on the steady growth of both reading and the number of printed texts available indicates very clearly that 'in sixteenth and seventeenth century England... the three media of speech, script, and print infused and interacted'.[43] As Fox amply demonstrates, by the Reformation period beliefs, sayings and stories were moving amongst manuscript, oral telling and print. There is at present no term that adequately designates the mixed literary, conversational and ideological sphere into which texts are sent and on which printed manifestations of wider debates draw. Throughout this study, though, this sphere of debate is significant and is referred to in several different, partially satisfactory, ways. When the terms 'folklore' and 'popular' and their derivatives are used it is with the intention of calling up this mixed sphere of print, polemic and protest as well as conversation and meditation.

Ovidian metamorphosis, liturgical transformation and transformation in nature are related yet distinct in the writing and reading of seventeenth-century English vernacular readers but they come to us, or, rather we return to them, in very different disciplinary frameworks. The logic of taking a horizontal slice of textual evidence on metamorphosis is that, although this study is disciplinarily grounded in literary methods, it engages with texts that in the modern world have been allocated to several disciplines. Historically metamorphosis might be studied specifically and incidentally by scholars working in disciplines including theology, history of religion, history of art, biology, anatomy, chemistry and literary criticism – to name a few. The necessity to attend to the pre-disciplinary period in terms not too over-determined by modern approaches has been widely taken up following path-breaking work by Bruno Latour.[44]

The constructed nature of the disciplines has long been established. In terms of 'natural history', Michel Foucault long ago wrote that 'for History to become Natural' the many layers of stories surrounding 'nature' must be removed. Foucault locates the start of this process in England and, albeit not quite accurately, in the 1650s, when 'Jonston published a *Natural History of quadrupeds*'.[45] For Foucault, the publication of Jonston's 'natural' history can symbolise the 'sudden separation... of two orders of knowledge'; from this moment onwards it was no longer the case that 'history was inextricable' from the fabric of the visible world.[46] However, as William B. Ashworth tells us, for all that Jonston's work eschews similitude, and for all that Francis Bacon seems to have refused to be drawn into the associational and storied understanding of the natural world as God's hieroglyphics, many of their contemporaries do not, as we shall see, seem to register a moment of shift. The fact that for historians of science this period is strongly associated with shifting perspectives on how to approach the world is part of what makes the place of metamorphosis in this specific period significant and throughout the study material with several, often overlapping, perspectives is represented. An example of mixed approaches is the work of Edward Topsell whose *Historie of Foure-Footed Beasts* (1607) is, in turn, a resource both for those writing in the period and for this study because of its account of the place of the animal in creation.[47]

The question of metamorphosis and disciplinarity itself is taken up in the Coda. For the present, within this disciplinary diaspora of metamorphic material, *Writing Metamorphosis* responds primarily to approaches within the humanities, drawing on interdisciplinary studies of the Renaissance, studies of reception, and to a lesser extent on the history of 'science'. The mixed world of seventeenth-century English metamorphosis is clear from the evidence.

My aims in *Writing Metamorphoses* are, then, twofold: to investigate the relationships amongst contemporary texts that put the idea of metamorphosis to work, and, in doing so to engage with, historicize and to an extent challenge, the dispersion of metamorphosis amongst the disciplines. What follows, therefore, analyses the presence of metamorphosis in five kinds of writing which seem, in modernity, to be separate. Each chapter examines metamorphosis in a kind of writing or situation: classical, sacred, physiological, oral-literate or 'folkloric', ethnographic.

Taking the reception of Ovid's *Metamorphoses* as its starting point, the first chapter explores the reception of classical discourses of transformation in texts that reach non-elite audiences. The second chapter takes up the question of sacred metamorphosis in a Reformation context. Starting from the translation of the baptismal liturgy in 1549, this chapter traces the address to sacred transformation made through animal events into the mid seventeenth century. Chapter 3 discusses the changed body and examines the vocabularies of transformation in the natural world by using the initial example of the monster. The werewolf stories of sixteenth- and seventeenth-century English print are contextualised in terms of readership and story in Chapter 4, and Chapter 5 engages with the question of what can be learned from a story – fable or narrative of exotic discovery – by analysing the tales of children found in the wild.

CHAPTER ONE

Classical transformation: turning Metamorphoses

1 Asse, Edward Topsell, *Historie of Foure-Footed Beasts* (1607).

> Of shapes transformed to bodies strange I purpose to entreat.
> Ye gods, vouchsafe (for you are they that wrought this wondrous feat)
> To further this mine enterprise, and from the world begun
> Grant that my verse may to my time his course directly run.
> Before the sea and land were made, and heaven that all doth hide,
> In all the world one only face of nature did abide
> Which chaos hight, a huge rude heap, and nothing else but even
> A heavy lump and clotted clod of seeds together driven
> Of things at strife among themselves for want of order due.[1]

So the complete Ovid's *Metamorphoses* came to English readers in Arthur Golding's translation of 1567. By 1632, when George Sandys published his translation, the *Metamorphoses* was an established resource in English culture. In the sixty or so years between the two texts, Ovid's 'turnèd shapes' were a live influence on many forms of writing and reading, 'turnèd' to the ends of, and reciprocally fashioning, their English users. As Raphael Lyne reminds us, translations of Ovid, by Golding in 1567 and Sandys in 1632, mark each end of a period in which Latin writers were 'rethought and rewritten by English imitators'.[2] Readers and writers set *Metamorphoses* to their own purposes and literary texts, though far from alone in using Ovid, seized on these stories of change as though heeding a long expected call. Reading metamorphoses in Shakespeare's *Midsummer Night's Dream* and *The Blacke Dogge of Newgate*, this chapter asks what literary uses of *Metamorphoses* disclose about the society that produced them. It does so in order to examine the mutual shaping of literary texts and Ovidian tales of transformation, and to understand and assess scholarly approaches to this relationship in both canonical and non-canonical texts. The chapter's approach to reception draws on and responds to work in reception studies, particularly the arguments made by Charles Martindale and Philip Hardie. As discussed in the introduction, Martindale and Hardie see reception as both diverse and active. As their arguments suggest, literary texts, and as we will see, cheap print and simple reading as much as folio editions, are a revealing point of entry and reworking for transformations.

I 'Mulberry shade': *A Midsummer Night's Dream*

A Midsummer Night's Dream offers a test case in the transformations undergone by classical metamorphosis. As a text for the popular stage which also has a highly self-conscious relationship to transformation, *A Midsummer Night's Dream* frames its action within the metamorphic potential of a dream on a particular night. The play, having no specific 'source', is understood as extensively intertextual with Latin and folkloric material, but how might this intertextuality work?

Ovid is on the play's agenda almost from the start. Quince, announcing 'The most lamentable comedy, and most cruel death of Pyramus and Thisbe' also introduces Golding and Ovid to those audience members equipped to recognise them.[3] This 'lamentable comedy' is to be the mechanicals' tribute at the wedding of the Athenian king, Theseus, and Hippolyta, his Amazon bride. The play that we witness, *A Midsummer Night's Dream*, takes place in the space of time the mechanicals have to adapt and rehearse Golding's story of the doomed lovers, Pyramus and Thisbe. The time of rehearsal is determined by the 'four happy days' which 'bring in / Another moon' after which Theseus will celebrate his 'nuptial hour'.

For Theseus, this time weighs heavy. He laments 'how slow / This old moon wanes' – like 'a step-dame or a dowager / Long withering out a young man's revenue' (1.1.1–5). The old moon is watery and changeable. Ruling over what should be a warm summer season, it blocks the path of change, though not as definitively as the masculine block constituted by the refusal of old-man Egeus to countenance young love.

The frustrating time between Theseus' speech and the wedding turns out to hold change. Thus, as the mechanicals meet, plan and rehearse, the lovers thwarted by age rebel and take to the woods, where visiting and local fairies wait to witness the marriage and redirect mortal lives. The woods signal a place and time of transformations. For the mechanicals, what starts as an after-hours rehearsal, and ends with their production of an anti-illusionist dramatic interpretation of Ovid's story, is interrupted by the transformation of Bottom into an ass and Titania into his lover – a change of magical completeness which is an antithesis to their own acting style.

Immediate and spectacular, *Midsummer Night's Dream* is nevertheless crammed with histories. It is haunted, as Helen Hackett notes, 'by the tragedy which it might have been'.[4] There are textual ghosts, too, as Peter Holland has explored; figures whose histories are fleeting semi-presences – Hippolytus as the future troubled child of the union between Theseus and Hippolyta; Egeus and the Minotaur.[5] Hippolyta's Amazon legacy, too, would be remembered by some in the audience.[6] Transformations inhabit and sustain the play in two interwoven ways, first, in the storied legacies of the transformations it presents and, relatedly, in the ambiguous sea-changes it works on the texts which it may, according to an audience member's or reader's apprehension, call up. Thus, in a play that has become a test-case for the nature and interpretation of 'source' and 'allusion' within the Shakespearean canon, that the Pyramus and Thisbe story uses Golding and Ovid's collaboration remains universally agreed. However, whether or not they are recognised by audiences, instances of transformation and intertextuality are bound together throughout the play in a way which constitutes a prolonged meditation on change and on the presence of texts as transformed in use: clearly the play takes metamorphosis as a project in two ways. *A Midsummer Night's Dream*'s reception (and transformation) of classical texts can be traced through the editorial approaches to the text, but for its first and many later audiences the *Dream* was and is primarily a text of theatre. Thematising metamorphosis and evoking it through differentially operating forms of intertextuality, the play also explores transformation in specifically theatrical discourses – as when, for example, the actors playing the mechanicals may well have undergone a kind of transformation in doubling for the fairies.[7]

The play's transformation of other texts finds detailed articulation in Harold F. Brooks' influential edition. Haunted, even troubled, by potential sources for the play and very focused on the text as read as opposed to performed, Brooks' edition offers a simultaneously complex and literal editorial strategy.[8] Responding to the fact that there is no single 'source' for the stories of *A Midsummer Night's Dream*, Brooks finds not none, but many, including Ovid's and Golding's *Metamorphoses* and Reginald Scot's *The Discoverie*. Brooks explores relationships between texts in terms of very specific linguistic borrowings and therefore, for all that much of what he finds resonates with the play, his tendency to list even general phrases as linguistic resemblances or 'sources' seems manufactured and, cumulatively, unconvincing as an interpretative strategy.[9] However, as Peter Holland notes, Brooks' source-hunting strategy recognises and responds to the text's shadowy intertextuality – its housing of allusions, but also linguistic and textual ghosts.[10] In this sense Brooks does address the play's evocative richness. Brooks embraces the presence of Golding's Pyramus and Thisbe while also taking on a less graspable set of splicings, borrowings, oblique references which seem (once noticed) to pull in other texts without offering a ready sense of how those texts might be at work – evocations which use, or seem to use, words and speeches from texts whose presence (like Seneca's *Medea*) are felt, if at all, in very different ways. For example, Brooks' understanding of Seneca's Phaedra – incestuous, extreme, libidinal – as a resource used in building Helena's 'abject' love acknowledges that the play's dense intertextuality is bound up with its repeated rededication of mythic and tragic material. Howsoever they are characterised, whether as 'source', absorption or appropriation, such tragic implications are in tension with the comic form of the play.[11] Thus, while the play of Pyramus and Thisbe (which makes sophisticated Philostate shed 'merry' tears, 5.1.69; play 5.1.108–334), is evidently putting to work Ovid's *Metamorphoses* in Golding's translation, many of the possible intertexts of the *Midsummer Night's Dream* have much more ambiguous relationships with the play. It is possible to trace transformation in one strand. Scenes which offer one thread in the play's interweaving of transformation and intertextuality include 1.2; 2.1; 3.1; 3.2; 3.3; 3.4; 5.1.

Brooks 'discovered' a significant quantity of dense intertextuality in sections of the play featuring transformation, and, unsurprisingly, these show us figures and places at the edges of Athenian society. Once the play is located in the wood – an acknowledged domain of transformation – we witness encounters between different groups from the borders of human society. The light-fingered local, Puck (apparently in this play a night fairy though also, as we shall see, associated with theft and with more sinister transformations), meets an alien fairy-retainer of Queen Titania, newly arrived to celebrate the nuptials.[12] The queen, through the derivation of her name from Ovidian references to Diana and other figures including Latona and Circe, brings with her Ovidian metamorphic associations.[13] Oberon (as fairy king associated with Ulysses, India, romance) and Titania meet and argue about another outsider – the 'lovely', 'sweet', 'changeling', 'Indian' boy (Puck, 2.1. 22–3). Puck and Oberon discuss the juice; the pair watch Helena's Ovidian pursuit of Demetrius. The scene ends with Oberon's plan to 'streak' Titania's eyes to fill her with 'hateful fantasies' (2.1.258), and his command to Puck to make Demetrius love Helena. Linked by their attention to the impact and fusion of worlds – the native fairy and the 'foreign', the Athenians and the apparently invisible fairies, the power of a changeling to disrupt the fairy world, and so the human – the scene sets up the transformations to come.

This scene introduces the heady mixing that is the order of the woodland world. The changeling boy seems to mix classical, romance and folkloric. In Puck's account to the fairy, the boy is 'stol'n' (2.1.23) from an Indian king; in Titania's version he is bequeathed by a human 'votress of my order' (2.1.123) but they each agree that he is from India which, as David A. Sprunger indicates, is where in the romances Alexander the Great meets wild men – as well as men of different sizes and shapes.[14] For those romances India is an extraordinary place, close to the edge of the world, and populated by hairy, angry, lustful and cannibal wild men.[15] Far from possessing the charm of the desirable changeling boy, these inhabitants of India nevertheless suggest some of the location's exotic connotations. At the same time, the wood in which they all find themselves is also the location of wild men as well as fairy folk and – appropriately enough in this play – lunatics and madmen. From these mixings transformation is to come. Yet, already, if these meetings can, for a moment, be understood as personified encounters between traditions, discourses and the possibilities of the woodland world, then the audience witness an indigenous, hybrid Anglo-Athenian fairy encountering an exotic shape changer; in the encounter of Oberon and Titania with Puck resides the juxtaposition of classical, exotic and homely.

Transformation, already clearly flagged as a concern of the play, is seen to be also that of the play's characters when Oberon, fresh from his fight with Titania, reminds Puck of a strange scene of transformation. 'Thou rememb'rest' (2.1.148), Oberon tells his servant, 'I sat upon a promontary' (2.1.149) watching a mermaid in the sea:

> PUCK: I remember.
> OBERON: That very time I saw (but thou couldst not),
> Flying between the cold moon and the earth,
> Cupid all arm'd: a certain aim he took
> At a fair vestal throned by the west,
> And loos'd his love-shaft smartly from his bow
> As it should pierce a hundred thousand hearts.
> But I might see young Cupid's fiery shaft
> Quench'd in the chaste beams of the watery moon
> And the imperial votress passed on,
> In maiden meditation, fancy-free.
> Yet marked I where the bolt of Cupid fell:
> It fell upon a little western flower,
> Before milk-white, now purple with love's wound;
> And maidens call it 'love-in-idleness'.
> Fetch me that flower (2.1.154–69)

Like the mulberry's tragic tale, earlier invoked by Quince and to be acted, this just-so story is bound up with human loves. It may also be dense with reference, explicit and shadowy. For some of the late sixteenth-century audience the 'imperial votress' would evidently indicate Elizabeth.[16] It might also suggest the political complexity of Elizabeth's later years as the virgin queen. Potentially operational, too, are, echoes of Seneca's *Hippolytus* – in which Phaedra's uncontrolled desire contrasts with her stepsons's overintense chastity – and his *Medea*.[17] The speech suggests both the priority of virginity and the power of sexual, even erotic, change – staining, but also transforming. The unruly sea seems to set the stage for Cupid's arrow and this, missing its intended aim, brings the storm to lodge in the 'little western flower' – flooding what we now know as the pansy with a desire so powerful (and dark) that in dream shapes it can overspill into the unguided human heart. Changed, and now itself an agent of transformation, the 'purple' flower also gives one person power to change another. It has become a witches' charm in all but name, allowing a third party to influence lovers' eyes and hearts.

The speech itself is at pains to transport the auditor or reader to an extraordinary world where Oberon sits on a promontory, elevated and observing. While Puck's inability to see the trajectory of Cupid's dart (he 'couldst not') obviously provides a pretext for Oberon telling him the story, it has further implications concerning questions of sight, knowledge and interpretation – if the mortals seem unable to see Puck he, himself, is unable to fully apprehend the world of Gods and, perhaps, the political world of the imperial votress. In this speech itself, for example, it is unclear how the intertextuality might work even for someone who recognised it. The agent of transformation, the flower, is changed in a story that again, depending on the auditor, may blend classical, political and folkloric implications. If we imagine that some members of an audience do recognise (recall or hear?) Seneca's *Hippolytus* and *Medea*, how they might bring that recognition to a comic play of fairies is intriguing, ambiguous and unstable. In the imprecise, evanescent atmosphere of popular theatre, and above all at the speed of production, even for an audience with ears trained from school and sermon, such fleeting references would have to be transformed, ambiguous, echoing.

While the nature and extent of such intertextuality must remain uncertain, Oberon's cruel aims are clear and return us to the nature of encounters in the woods. Oberon's is jealous magic. He wishes that Titania wake to take for her true love a 'vile thing' – 'ounce, or cat, or bear, / Pard, or boar with bristled hair' (2.2.33; 29–30). When she awakes it is not, in fact, wild creatures but Bottom-as-ass – a man hybridised with a domestic animal – whose looks captivate her. Exploring the relationships amongst fairies, animals and humans, animal transformation, the status of love, the mind transformed, differences in status, beauty and perhaps size, the Titania–Bottom romance, though arguably playing little role in the plot, is revealing in terms of the play's use of transformation. Isolated from his peers by Puck's chase – 'sometimes a horse I'll be, sometime a hound, / a hog, a headless bear' (3.1.104–5) – Bottom experiences the full fear of the wood as well as realised fantasy delights.

Bottom's fear and fairy delight, at the centre of the play, juxtaposes several forms of transformation. The rehearsal–reception of Golding's Ovid in which the would-be actors 'disfigure' (3.1.56–7) their play gives way to the contrastingly complete, precise and pointed change in which Bottom is hybridised, 'translated' into a singing ass, encounters the potion-transformed Titania (3.1.113–14; 115–41). Within the first scene, Bottom reminds us of the metamorphic power of the actor, as he promises to play all parts. Holland notes Bottom's delusion that he is a 'master of metamorphosis' – yet, his (donkey-brained?) fantasy of change is both fulfilled and, itself, changed, when he acquires the ass head.[18] Bottom, as lion, offers to 'aggravate his voice so, that I will roar you as gently as any sucking dove; I will roar you and 'twere any nightingale' (1.2.76–8). Bottom, though,

'Mulberry shade': A Midsummer Night's Dream

is not Philomel; as Leonard Barkan's fascinating argument suggests, he is closer to a 'disfigured', or grotesque, Actaeon, Titania (as we have seen) a naughtily reworked Diana.[19] Through his donkey-nose he is singing of male birds when he wakens Titania – '*The ousel cock, so black of hue*', '[*t*]*he throstle, with his note so true*', the '*wren with little quill*' and, appropriately, the '*cuckoo gray*' (3.1. 120–3; 126). Rather than the '*plain-song*' of the cuckoo, the scene offers a counterpoint and mixture. Appropriately, Brooks relates this scene in relation to the 'fantesey and enchauntments' of Oberon's woodland domain in *The Boke of Duke Huon of Bordeaux*.[20] At the play's heart, change and transformation rule producing new and alarming shapes but also, in the union of artisan, donkey, classical fairy queen suggesting the scandalous pleasures of mixture. As such, Bottom's 'translation' does not seem to suggest exactly the falling away to the ever-ready lower level of beastliness. Rather, it is closer to what Caroline Walker-Bynum discusses as a metamorphoses of addition, or over-layering – here human beastliness is understood as a supplement, just as Bottom's head is added, foregrounding his bestial side and its sexual dimensions (literally) and over-layering his human aspect.[21] This makes his scene with the fairy queen complex because although, arguably, physically hybrid he is not wholly degraded. Beastliness added and emphasised at one level realises his donkey-like being, but it also catapults him into the play's most intense visionary experience. Improper as a lover of a fairy queen in terms of mortal and artisan status, size and shape, Bottom is not a wholly unworthy object of adoration, remaining, head notwithstanding, his ever-ready self: as he says when he awakes, 'When my cue comes, call me, and I will answer' (4.1.199).

When, at the end of the fourth act Bottom finally returns from his 'rare vision', he seems to remember it. However, rather than 'discourse of wonders' (4.1.203; 4.2.28), he holds his tongue like 'a true Athenian' (4.2.29). The possible reasons that the night with the fairy queen escapes disclosure to the adult world multiply in proportion to his silence. Is it that the logic of dream is untranslatable? The fairy spell? Social inhibition? The unspeakable, or at least unspoken, dream may also have a traumatic or sinful implication. Unarticulated, the dream of change is nevertheless an influence in the rest of the play. It is acknowledged in the description of Bottom's absence – his having been 'transported' (4.2.3–4). Bottom returns from both a realised erotic fantasy and from fear, madness and animal addition in the wood. His return to the world of the rehearsal and his self-identification as 'Athenian' signals a resurfacing in the play, yet, it also inaugurates an episode with its own logic and one which some critics see as happening after the traditional shape of comedy is completed – taking place after the completion of the 'telos' of marriage.[22] Theseus and Hippolyta have heard the stories of the lovers – 'strange', 'antique fables', 'fairy toys' to be believed, Theseus says, 'by lovers and madmen' (5.1.1–4).

Thus, the forest experiences, while remaining operational in the world, are distanced as though in time and in narrative mode – they are, for Theseus though not, it seems, for Hippolyta (both, themselves, fabulously antique), outdated tales.[23] The play's linking of the 'antique' and transformation – change – in the description of the telling of the lovers' dreams is significant. Although texts of the 1590s can evidently be considered 'late Elizabethan', that general designation tells little about the way texts like this one imagine their future by calling up and reworking the past. In dramatic terms, the association between the antique and transformation sets up the mechanicals' playing of classical, specifically Ovidian, material. Both the mechanicals' and the play's own evocation and use of the antique also, paradoxically, acknowledges change and a changing world. As so often in this period, material that seems to be bound up with the archaic is also, simultaneously, oriented towards an anticipated future. We can turn, now, to the pansy's parallel, or responsive, scene – that of the mulberry.

Like and unlike the trees under which met lovers, fairies and mechanicals, the 'mulberry shade'(5.1.146) below which Pyramus and Thisbe plan to rendezvous looms over a realised disaster. Within the frame of the lamentable comedy, Quince's opening to the play situates it in relation to Golding's version as the lovers plan 'at *Ninus* Tomb to meete without the towne'.[24] Pyramus has his big scene:

Enter PYRAMUS
PYRAMUS *Sweet Moon, I thank thee for thy sunny beams;*
I thank thee Moon, for shining now so bright;
For by thy gracious, golden, glittering gleams,
I trust to take of truest Thisbe sight.
  But stay! O spite!
  But mark, poor knight,
  What dreadful dole is here?
  Eyes, do you see?
  How can it be?
  O dainty duck! O dear!
  Thy mantle good,
  What! Stain'd with blood?
  Approach, ye Furies fell!

> O Fates, come, come!
> Cut thread and thrum:
> Quail, crush, conclude and quell.

THE. This passion, and the death of a dear friend, would go near to make a man look sad.
HIPPOLYTA. Beshrew my heart, but I pity the man.
PYRAMUS O wherefore, Nature, didst thou lions frame,
  Since lion vile hath here deflower'd my dear? (5.1.261–81)

Ambiguously received, the play also carries through the darker logic of the star-crossed lovers. If comedy, marriage and the triumph of youth are presented as 'modern', the tragic histories that the play knows, while being kept at a distance by the language and aristocratic commentary, are also strongly present.[25] Similarly, while archaic language and acting style, as well as Theseus' mediating commentary, forcibly distance the horror of this scene from the audience, it nevertheless follows through and realises the logic of the tragic play that haunts *Midsummer Night's Dream*. The archaic language and dramatic convention so much remarked upon call up the question of time and change and, through Bottom as Pyramus, '*Furies*' and '*Fates*' (5.1.273, 274) are finally admitted into the text and play. Brooks pounces on these furies as Senecan – from *Medea*, or *Hercules Furens*, or *Agamemnon*.[26] While Brooks' specific allocation of the Furies may be over-zealous, there is no doubt that Bottom as Pyramus does make explicit the tragic potential of events. It is in some ways the case that – at bottom; ultimately; in, or at least at, the end – the events are arranged tragically (though, of course, comically and – as always with Bottom, scandalously as when he reactivates the imaginary scene of human–animal sex, opining '*lion vile hath here deflower'd my dear*' (5.1.281)).

The Fates, with '*hands as pale as milk*' (5.1.325) have cut Pyramus' thread. In Golding, preparing her suicide, Thisbe castigates the tree:

> 'Black be the colour of thy fruit and mourning-like alway,
> Such as the murder of us twain may evermore bewray.'
> This said, she took the sword yet warm with the slaughter of her love
> And, setting it beneath her breast, did to her heart it shove.
> Her prayer with the gods and with their parents took effect.
> For when the fruit is thoroughly ripe, the berry is bespecked
> With colour tending to a black;   (Bk IV. 194–200)

At her behest nature is changed; the stained fruit memorialises the double suicide. If, as Patricia Parker explains, the Latin 'mora' allows the mulberry to be associated with the 'ass, or fool', like Bottom, it also suggests 'moriens' – the dying of Pyramus which transforms the berry.[27] And whereas in the preceding comedy the juice of an empurpled flower allows the productive transformation of human lives, in the tragedy human life ebbs away fruitlessly, or is channelled into the changing of the mulberry and its story.

Playing out the tragic logic which has haunted the play, the tragedy of Pyramus and Thisbe takes us directly to Golding's version of Book IV. If Shakespeare, though not necessarily his audience, read the story of Pyramus and Thisbe in Golding then it is likely that, though it is excluded from the play, he and some of his audience knew the frame narrative. The tale is told by a group of women who, led by Minyas' daughters, reject the priest's bid to 'holiday' (Bk IV. 5) in celebration of Bacchus, a new-fangled God to whom 'obeyeth all the east as far as Ganges goes, / Which doth the scorchèd land of Inde with tawny folk enclose.' (Bk IV. 26–7).[28] They stubbornly remain in their houses, 'spinning yarn or weaving in the frame' (Bk IV. 44) and the story we hear is in the service of 'Minerva' – 'a better saint' (Bk IV. 57) and herself sometimes associated with weaving.[29] The darkening of the mulberry is juxtaposed, for Ovid's reader, with the dark wine of Bacchanalian feasts. The tellers are overzealous weavers and unlawful resisters of Bacchus, whose realm is specified as extending to 'Inde'. It is within this complex frame that Pyramus and Thisbe are horribly punished. Ultimately, Minyas' daughters feel the power of Bacchus. Weaving after the storytelling 'In spite of Bacchus, whose high feat they break contemptuously' (Bk IV. 483), the women are taken by surprise when 'the web they had begun / Immediately waxed fresh and green' (Bk IV. 488–9) and, in an exciting vision, 'part thereof did run / Abroad in vines' (Bk IV. 491). Bacchus' power is felt as the house 'seemed to shake' (Bk IV. 497) and 'likenesses of ugly beasts' run about (Bk IV. 499). Worse, they themselves 'how they lost their former shape, of certainty to know / The darkness would not suffer them. No feathers on them grow / And yet with sheer vellum wings they hover from the ground.' (5.1.505–7). The refused Bacchanalia has asserted itself in any case and, their weaving alive and spreading, Bacchus' victims shriek their mourning – as bats.

Although the contexts of Bacchanalia, weaving, disobedience and punishment are absent from the explicit narrative of the play, Bottom is a weaver; the realm of fairy and the realm of Inde are associated if not coextensive; the shortcomings of parental rule are clear, and, crucially, the mechanicals' play and Bottom's words within it foreground the fateful consequence of rejecting the transforming power of desire. The 'tawny folk' of 'Inde' (Bk IV. 27) and Bacchus' power over animals (Bk IV. 31–5) seem to find shadow counterparts in the play – Inde is there, but so are the frightening phantom animals that Puck promises throughout, of which Bottom sings, and into which he is partially changed. These echo the rule of Bacchus. More significantly, though, the furies' harsh parental refusal, banished from the comedy, are worked out in this comic–tragic addendum-finale – the tragedy beyond, and up to this point held within, but also promised by, the play.

As a crucial 'answering' scene to that staging-in-language of the arrow falling into the 'little western flower', the tragedy of Pyramus and Thisbe is appropriately positioned *after* the couples are joined. A tragedy of marriage ruined follows a comedy of desire fulfilled, and as we will see, much of the material concerning marriage and its discontents recurs in *A Winter's Tale*'s exploration of change, wild children, jealousy and marriage. The evidence suggests that this scene can also be read as a kind of fulfilment of the play's engagement with metamorphosis – weaving together and joining, at the very least, the comic and tragic potentials of the plots.

At the core of *A Midsummer Night's Dream* is a question about change and constancy. Investigating what it implies to experience change, the transformations in the play set the constant and true against the changed and wandering. If metamorphosis is part of the play's agenda, as suggested earlier, it is as importantly part of its textual and theatrical practice in changing the very text of change, Ovid's *Metamorphoses*. Transformation is thematised, represented and part of the material from which the play is made. Associated with transformation, imagination both deceives – 'How easy is a bush suppos'd a bear' (5.1.122) – and allows a process of change. If, therefore, the play indeed uses transformation, as Caroline Walker Bynum suggests, to explore identity, at the same time it is deeply embroiled in the different ways of telling, showing, evoking the story of change – classical, theatrical, folkloric. For an audience, the changes and the questions those propose surely dominate, whether or not the play's rich intertexuality is activated.

Let us revisit the opening question of how the play is using transformation. There is a further dimension to the play's engagement with classical metamorphosis. Even as the final show demonstrates a process of strong reading, and misreading, in the mechanicals' dramatisation of Golding, *A Midsummer Night's Dream* is alert to the ways in which classical transformation was received and in part thematises differentials in cultural capital held by the audience. If some audience members were as likely to know Pyramus and Thisbe, if at all, from a 'ballad' in *Handefull of Pleasant Delites* (1584) where 'You Ladies all' are invited to 'peruse' and see 'bright' Thisbe's faithfulness to 'Pyramus this noble knight', then the play knows and acknowledges this in two ways – in shaping the metamorphoses in the play and in mocking the mechanicals' interpretation even as it brings to fulfilment the tragic potential. Both plays – that is the mechanicals' play and *Midsummer Night's Dream* – are aware of distinct apprehensions of transformation in different parts of society.[30]

Taking a step back from the text to the context of interpretation, clearly some of the audience would indeed have had a relationship with Ovid very similar to that of the mechanicals. As Adam Fox argues, by the 1590s print and unlettered culture overlapped, and mixed. Print had actually boosted the popularity of some genres – and Fox cites ballads. Enthusiasm for ballads specifically, one preacher thought in 1595, was an 'evil disease' now 'renewed, and commeth on a fresh againe, so that at every Faire and Market almost you shall have one or two singing and selling of ballades, & they are bought up a pace'.[31] Fox's argument that the growth of print gave some old fashioned parts of culture fresh currency is suggestive with regard to the old-fashioned engagement of the mechanicals with Golding – perhaps old-fashioned forms were being heard once more. An intriguingly similar point is made by Siobhán McElduff, writing on the Irish hedge-schools of the nineteenth century. McElduff finds ballads a key location of classical narrative, observing the way they efface chronology and 'had no problem tossing in' together Latin stories, Christian and Irish myth. Similarly, she finds the hedge-school pupils moving chaotically, as it seems to us, between Irish rogue literature and Ovid.[32] *Midsummer Night's Dream* imagines a cognate encounter between Golding and the mechanicals, with Ovid playing a minor part. Although we cannot tell how often, or how, Golding's Ovid met unlettered readers, we can see clearly that it would have done so through texts like, for example, *A Midsummer Night's Dream* itself which brings Ovid, and Golding, to the exchange between play and audience.

The encounter between Ovid and simple readers, like the question of translation, is re-enacted in the mechanicals' play and elsewhere. The play explores encounters between unlettered readers and classically derived texts, and between different kinds of stories. Where, in the play, the mixing of folkloric and classical, the miniaturising of Ulysses to become Oberon, and the mixing of Ovidian and English flowers is artful, the mixing in audience reception might not be. Such a description might seem close to the ancient wisdom that Shakespeare 'put in something for everyone' but a very substantial corrective to any such generalisation exists in the way the play may hint at tragedy throughout but it is in the mechanicals' scenes that the language and genre of tragedy (mixed with archaism, ballad, lament) finds its most linguistically complete, though ravaged, expressions.

Discussion of the play's transformations in terms of how it is using its sources remains subject to endless revision in the light of specific audience responses. It is, as Jonathan Bate puts it, 'deeply but not directly Ovidian'.[33] Yet, this point of view is illuminating in terms of both the kinds of transformation the play presents and the ways in which it transforms its sources; as Peter Holland notes, its engagement with Seneca's *Hippolytus* may not be diegetic, though as the offspring of Theseus and Hippolyta, as Holland puts it, Hippolytus is a shadowy presence – 'is and is not there' and as the unborn child at the end of the play threatens the future.[34]

In the critical reception of *A Midsummer Night's Dream* the obsessions of its foundational editor, Harold Brooks, with the detailed integration of phrases from 'sources' has been influential in forming our understanding of the play's intertextuality (or perhaps more accurately, sources). However, it seems that while it is possible to read, for example, tragic materials from Seneca as pointing up comedy by contrast, and this possibility is reinforced by other, overt, aspects of the play inviting readers to make such comparisons, yet it is not clear that the pervasive reference strongly directs or requires such discrimination between 'sources' or validates a thematic interpretation of their influence. Ultimately, *A Midsummer Night's Dream* sheds light on the way the different treatment of kinds of texts, and authors, has very substantially shaped understanding of the reception – that is use – of the idea of transformation in texts. On the one hand, *Midsummer Night's Dream* makes it evident that we need to see classical metamorphosis as hybridised in its Englishing – both classical and folkloric; oral and literate. At the same time, the influence of editorial practice; the very intensity of editorial and critical scrutiny; the isolation of the text as 'Shakespeare' also very evidently mark its reception. This is illuminated clearly when we set it against other, contemporary, texts.

Finally, to return to the question of critical approaches to transformation, *A Midsummer Night's Dream* makes it clear that the editing of the Shakeapearean text brings the modes of textual reception into focus. It does so, as we can see in the careful and close focus on the text, in relation to, first, the interpretation and transmission of the Shakespearean text and secondly, the Shakespearean canon. *A Midsummer Night's Dream* has been intertextually excavated to reveal, I would argue, a dense saturation of metamorphic material which is in varying degrees likely to be present to auditors. Perhaps, after all, Brooks has a point when he understands them as sources, because their active presence, and so function, varies from explicit to highly enigmatic, and shadowy. To rudimentarily model audience reception, we can easily see they might be in the mix but the audience's relationship to them is harder to judge. That metamorphic references of the play have been so mined is a function of the play's enduring importance in the Shakespearean canon. In the end, Brooks is interested in the sources because they are likely to have a bearing on *Shakespeare*'s thought and the development of his writing. The density and range of material in some way at work seem to be naturalised by association with a figure whose writing and career are monumentalised as extraordinary. Yet, it may be partially possible to turn this material towards a wider culture of thought and literature.

Considered as a starting place for a study of transformation in the writing and culture of seventeenth-century England, this late Tudor text both tells a story of literary transformations and suggests a centrality of Ovidian transformation to foundational concerns of a troubled society. For as we have seen, even within this one text, metamorphosis suggests, almost names, things that need to change in a social world. Thus, the story of change reminds us of the social stasis of the opening; animal additions remind us of hierarchy and its tendency to be transgressed by desire; the mingling of fairy worlds with human suggests some of the conflicts inhabiting social relations. Yet such allegorising is not needed to understand that the play offers evidence that the vocabulary of metamorphosis was very fully available and mobile to articulate a range of experiences. Two avenues of exploration which can yield further evidence about the literary reach of Ovid in late sixteenth-century literature are comparison with other texts and analysis of the mechanicals' Bible – Golding's Ovid. If the use of transformation to articulate a range of experiences is not restricted to Shakespeare, this literary evidence suggests something about literature but also about the social world of the audience and idea. In order to test this we can turn to a text that, whether or not it inhabited a wholly different location in culture as a pamphlet, has certainly been accommodated to a very different position in our understanding of the past.

II Popular metamorphosis? Ovid goes to the *Dogges*

> When as blacke Tytan with his duskie robe,
>   Had *Tellus* clouded with his curtaynes nyght,
> Fayre *Phebus* peering underneath earthes globe,
>   With wingèd steedes hence takes his course a right,
> Tytan he leaves to beare imperial sway,
>   Commaunding nyght as Phoebus did the day.

So begins *The Blacke Dogge of Newgate* (1596).[35] What does this text tell us about the literary and cultural work done by classical forms of transformation? This strange and composite text is part metamorphic dream-vision, part coney-catching narrative set in Newgate, London and Hell. Marketed as a cheap pamphlet, the text sports a woodcut placing metamorphosis in the London streets (see fig. 2) and was reprinted and reworked several times. Entering the public domain just after *A Midsummer Night's Dream*, like that play Hutton's *Dogge* explores night and darkness; time; transformations. Unlike *A Midsummer Night's Dream* scholarship on this text has focused primarily on its role as cheap print, with very little discussion of its use of metamorphosis. However, read in detail, the text and its immediate recensions offer a test case in the potential of Ovid to communicate intense personal and social experiences. Accordingly, we here examine three imbricated aspects of the text: its Ovidian and Dantean uses of transformation; its use of transformation to articulate penal suffering and its relationship to other, later, 'prison writings'; and the relationship between Ovidian transformation and the sufferings of the 1590s.

For readers of *The Blacke Dogge*, Newgate, cony-catching and Ovidian interests were interlaced with the celebrity of its enigmatic 'author'. Luke Hutton, closely identified with the text's protagonist, was Cambridge-educated, possibly a member of a prominent church family, and had spent time in Newgate. He was a convicted thief, executed at York in 1598. So, two years of the publication of the *Dogge* some readers, at least, would have known the poem also attributed to him – 'Luke Hutton's Lamentation', supposedly penned as he awaited execution. For readers that ballad could only enhance the *Blacke Dogge*'s poignant, piquant, criminal provenance.[36] Whether or not he truly wrote *The Blacke Dogge of Newgate*, and it seems likely that he did, Luke Hutton's contradictory affiliations lead us to the world of his last decade – London in the 1590s. In a decade which began with the impulsive political challenge of Essex's rebellion, and contained plague (1592–3), the failure of harvests, and social disorder, Luke Hutton is no Thomas Nashe to evoke a nightmare world, but the text, like *A Midsummer Night's Dream*, does evoke disturbance, night, change and danger.[37]

If Hutton was a character who sparked fascination, Newgate too had a history and fearsome reputation that also gave the pamphlet a frisson of horror. As Ian Archer informs us, throughout this period there were between ten and twelve gaol deliveries to Newgate each year; as the carts took prisoners in and brought out the condemned for execution, Londoners were witnesses.[38] The prison itself was on the edge of the City. Built, or adapted, by Henry II in 1188, Newgate included part of the gatehouse and its dungeons. By the Tudor period it was rotting. According to one analyst, it was from the first a prison for 'the very worst types of criminal', besides 'rebels, traitors, heretics, spies and debtors'.[39] Newgate's keepers (appointed by the sheriffs of London) left records in the Court of Aldermen, which made repeated attempts to halt abuses such as the shackling of prisoners who could not pay.[40] In 1544 a clergyman was appointed, with duties to visit, provide services and sentences from scripture, and to persuade the prisoners to give up the names of others.[41] Henry VIII used Newgate to house heretics, and Foxe uses scenes from Newgate to dramatise Protestant martyrs, giving the prison a life in print.[42] Elizabeth used the prison for state affairs. Abuses continued – with further measures taken by the aldermen in the 1570s and 1580s.[43] This grim dark world is evoked by descriptions (for misdeeds, a prisoner 'shall be put in a place called Limbo'), or the 1574 ruling that prisoners should be allowed 'sufficient lights, with trays, tubs and hoopings of the same'.[44] Archer suggests that an anxiety to exert control over London meant that in the 1590s the disciplinary reach of justice extended to new groups; as plague struck in 1593, bear-baitings became a target, and the riots in 1595 prompted a disciplinary drive which resulted in the appointment of provost marshals in the City.[45] Correspondingly, in 1593 the Court of Aldermen agreed that the fabric of Newgate should be examined. Linking pain and justice, Hutton uses a dedication to Lord Justice Popham, a significant figure in the policing of London in the 1590s, with the appeal of the prisoner as penitent and victim.[46] It seems likely that the 1590s were a significant decade in the formation of Newgate's extraordinarily rich, if horrific, mythic status and presence in print, and Hutton's text seems to register and respond to this context. However, as we will see, although Newgate was to become synecdochic for prison literature with its own associated pamphet imagery and genres, the main Newgate and penitent pamphlet industry slightly post-dates *The Blacke Dogge*.

Any reader drawn in by the fascinating woodcut would find themselves plunged into a poem that opens in a Romanised night, ruled by nocturnal gods, *The Blacke Dogge* foregrounding its relationship with classical texts of transformation. The arrival of 'blacke Tytan with his duskie robe' as Phoebus disappears, sets the scene for the imperial rule of monsters. Saturn, a remaining Titan, pulls the curtains of night past Tellus, goddess of the earth and Phoebus (Apollo, Diana's brother) disappears round a modern globe. Saturn and night rule.

'The Earthes Cell cole blacke' (st. 2), Morpheus summons the world, but our narrator lies awake:

> Layed in my bed I gan for to recount
>   A thousand thinges, which had been in my time;
> My birth, my youth, my woes which all surmount
>   My life, my losse, my liberty, my crime.
> Then where I was unto my mind recalling,
>   Methought earth gaped and I to Hell was falling.
>
> (st. 3)

Following Hutton in his plunge to Hell, we find an exploration of guilt, innocence and pain articulated in the opening excursus of some eighty stanzas. The narrator, '[a]midst these fears that all my senses cumber' (st. 4), finally falls asleep and dreams, 'beholding Hell and Devils' (st. 5). As if looming up from the fog of hell, 'One anticke monster, hidious, foule, and grim, / Mee most appayld, and most I lookt at him' (st. 5). This, the transformative – and, for the narrator, transfixing 'dogge' of the title and the figure illustrated on the frontispieces to the 1596 and 1638 texts, is the narrator's adversary and, in part, his subject. It is also in some sense his mirror – a monster in which he sees his own profligacy registered and avenged.

The dream-vision embraces Christian and Classical Hell. Thus, a voice, 'like an Angel' tells him '"*Hutton*, be bolde, for thou shalt see and heare / Men Devils, Devils men, one both, both all deluding"' (st. 6) and before long, having seen 'furies affrighting' Hutton, 'waking with dread' (though not, it seems, from the vision), is visited by Minerva who gives him the task of deciphering this 'Curre'.[47] 'Light thy Lampe, and take thy Pen in hand' she commands, 'Write what thou sees, thy visions all unfolding' (st. 9). Wisdom's command to write seems bound to the poem's genre as a vision to be told, as well as to the subject's excessive knowledge and suffering. At the same time, the order conveys an urgency to capture in written words a being not only a devilishly double shape-shifter, but one that has also hitherto escaped formal articulation. Introducing Time, '"who mourns to see these helhounds, Tymes abusing"' (st. 15), Minerva insists, '"Resolve the wise that they have been deceived"'. '"Many Blacke dogs have walkt in shapes of men"' (st. 16) pretending 'service' (st. 15) Hutton is to expose his 'divers secrets' in the service of 'Time' who himself urges Hutton to 'Unmask this beast'.

The experiences produced by such a creature, his terrifying power and wickedness are in themselves metamorphic, and have a transforming effect on the teller. As we will find, such searing effects require stabilisation in writing, and Time needs to reveal truth. For the present, though, the narrator is both vulnerable and implicated:

> Then did I fix mine eye upon this Beast
>   Who did appeare first in the shape of Man,
> Homely attyrde, of wonders not the least,
>   A Broome-mans song to sing this Dogge began,
> From street to street trudgeth along this groom
>   As if he would serve all the worlde with Brome.
>
> But in a trice he did transform his shape,
>   Which stroke a trebble horror to my hart.
> A *Cerberus*, nay worse, he thrice as wide did gape,
>   His ears all Snakes, curling, they will not part;
> Coal blacke his hew, like torches glow his eyes.
>   His breath doth poyson, smoke from his nostrels flies.
>
> (st. 9, 10)

The initial evocation of the monster-dog conveys its nightmarish, transforming power and does so in ways that evoke wider implications of transformation. The narrator first encounters the dog in the open street, apparently working as a lowly crossing sweeper who seems to be a servant.

Clearly, Hutton's ability to recognise, and so disclose, the dog is bound up with knowledge of the forbidden. His identity – 'life', 'loss', 'liberty' and 'crime' – makes him a valuable witness but is tied to what makes him vulnerable to the dog's power. As Leonard Barkan argues about the myth of Diana and Actaeon, the subject is transformed because he or she comes to have sacred, forbidden knowledge. In Renaissance interpretations, moreover, Actaeon's keeping of a huge pack of hounds came to be read as a metaphor for excessive, destructive, consumption, as Actaeon's being consumed by his hounds becomes a metaphor for profligacy.[48] Barkan's more general suggestion, that '[m]etamorphosis becomes a means of creating self-consciousness because it creates a tension between identity and form', also has resonance.[49] Both profligacy and self-consciousness shape the text, but the narrator's transformation also has implications which extend beyond personal identity to the wider society.

In *The Blacke Dogge* such engagements with the myth of Diana and Actaeon have a similar status to the place of Hipplolytus in *A Midsummer Night's Dream* – for a reader who knew that story they might recall it. Actaeon and Diana may or may not haunt the poem, but it is clearer that, like *A Midsummer Night's Dream*, the *Blacke Dogge* engages Book IV of the *Metamorphoses* as several of the personnel inhabit Hutton's poem – Medusa, Cerberus, the Furies. As Golding Englishes part of Book IV, 'The way doth directly lead him to the Stygian city / Or where black

2 Title page of *Blacke Dogge of Newgate* (1596) showing broom-man/dog metamorphosis, Newgate with prisoner and London.

Pluto keeps his court that never showeth pity' (Bk IV. 542–3) and here Ino encounters Cerberus 'with three fell heads which barked all together' (Bk IV. 559) and the Furies, 'a-kembing foul black snakes from off their filthy hair / Before the dungeon door, the place where caitiffs punished were' (Bk IV. 561–2).

As Minerva reminds 'Hutton', 'many black dogs have walked in shapes of men' (st. 16) and the narrator is to 'disclose' both the individual and the metamorphic 'deceits' (st. 16) of his terrifying type – for when transformed:

> His countenance gastly, fearfull, grim, and payle,
>   His fomie mouth still gapeth for his pray:
> With Tygers teeth he spares none to assayle,
>   His lyppes Hellgates, o'erpaynted with decay,
> His tongue the clapper, sounding woofull knell,
>   Towling poore men to ringe a peale in hell.
>
> Like Sepulcher his throate is hollow made,
>   Devouring all whom danger makes a pray,
> Brybrie his hand, spoyle of the pore his trade,
>   His fyngers Talentes ceazing to betray.
>
> (st. 21, 22)

This creature is so terrifying because of its powers of transformation, conveyed in its ability to move between animal and human form, but also because it is effective, deadly to its victims. The poem expresses the metamorphosis from meek crossing sweeper to seizing animal as a hellish vision which conveys the deceitful power as exceeding human limits – demonic in both its force over those it grasps and the way it is concealed behind and within worldly shapes. The huge 'sepulcher' of its swallowing throat evokes, perhaps, the newly stripped ossuaries of the Reformation – now, like that of St Paul's, gapingly emptied of the dead.[50] If the dog's throat is a sepulchre, his belly 'a scalding furnace' (st. 23), the ravening beast leads his prey to the very bowels of hell – to 'blacke *Plutoes* cell'; 'in Limbo cast, / A Stygian lake, the dungeon of deep hell' (st. 25).

At this point, just under halfway through the poem, we are finally given an earthly mapping of this mysterious and frightening place. The dog 'like *Madusa* doth he shake his locks' (st. 26) before leaving our 'author', chained and trussed, 'Bound for the slaughter, lying like the Lambe' (st. 32); 'Robbed of the sky' (st. 27); in the deepest dark. Elsewhere in the poem the potential pun on 'bolts', bolted in and striking victims of divine anger, seem to link Newgate to its Ovidian intertext. Here, the locks seem to be both hair and keys and tie us to a specific place: '"This house is *Newgate*,"' and '"this place, Lymbo wherein now thou art'" (st. 34), we and Hutton are told. The story Time has commissioned, then, has several levels: it is the story of terrifying metamorphosis – the story of the dog; it is in part the story of disclosing the deeper meanings of the hell of Newgate and time bringing truth to light; it is the story of this prisoner but also of the other prisoners of Newgate. Finally, the story is also of the process of communication in which the prisoner's experiences are transformed into a narrative – the story of writing, making known and reading which makes understanding possible. The myth of a black dog that haunts Newgate opens the poem to supernatural implications and these are enriched by the hellish terminology for Newgate such that Limbo stands simultaneously in the metamorphic and the literalised narrative – as a colloquial term for Newgate's various decayed, cramped, unlit, underground areas.[51] At the same time, part of Time's commission seems to be to explain the unarticulated part of the story – to put into writing that which has not been previously adequately known.

It is in respect of the heroic tasks of witnessing and above all writing, in delivering the dog into words in time, and to justice, that the narrator becomes the hero of his own story. In his attempt to write what has been done to him, rather than in any barely present and highly compromised identification with Perseus as the enemy of the Medusa, the role of the narrator is foregrounded. And, in telling the tale of the dog, a Cerberus who takes him into Hell, the narrator explores the different levels of Hell. A man tells him (and us) where he is, and he 'offered me both fyer, bread, and drinke / Leaving a Candle by me for to burne' (st. 38), leaves. Immediately, 'A Rat doth rob the candle from my handes', the narrator battling 'a hundred rats' (st. 39) in a vain attempt to retrieve it. Food, clearly, is at a premium in this new hell.

Plunged once again into darkness and despair he exclaims 'Woe to that Dogge made me to woe a thrall!' Perhaps unsurprisingly this is the moment at which '*Lymboes* dore' opens and the candle-giver returns, in a surprise alliance, accompanied by 'the Dogge' (st. 44). Although the scene is not explicitly shaped as the appearance of the devil to a human deep in despair and so ripe for harvest, yet it has the contours of such a scene even as it remains allied also to the metamorphic narrative and to the now explicit Newgate location:

> But now this Dog is in another shape,
>   In every point proportioned as a man:
> My heart did throb not knowing how to scape,
>
> (st. 45)

Grinning, the dog-man rejects his 'fee' insisting, 'Thy fault is such, that thou shalt surely dye' (st. 46) and says that 'in time' (st. 46) he hopes to have all such as our narrator in Newgate. 'When he namde *Tyme*, then I on Tyme did thinke' (st. 47) but, in the present, the storyteller is forced to bow before the dog:

> Like as the child dooth kisse the rod for feare,
>   Nor yet dare whimper though it have beene bet:
> So with smooth lookes this Dog approach I neare.
>   Before the Devil, a candle do I set.   (st. 48)

The dog decides who is subject to the room's implements of torment – 'Bolts, shackles, colors, ... Iron shears ... / Thumbstalls, wastbands' (st. 51) – he chooses who is and who is not laden with chains. A 'feend of hell' who thirsts 'for angels', 'Mans life and soule this dog seekes to subdue' (st. 53).

At this juncture another character, a 'sorry soule without a ragge' (st. 55) enters the narrative. '[H]urokling for colde' this prisoner of nine years' standing (or shivering) takes the narrator on a tour – of hell. As the narrator tells us, 'I followed him, as he that in a wood, / Hath lost himselfe', apparently renewing the fusion of the topographical and supernatural, metamorphic, narratives through a Dantean intertext. The narrator may be modelling his experiences on Virgil, and it is hard to know how far Hutton, though university educated, might know the *Inferno*, important as that text is for the European reception of and answer to Ovidian metamorphosis. The expression here, though, seems much closer to Dante's vivid evocation of Hell, apprehended in the lost moment in the middle of a life, than to Virgil. As in Dante's hell, the *Black Dogge*'s narrator inhabits a place and an experience.[52] Dante, too, invented his own monster – the huge Geryon transports the narrator and Virgil to Maleboge at the end of Canto XVI, again, appropriately enough, the circle of fraudsters.[53] There are obvious resemblances, too, between the *Inferno* and *Blacke Dogge*, in genre and use of first-person narrator. As Marina Warner indicates, one of the trajectories of the 'scandalous behaviour of the deathless but nevertheless superseded gods' was into hellish images of protean transformation.[54] Yet the reach of Dante's extraordinary text into English culture remains less clear than that of Ovid or Virgil, the *Inferno* remaining a shadow presence evoked for a reader who knows. Just as Hutton might have known the *Inferno* he might, equally, be like Dante responding to Virgil.

No sooner has the text offered a Virgilian or Dantean frame for our narrator's tour of hell than the terrifying actuality of Newgate geography and events is again pitched before a reader. E. D. Pendry has traced this journey from the Partner's Hall upstairs to the chapel.[55] Located physically, the tour allows the narrator to recognise Newgate's moral landscape at the same time as the sufferings of the condemned illustrate the full depth of hell: 'O Lord thought I, this house will rend in sunder, / Or else there can be no hell this hell under' (st. 60). The tour begins with a scene of preaching. 'Hutton' asks his guide, 'What's this?' – and the 'deeper secret' (st. 63) of the sight, so frightening that it dims his senses, is rapidly disclosed as the final comforts of men, '"pale and wan"' (st. 64) to be taken to the gallows – judgement given 'that corde shall stop their breath' (st. 64) and he witnesses them as, 'ropt and corded, they discend the stayres' assisted by the torments of the black dog, and they are 'bound to the cart' and carried 'to be hanged' (st. 66). If the 'emotional force of the gallows' anchors execution and the condemned at the centre of the study of early modern imprisonment, it performed the same function even more powerfully for sixteenth-century witnesses of imprisonment.[56] One traveller observed the 'criminal, seated in the cart,' with 'one end of a rope tied round his neck, and the other is fastened to the gallows'. As the cart moves, 'the condemned wretch is left hanging; friends and acquaintances pull at his legs, in order that he may be strangled the sooner.'[57] Such desperate scenes were known to those about to die and the text seems to blend epic, Christian, evocations of Hell, and the experience of witnesses in evoking a scene of horror in a claim on the reader that oscillates between gritty realism and myth.

In the reader's negotiation of the dual dimensions of the poem, the dog, simultaneously quotidian and supernatural, links figural and literal landscapes. He turns from assisting at the despatch of prisoners to again harass our narrator, and 'plays the gripe one Tityus intended / To tire his heart', preying on 'Hutton' until 'quite consumed my golden angels be' (st. 69). Tityus returns us to Ovid, possibly to Book x but, more likely, to Book IV where Juno visits the Furies in Pluto's court. There we have already met Cerberus and the cruel Furies combing their snaky hair. 'Before' Pluto's 'dungeon door' (Bk IV. 562), in company with Sisyphus and Tantalus, we find 'Tityus, stretched out at least nine acres full in length, / Did with his bowels feed a gripe that tare them out by strength' (Bk IV. 566).

Swinging back from Ovid, we find the impoverished narrator once again despatched below:

> I lye me down on boordes as hard as chenell.
> No bed nor boulster may affoord releefe,
>   For worse than Dogs lye we in that foule kennel.
> What might I thinke but sure, assure me then,
>   That metamorphosd we were beasts not men.
>
> (st. 71)

So squalid are conditions that as a man 'his last lives breath dooth blow', 'ere the sorry man be fully dead' (st. 72), in another kind of transformation, rats feed on him. Thus far in the text the reader is required to be agile in making repeated accommodations to shifts from the writing present to the streets and Newgate and on to Hell and Ovid. At this point, night once more, Time makes a decisive appearance and Hutton presents the book to him:

> Yea, but sayth Tyme, thou must discover yet
>   Who this Dog is, who else will be excused.
> For albe I so cleard thine eyes to see him,
>   So may not others, yet Tyme would have all flie him.
>   (st. 74)

However, Time responds that while 'thy verses covertly disclose, / The secret sence, and yet doth shadow trueth' (st. 75), Hutton must disclose who the black dog truly is – 'Explaine this Black Dogge, who he is, in prose' (st. 75).

Prose is appropriate, Time asserts because, 'Truth needs no coulours' (st. 76). Before examining responses to this poem, including the narrator and author's own prose version which forms the second part of his text, we can pause to consider how the poem puts to work Ovidian metamorphosis. The poem seeks to present and elaborate the experience of unjust imprisonment using overlapping Christian, secular and experiential modes of expression within an overall narrative of metamorphosis in which transformation articulates the experience of the law's deceit: capture, imprisonment. Identified particularly with Cerberus, hinting at Medusa and the Furies, yet disguised as a broom-man, the creature at the centre of the drama is enigmatically both familiar and monstrous. Drawing on Book IV of the *Metamorphoses*, possibly in Golding's translation, to evoke prison and darkness, it is not until halfway through the poem that the narrative of transformation is explicitly joined by the 'real world' Newgate location. Yet, following this, the characterisation of Newgate as hell is developed and it seems at least possible that the reader is encouraged to read the location through Dante's *Inferno*.

Ovidian metamorphoses articulate the pain of the subject which the poem is keen to assert as 'real' in itself and legitimately expressed, but also requiring clarification.[58] Although, at the end of the poem, Time intervenes once again to impel the narrator to disclose the 'truth' in prose, he also asserts, 'Twas no illusion movde me this Poem to make' (st. 80). From this point the contemporary reception of the poem is illuminating in terms of both how classical reception was expected to be understood by writers and booksellers, and in terms of the problems of how to convey the experiences on which Hutton is focused. The poem chooses to put before us both metamorphosis and doubt about metamorphosis as a mode. Only after offering the reader metamorphosis and poetry does it shift to retell the whole story in the form of a coney-catching dialogue between 'Zawny', a Newgate prisoner, and the 'author'.

This prose telling of the story supplements the poem and ambiguously both supersedes it and acknowledges its primacy. The emphasis shifts decisively to explanatory detail and disclosure of secrets. So, opening this dialogue 'Author' explains to Zawny why he called his book after the Black Dog:

> in that tytle shadow the knaverie, villanie, robberie and Cunnicatching committed daily by divers, who in the name of service and office, were as it were attendants at Newgate. Againe, I did choose to give my booke that title, aswell to satisfie some who yet thinke there is some spirit about that prison in the likeness of a black Dog; of which fond imagination to put them out of doubt, I thought good to give them to understand that indeed there is no such matter. The third reason was, for I being in Newgate a prisoner, and overthrowne by these kind of bad people with their cunnycatching in most vile and wicked manner, in so much that, whilest I there languished in great extremitie, I did both hear and see many outrageous injuries by them committed on diverse sorts of people.[59]

Three justifications for the title emerge – first, the legend that a spirit of that name lurks within the prison; second, paradoxically, to clarify that there is in fact 'no such matter'. Thirdly, however, the image was chosen because 'I being in Newgate a prisoner, and overthrown by these kind of bad people with their cony-catching in most vile and wicked manner' – the text expresses his 'extremitie'.

This explanation does make clear that, in the world of Newgate, the broom-sweeping dog supplies an identity for a kind of double agent who roams streets and taverns. As the author explains, 'if a man be robd by the way, they will help the party to his money again' and to do so they get a warrant 'from some justice' and, by this, 'take up all suspected persons' – that is, they round up known criminals taxing them with the crime abusing both the justices (or so the pamphlet claims) and those taken up.[60] Naming and explaining in detail the dialogue examines specific figures. Claiming to rescue the victims of crime (for a fee) and bringing known cutpurses and thieves before the justices they are fearsomely powerful double-dealers in a system where, one traveller to England comments, '[i]t is the easiest thing in the world to get a person thrown into prison in this country; for every officer of justice, both civil and criminal, has the power of arresting any one, at the request of a private individual, and the accused person cannot be liberated without giving security' and, moreover, 'nor is there any punishment awarded for making a slanderous accusation'.[61] In prose the Black Dog is disclosed as something close to the thief-taker whose trade 'lay in brokering the return of stolen goods to their owners', and about whose symbiotic criminal and official connections Tim Wales has written so illuminatingly.[62]

The 1590s prose pamphlet illuminates as monstrous precisely the thief-taker's ability to make crime pay by, simply, extorting money from the victims of the crime in securing a conviction from known criminals who may or may not have committed this particular offence. Patricia Fumerton's insight that many pamphleteers found a way to write about economic fear and change 'by transforming the *fact* of a vagrant economy grounded on a shifting mass of itinerant labor into the *fiction* of role-playing rogues' is helpful in considering both the *Blacke Dogge*'s shift from metamorphic poetry to the more concrete form.[63] While *The Blacke Dogge* shares with other cony-catching pamphlets a fascination with the power of role play and transformation, even as far as inviting the reader to identify with the victim of transformation, the poem, at least, takes the issue substantially beyond the finding out of role-playing thieves; transformation is represented on an altogether larger scale, with classical and metaphysical metamorphic dimensions. The plight of the poor and criminal is dramatised in terms of the metamorphic, even demonic, powers unleashed by the alliance of crime and justice. For Hutton, the interdependence and complicity between justices and such criminals and the ability of the dog-sweeper-thief-taker or cutpurse-trickster to control these relations involves a diabolical manipulative agency; the hellish dog of the poem is made literal in the prose piece but remains an agent of Satan articulated in a different register.

Once in print, the relative importance of the poem and the cony-catching dialogue changed rapidly. That the poem was considered enigmatic is suggested by an adapted re-issue of 1612, issued again in 1638. *The Discovery of a London Monster*, attributed to Samuel Rowlands who wrote other prison materials, reminds us that '*Time bringeth all things to light*' and opens with a narrative called 'The Discovery of A *London* Monster, called, The *Blacke Dogge* of New-gate'.[64] This pamphlet concentrates its opening efforts on the clearly fascinating question of the legend, or rather legends, of the Black Dog. The scene is set by an inn-sign:

Popular metamorphosis? Ovid goes to the Dogges

> A Wonder, a wonder, Gentlemen, Hels brooke loose, and the Blacke Dogge of Newgate is got out of Prison, and leapt into a Signe: What the Devils here (quoth a mad fellow going by) seeing the Black Curre ring'd about the nose with golden hoope, his two sawcer-like eyes, and an iron chaine about his necke, this cannot choose (said he) but be a well customed house, where such a Porter keeps the doore and cals in company.[65]

Here, drinking with 'a poor Thin-gut fellow, with a face as red as the gilded knobs on an Aldermans nose,' they begin 'to argue of the Blacke Dogge beginning and how he came first to be called the blacke Dog of Newgate'. Two versions are offered. First, our author gives us a supernatural version from 'an old Chronicle', where he read of 'a walking spirit in the likeness of a blacke Dog, gliding up and downe the streets a little before the time of Execution and in the night whilst the Sessions continued, and his beginning thus'.[66]

He offers the story behind this as one from the reign of Henry III when London was enveloped by 'famine' so intense that 'the Prisoners in Newgate eat up one another alive, but commonly those that came newly in, and such as could make but small resistance'. Into this '[d]enne of misery' was sent 'a certain Scholler brought thither, upon suspition of Conjuring, and that by Charmes and devilish Witchcrafts, had done much hurt to the king's Subjects'. This scholar, 'mauger his Devils Furies, Spirits and Goblins, was by the famished Prisoners eaten up and deemed passing good meate'. However, the cannibal deed done (another kind of human transformation and one that Ovid associates with the tyrant Lycaon), collective guilt ensues.[67] A 'conceit possessed the mindes of the poore Prisoners that they supposed nightly to see the Scholler in the shape of a black Dog walking up and downe the Prison, ready with his ravening Jawes to teare out their bowels'. They hear groans as of a human in torment, and a 'nightly feare grew amongst them, that it turned to frenzie, and from a frenzie to Desperation, in which desperation they killed the keeper, and so many of them escaped forth'. But wherever they went the black dog followed. There was no escape from the wicked deed.[68] The food shortages and grain riots of the 1580s and 1590s might have meant that for readers this version had a worldly as well as supernatural impact, potentially resonating with knowledge or even experience.[69]

Countervailingly, 'Signior Thin-gut' proposes an entirely topographical clarification, albeit one with a gory, real-world narrative attached:

> there is no other blacke Dog that I ever saw or heard of, but a great blacke stone standing in the dungeon called *Limbo*, the place where the condemned

Prisoners be put after their Judgement, upon which they set a burning candle in the night, against which, I have heard that a desperate Prisoner dashed out his braines; and that is all the Blacke Dogs that I know, or heard of.[70]

To clarify, simply, 'Sir (quoth he) the Blacke Dog is a black Conscience, haunting' such as 'Newgate may challenge to be guests'. And from this we are led into a sequence of cony-catching narratives. Much less sophisticated than Hutton's dialogue, these deal, simply, with thieves rather than with the complex psychological problem of the thief-taker. They are followed by the dialogue between Author and Zawny and, finally, by '[c]ertaine fearfull Visions appearing to the Authour of this Booke, most worthy to be noted' – Hutton's poem.

The addition of material and the reversal of the ordering tells us a little about contemporary interests and about perceptions of the poem, dog, and perhaps of Newgate. The poem, a 'vision', is both enigmatic and disturbing in revealing not necessarily the literal nature of the thief-taker's art but the power and associated images generated by the close alliance of authority and criminality as one turns into the other and both inhabit one shape. If, as seems to be the case, the ordering of 1612 implies a perception of the poem as enigmatic and so problematic to market, then the insertion of the prefatory material concerning the legends and lives of the dog suggests that figure was highly saleable in itself. The cultural life of Newgate's legendary black dog – as inn-sign, ghost, compulsion, history, fearful boulder – in turn suggests the fear and fascination of the place, its nightmare quality, its association with rumour and local knowledge, and its traumatic history. Perhaps the expansion of the Black Dog's role is best understood as giving symbolic form to the many layered feelings about penal justice (and injustice) condensed in the problem of Newgate.

At the turn of the century the images of the black dog and of Newgate evidently resonated in a world of mixed written and oral culture, an index of the development of 'Newgate's' symbolic, mythic and literary, life. Appearing at a moment before the full fashion for penitential narratives, *The Blacke Dogge* draws on Newgate's stories, legends and ghosts and was published in a period of attempted reform – a cause to which it is partly attached. Although, as Lee Beier notes, four editions of Thomas Harman's *A Caveat or Warening for Common Cursetors* appeared in the Elizabethan period, it was under James that the penitent narrative grew in importance and took on particular forms.[71] In the seventeenth-century streets pamphlets jibed in horror at Newgate. As a jest book of 1607 asks 'what is prison but the very next door to hell? It is a man's grave wherein he walks

Popular metamorphosis? Ovid goes to the Dogges 43

> # The Discovery of a London
> Monster, called, *The Blacke Dogg*
> *of New-gate*;
> Profitable for all Readers to take heed by.
>
> *Vide, Lege, Cave.*
>
> Time bringeth all things to light.
>
> Printed at London by *M. P.* for *Robert Wilson,* at his Shop at Grayes-Inne Gate in Holborne. 1638.

3 Reworked design for title page of Samuel Rowlands attrib., *The Discovery of a London Monster* (London, 1638). In comparison to the earlier design (see Fig. 2), Newgate's status as a prison is clarified visually and two doors represent the entrance and Hell's mouth. The broom-man is removed and this allows clear focus on what was probably the main selling point, Dogg.

alive', and William Fennor's *Compter's Commonwealth* (1607) also evokes prison as hell. Prison as hell was part figural, part topographical common currency in the early seventeenth century. As implied by John Leon Lievsay's painstaking research into the recycling of penitent narratives, by the early seventeenth century, the shared tropes and vocabulary of crime and prison was in part a function of the splicing in of chunks of borrowed text, producing the new narrative as the same and different.

The Blacke Dogge is distinct from cony-catching pamphlets in terms of the highly specific qualities of the narrative; use of literary modes of dream vision, journey to Hell and metamorphosis. It seems that the establishment of Newgate in imaginative printed texts and the corresponding emergence of a known descriptive and imaginative lexicon for prison, slightly postdates *The Blacke Dogge*. If the text belongs with cony-catching pamphlets, it is also a literary evocation of the social and literary turmoil of the 1590s and shares as much with *Midsummer Night's Dream* as the emerging cony-catching literature. That very soon after the poem's publication the figures of the 'Newgate experience' were to be familiar has perhaps obscured the extent to which Hutton's text was innovative, perhaps, but crucially registering concerns shared in other texts of the 1590s in its use of a metamorphic dream vision. The Blacke Dog's first, and so, arguably, primary, presence is as a shape-shifter and this figural complexity indicates a depth in the poem's search to articulate imprisonment.

The 1590s undoubtedly saw social and political tensions and suffering and literary genres register this. Georgia Brown writes about literary culture of the 1590s in terms of fragmentation, dismemberment and recycling of cultural remains.[72] Metamorphosis, too, was experienced as an appropriate figure with which to consider what many see as a crisis but one which indicates vigorous anticipation of a future as much as complicated memory of the past. In the 1590s the 'reinterpretation of Ovid' was the 'catalyst for cultural change', used repeatedly to signal a claim to be modern, innovative – through the invocation of ancient authority supplying 'classical sanction for self-proclaimed modernity' and experiential authority.[73] Thematically Hutton's journey emphasises the writing subject as both undermined by error – particularly by prodigality – but also gaining a paradoxical, subjective authority from that experience. The status of the narrator as guilty yet an object of empathy is closely tied to *The Blacke Dogge*'s use of shards of myth, parts of Book IV of Ovid and their blending with folk beliefs, legends and history as well as the two complementing and competing discursive modes of lament and cony-catching dialogue. In the specific case of *The Blacke Dogge* and *A Midsummer Night's Dream*, metamorphosis takes on the role of mediating between past and present and strongly imagining change. Metamorphosis in this text seems to be invoked as a response to change and even crisis.

The place of metamorphosis in articulating social turmoil is made clearer by the juxtaposition of *A Midsummer Night's Dream* and *Blacke Dogge*. Without abandoning its individual significances it is possible to recontextualise *A Midsummer Night's Dream* as part of a shared turn to Ovid as a source of reflection, transgression and anticipation – tied to literary fashions but also evoking a sense of foreboding and anticipation of change. Attending relatively closely to Hutton's poem and prose, rather than assuming that their significance is accounted for by generic designation as cony-catching texts, also shows a complex use of Ovid to voice social and political pain and to invite change. Together, the texts clarify some of the uses of classical metamorphosis in English vernacular writing, suggesting that contemporaries apprehended Ovidian transformation as enabling articulation of their social experience. However, in each case, the limits of metamorphosis to articulate, rather than powerfully evoke, change are denied – the trivial example of Bottom's refusal to 'tell' suggests the necessarily figural, illogical status of metamorphosis in a different way from the cony-catching explanation of *The Blacke Dogge*.

Brown's foregrounding of the importance of the *Metamorphoses* as a perhaps dubious but also powerful resource with which to imagine change and modernity is illuminating in distinct ways with regard to *The Blacke Dogge* and *Midsummer Night's Dream*. The *Dogge*'s hybrid generic structure pits against one another the complexity of subjective experience and the formal categories of dream vision and cony-catching narrative, even poetry and prose. The 'discord' of *Midsummer Night's Dream* is both resolved as 'concord' in marriage, and threatening in the status of the mechanicals' play as addendum and the frightening potential of the marriage of Theseus and Hippolyta. Yet, if *The Blacke Dogge*'s use of dual, arguably contradictory, genres makes it 'fragmentary, disjunctive and self-subverting' and *A Midsummer Night's Dream* is contrastingly coherent in its careful play on concord and discord, yet the material it presents is also deeply, and emphatically, disjunctive between the foregrounded possibilities of tragedy and comedy.[74]

The evidence presented here has several implications. The logic that links these two texts as uses of classical transformation also invites us to look again at the critical field in which they have been received. If, as Charles Martindale argues, '[w]hat else could (say) "Virgil" be other than what readers have made of him', the active, if arguably indirect or highly mediated, use of classical texts must imply both close study of examples and analysis of their implications.[75] While the theoretical aspects of reception studies wholly endorse drawing together texts that put to work classical texts such as Ovid's *Metamorphoses* and in so doing hybridise those materials in such a way that the reception of classical texts is not, necessarily, separated from vernacular and religious questions, nevertheless the practice of reception studies tends understandably to isolate the classical text as the one read and works with texts located as elite culture. Liz Oakley-Brown and Siobhán McElduff extend this analysis beyond the boundaries of masculine high culture. Oakley-Brown pursues questions of reception to previously unexplored areas of early modern culture, looking at the reception of Ovid in, for example, needlework. McElduff examines the readers in eighteenth-century hedge schools.[76] Such work productively turns away from an agreed canon of reception towards an investigation of what is more often understood as 'popular' or vernacular culture.

If, as this suggests, we can track metamorphosis far from any imagined point of origin, then *Midsummer Night's Dream* and *Blacke Dogge of Newgate* both use metamorphosis directly and evoke it as a sketchy, uncertain, presence. They use it to articulate experience. Each is a text that seems to imagine an audience well beyond an elite and we know that both theatre audiences and the recipients of pamphlet news and stories included many who could not read in the vernacular – both texts were potentially heard and read, mixed with other kinds of stories, verbal and – in stage play and wood-cut, visual in their intertextuality with other known stories and images. With others, Ovidian stories clearly carry ideas far beyond the reach of Latin texts or even of vernacular versions. We see the mechanicals reading and using Golding's Ovid for themselves and re-presenting it to a sneering elite. At the same time as witnessing a circuit of reception, mediated by Golding's Ovid, our own encounter with the play is with a fairly promiscuously mixed set of stories – classical, folkloric and courtly. Perhaps such an encounter is akin to the fluid mixture of classical and other influences McElduff finds in the hedge-school as we move amongst the folkloric, fairy and frightening. At the same time, in working with Ovid both texts were aware of and probably use Arthur Golding's translation of Ovid's *Metamorphoses*. Before moving on to other texts of transformation, literary and non-literary, Golding's influential Englishing, shaping or ornamenting so many texts of transformation, demands discussion.

III Golding, Ovid and a 'dark philosophy of turnèd shapes'

'Of shapes transformed to bodies strange I purpose to entreat' (Bk I. 1). If poetry can be considered famous, this line famously begins Ovid's *Metamorphoses*. That this line is so well-known, though not this version, is substantially the work of Arthur Golding who delivered a full text to vernacular readers in 1567.[77] What Golding's motivations and markets might have been is a complicated question. The questions of classical reception raised by Golding's, and later George Sandys', Englishing of *Metamorphoses* have generated a large body of scholarship. Critical discussion is at present framed by Jonathan Bate's contribution to a long tradition of discussion of Shakespeare and, in a wider investigation, Raphael Lyne's illuminating reconsideration of the terms of Golding's work on Ovid. Lyne's discussion conveys Golding's achievement – the specificity and completeness with which Golding imported *Metamorphoses*, the nature of his paratextual and expanding interventions, and the 'distinctive flavour' of the vernacular.[78] To restate a key point, for this present project Golding's *Metamorphoses* is significant not in terms of a politics of Englishing (important as that is), but as material that was absorbed into, augmented and ignited other imaginative resources. It is significant as a complex, and for early modern readers, disturbing matrix of possibilities for the fate of the self and the body; as a resource of stories, and specifically stories of change. Moreover, as we find in subsequent chapters, Ovid in Latin and English was also a source of knowledge in the sense that what happens in the *Metamorphoses* could be taken very seriously and literally. For instance, it could be cited by investigators of the natural world as almost forensic evidence.[79] As we have already seen, the transformations described and enacted in the *Metamorphoses* took on a life of their own for audiences, who, clearly found them compelling and ensuing chapters explore these other kinds of writing on transformation. However, before plunging into the many other understandings of metamorphosis, we can briefly examine the issues and problems that concerned Golding and Sandys, and their attempts to regulate the ways on which readers took hold of these amazing tales.

One of the most significant ways Golding set the terms on which the texts were used was his movement of the *Metamorphoses* to England, with English fruits and flowers.[80] This decision to translate the world as well as the word is a distinctive feature of Golding. We can speculate, of course, on the relationship between Golding insisting Ovid be at home in the English countryside, so that bacchants rub shoulders with native fairy folk, lying at the heart of his being so at home for the mechanicals of *A Midsummer Night's Dream*. We can also speculate that the decision to relocate the text so fully may have been a factor precipitating Golding's consideration of readers and reading in his framing and introducing of his text.

In his preface to the 1565 translation of the first four books Golding described Ovid's work as 'outwardly most pleasant tales and delectable histories, and fraughted inwardly with most pithy instructions and wholesome examples'.[81] However, Golding later felt the need to comment on the terms on which pleasure might legitimately be taken from such tales; its nature; his own role as promulgator. For all that the *Metamorphoses* was made up of both 'exquisite cunning' and 'deep knowledge', in the 1567 translation of the whole work he chose both to give another, long, poetic dedication to Leicester and to supply an orientation 'To the Reader'. The Epistles of 1565 and 1567 were both dedicated to the Earl of Leicester and appeared before the address 'To the Reader'. The patron was encouraged to enjoy 'this same dark philosophy of turnèd shapes', 'wonderful exchange / Of gods, men, beasts and elements to sundry shapes right strange' and to understand that Ovid's argument concerning change is, first, that 'nothing under heaven doth aye in steadfast state remain' and 'that nothing perisheth, but that each substance takes / Another shape than that it had' (Bk VII. 14–15, 10–13). As Lyne argues, in responding to this idea, Golding's work produces a text that is moralised, in part, but in ways that are distinct from the medieval tradition of moralisation.[82] Golding's concern has been debated, particularly because of his revisiting of the 'Epistle' to his patron, and his attempt to give a compass to interpretation in his address 'To the Reader'.[83]

Golding does not, exactly, seek to play down the force of what metamorphosis can mean. Thus, where contemporary commentators on Ovid see the Pythagorean interlude as ironically framed, Golding's readers encounter Pythagoras as a strong statement of the thesis as before.[84] On the other hand, as we saw in the introduction, Golding was careful to integrate Pythagorean shifts into the Aristotelian three-soul model, carefully reserving man's special place in the Christian universe. As in the tendentious case of Pythagoras, Golding works to anticipate, even circumnavigate the problems his translation might generate. Insisting, 'I would not wish the simple sort offended for to be / When they in this book the heathen names of feignèd gods they see', reminding his actual readers, that the 'paynims' were ignorant of the 'true and everlasting God', and so 'bestow' the 'name of gods on creatures' (1–4). Of course, the paynims might have been unaware of God, but nonetheless they were existing in Christian time and one of the results of Adam's fall was the falling away of religion such that birds, strangely shaped rocks, ghosts and 'every strange and monstrous thing for gods mistaken were' (17). Recognising this parlous situation the one true God allowed men to sink into their own sin which includes a wanton wallowing in such stories and the bad behaviour of the gods. By reminding the reader of the true, Christian, time-scheme of the *Metamorphoses* Golding simultaneously institutes a moral framework and emphasises that his readers, aware that they live in Christian time, have a responsibility to interpret both the world and the text.

Golding's vernacular readers are Christians, but potentially 'simple', too. His discussion begins by imagining 'simple' readers. Clearly, an address to a vernacular reader belongs with the translation of a full text because such readers need the whole. The development of the connotations of 'simple' suggests a mildly moral, ecclesiastical, force in the word in the medieval and Tudor period. Simple readers and listeners were at the heart of the church. Golding seems to see these readers as a cohort within the body of readers who lack Latin, and ensures that any reader would find the full-text vernacular *Metamorphoses* addressed to and framed for both an aristocratic patron and the vernacular reader. As Eugene Kintgen's work implies, Golding was probably right to see it as hard to gauge and anticipate the training of a 'simple' vernacular reader – such readers were, indeed, diverse.[85] As Latinate readers would be aware, a vernacular readership also lacks the reading disciplines and comparative range supplied alongside education in the classics. So, from a marketing perspective Golding shows the reader that a translation is for all; invites vernacular, 'simple' readers to participate in the classical club while warning them that it is not intended for them and offering models for reading. He also shows the Latinate readers that they are discriminated from the simple, but the simple readers face the same problems of moral navigation of the text.

Interpretation and the stakes of reading are the terrain of paratexts. However, Golding's discussion of the topic is markedly prolonged. We readers are reminded that, besides offering a reminder to remember the true God and his laws, the gods of *Metamorphoses* express qualities. Mars, for example, stands for 'valiant men of war' (62). Above all, how a contemporary reader responds is a test. Thus, 'whoso doth attempt the poets' works to read' needs a steady judgement (139–40):

> Some naughty person, seeing vice shewed lively in his hue,
> Doth take occasion by and by like vices to ensue;
> Another, being more severe than wisdom doth require,

> Beholding vice (to outward show) exalted in desire,
> Condemneth by and by the book and him that it did make
> And wills it to be burnt with fire for lewd example sake
>
> (143–8)

A better reader, though, Golding insists, understands that 'when thou read'st of god or man, in stone, in beast or tree, / It is a mirror for thyself thine own estate to see' (81–2). Thus, for the illumination of those who 'give themselves to filthy life and sin', the *Metamorphoses* shows immoral behaviour as leading to transformation to beastly shapes, 'So was Lycaon made a wolf' and 'Jove became a bull' (94–5). For, indeed, men are not beasts – 'Our soul is we, endued by God with reason from above' (103).

In a brief animal simile Golding fables clever readers as bees and spiders. His prescription is for the reader to gather wisdom like a bee, taking 'these works as fragrant flowers most full of pleasant juice.' These fertile drops 'the bee, conveying home, may put to wholesome use /And which the spider, sucking on, to poison may convert' (164–5). Golding clearly situates responsibility for the use of the text with the reader, but in a notably active process. Both spider and bee readers carry the text's fruits away to another context, reprocessing them to put them to 'use'. The moral use of Ovid is external to the text – 'to the pure' all is 'clean', whereas the 'corrupt' can taint even the best (167, 170). The text itself demands readers because, as Golding conveys, reusing the phrase 'turnèd shapes' we found in his address to his patron, it is full of mysteries, advice, examples and pleasure:

> ... in no one of all his books, the which he wrate, do lurk
> Mo dark and secret mysteries, mo counsels wise and sage,
> Mo good examples, mo reproofs of vice in youth and age,
> Mo fine inventions to delight, mo matters clerkly knit,
> No, nor more strange variety to show a learnèd wit.
>
> (186–90)

Using an example from Ovid, Golding ends by emphasising that the responsibility of reading rests with the interpreter alone:

> If any stomach be so weak as that it cannot brook,
> The lively setting forth of things describèd in this book,
> I give him counsel to abstain until he be more strong,
> And for to use Ulysses' feat against the mermaids' song.
> Or if he needs will hear and see and wilfully agree
> (Through cause misconstrued) unto vice allurèd for to be,
> Then let him also mark the pain that doth thereof ensue,
> And hold himself content with that that to his fault is due.
>
> (215–22)

Strangely, of course, the logic here produces Ulysses, who (wisely) refused to hear the sirens' song, as both the weakest and strongest reader. Intriguingly, though, Golding does seems to in part anticipate the many spheres of knowledge which his text would enter – from 'wit' to natural philosophy. Golding's strong and literal insistence on the moral pedagogy of the *Metamorphoses*, his Christianising of temples and adaptation to Christian vocabulary was accompanied by a verse form found by critics to be unwieldy and a very specific and located vernacular which expands the range of language used. Besides the explicit emphasis on the reader's responsibility, Golding's thoughts about his reader convey subtler messages: he shows by example that Ovid's own stories can be used to make moral points. At the same time, he allows the richness, ornamentation, copious and even excessive nature of Ovid's text to emerge (more dark, wise, full of examples) and feels the dangerous yet beneficial pleasures of strangeness and 'turnèd' shapes. The nature of Golding's response hints at the possibility that readers will see him, as well as Ovid, as the agent of their corruption (corruption being something which his forceful denials strongly suggest he saw as a potential of the text) and, as we will explore, Golding was right to anticipate that the stories in the English form he gave them would reach a huge number of readers, fit and unfit in Golding's terms, but also listeners, storytellers, dreamers, natural philosophers, doctors, travellers.

In what follows the *Metamorphoses* is often present, often in Latin or in Golding's version, and applied to a situation. For the texts in ensuing chapters, just as for *Midsummer Night's Dream* and *Blacke Dogge of Newgate*, the *Metamorphoses* offers vernacular knowledge in many registers – forensic, philosophical, poetic. We will see Ovid cited and explored. Whether the users are spiders or bees is hard to judge but, certainly, their relationship with the text is one focused on the work it can do for them.

The texts encountered in the chapters that follow have absorbed Ovid and quite often show their readers Ovid in Golding's version. Sandys' version is, in a way, for the purposes of this study one of those responses or uses. Almost a century after Golding began publishing, George Sandys translated the *Metamorphoses* at sea, and in the startling new world of Virginia, and he, too, sought to shape text for readers and readers for Ovid within a significantly different, though overlapping, sense of Englishing. For Sandys, the main aim of 'publishing of Books' is 'to informe the understanding, direct the will, and temper the affections.' Accordingly he finds in 'Ancient authors the Philosophicall sense of these fables of Ovid'.[86]

He writes that, '[A]s they expressed their Conceptions in Hieroglyphickes, so did they their Philosophie and divinitie vnder Fables and Parables'. This use of fable was 'not untried by the sacred Pen-men, as by the prudent Lawgivers, in their reducing of the old World to civilitie, leaving behind a deeper impression, than can be made by the little precepts of Philosophie.' Sandys here makes fable into a powerful educational and ideological tool, able in the past to discipline whole states.

The twin questions of 'fable' and of visual or plastic presence, are crucial for Sandys and the busy plates expressing the episodes of each Book are vital testimony to the way the stories had come to life in English culture:

> For thy farther delight I have contracted the substance of every Booke into as many Figures (by the hand of a rare workman and as rarely performed . . .) since there is between Poetry and Picture so great a congruitie; the one called by *Simonides* a speaking Picture, and the other a silent Poesie: both Daughters of the Imagination, both busied in the imitation of Nature, or transcending it for the better with equall liberty[.]

For Sandys, the painter is able to represent not only actions but, 'making their Passions, and Affections speake in their faces; in so much as he renders the lively Image of their Minds as well as of their Bodies'. Certainly, the densely peopled scenes of the illustrations offer a development of the interior effects of transformation which sometimes exceed the enigmatically concise comments of the text.

Sandys is with Golding in seeing Ovid as 'shewing the beautie' of 'Vertue' and the 'deformitie' of 'Vice'. By contrast with Golding, he even asserts that it is 'apparent' that 'the Heathen preserved the truth of the immortalitie of the Soule' and as a negative counterexample he gives Epicurus, characterised as opposing the immortality of the soul and as having favoured a ban on poetry. In response, while Sandys has consistently tried to demonstrate the fabular value of the stories, he has not done so by close and analytical method but by drawing on the different ways in which the stories have been taken. Sacred history, he suggests, has been his guide to making clear the 'loose and broken fragments' of the actual historical narrative bound up with 'instructing Lythologies' by the ancient poets. For him, both 'Heroycall,' and 'Fabulous' tales can by this be situated in the period between the creation and the flood. Thus, he has (as appropriate) 'given a touch of the relation which those fabulous Traditions, have to the divine history' at the same time as maintaining commentary as neither excessive for 'the ordinary Reader' nor 'too obvious' for the learned. A similar approach governs the translation where he seeks neither to overfreight the text nor deprive the 'mere English reader' of clarifying marginal notes. Finally, as with Golding, he acknowledges the text's pleasurable copiousness.

The attention each writer pays to shaping the path of the 'turnèd' bodies and 'fabulous deformities' into English culture foregrounds as a major concern of contemporaries two of the main themes of this book – the interrelationship of sacred, classical and vernacular (oral, folkloric but also printed) tales of transformation and, secondly, the diverse ways in which the Latin tale of transformation might be put to work dynamically, and uncontrollably, within that culture. Golding seems to have known, or felt, more intensely than Sandys that any and many sorts of readers, could and would use his text. Just as Ariel in *The Tempest* blends natural and supernatural transformations of the body in death, there were readers who might use Ovid to work a linguistic magic of their own. Golding, particularly, struggled with the knowledge that readers of an Englished Ovid were indeed going to read and be damned – that is, take the text and its pleasure on their own terms. Golding, particularly, was aware of what Charles Martindale's discussion has more recently reminded us to keep in mind – the use of a text is transitive – active – and, in Golding's terms (though not Martindale's) such taking up of the text is likely to be unruly.

The powerful quality of Ovidian narratives of transformation for '*the mere English reader*' was recognised by both Golding and Sandys who in their different ways tried to anticipate and shape readers and users of the work, while at the same time offering them delight in change. Each recognised that change as found in the *Metamorphoses* is far, far from the limits and possibilities of change prescribed by Christian doctrine. The texts using them, as we see, are less concerned with limits and strictures than possibilities. As a decade when, while Elizabeth aged, social and political change was anticipated, the 1590s supply a logical starting place for the study of transformation. In social, political and literary terms, both the reception of Ovid specifically and the cataclysm of the Reformation, or Reformations, earlier in the century underlie these developments in enigmatic but shaping ways. Golding was, himself, deeply engaged with the project of reformation. The effects of the Reformation were inescapable and some of these are explored in the next chapter. Golding's Englishing of Ovid provides perhaps the most significant point to start discussion of the ways in which classical transformation was used and how the influence of his translation, conveying the whirling shapes of Ovid's bodies changed, clearly extended and reshaped the imaginative resources of vernacular writing.

IV Turning Ovid

Let us return to the question of what literary evidence suggests about the presence of metamorphosis in late sixteenth-century culture and society. The vernacular use of classical transformation in *A Midsummer Night's Dream*, *The Blacke Dogge of Newgate* and Golding's vernacular Ovid invite both re-evaluation of the work that material did in culture and consideration of how it is approached. Each text has been the object of literary study, but from very different points of view. Each text suggest, in different ways, that Ovid's *Metamorphoses* was culturally significant both in terms of citation (referentiality, quotation, ornamentation) and absorption ('sources' and hauntings in *A Midsummer Night's Dream*; the use of metamorphosis to link subjective and social pain in *Blacke Dogge*; Golding's movement to make Ovid an English voice). The texts can be contrasted in terms of Golding's endeavour to keep control over the terms on which metamorphosis was read.

Golding meditated on Englishing and attempted to know and, to an extent, control his readers, particularly his unlettered readers. Both *A Midsummer Night's Dream* and *The Blacke Dogge of Newgate*, in different ways, give evidence that Ovid, mainly but not only through Golding, was indeed taken up by a wide audience. *A Midsummer Night's Dream* arguably 'Englishes' Ovid in its own way, whereas in *The Blacke Dogge* we see metamorphosis experienced as an imaginative and literary correlative for the pain of the subject, in the prose reworkings we see uncertainty about how far a vernacular audience is ready to receive the message of pain through the medium of metamorphosis. In each case, we see Ovidian metamorphosis understood as potentially available to the very widest range of readers and auditors.

The most fruitful critical debate on vernacular reception theory attempts not to control but to comprehend the scope of reading and this has facilitated this chapter's concern with the specific question of changes in the thinking on the 'reception' of classical texts of transformation in sixteenth- and seventeenth-century English thought and writing.[87] As Charles Martindale reminds us, the strand of reception studies which focuses on classical reception responds to the intensity with which classical scholarship had embraced the earlier critical orthodoxy of a desired encounter with 'the reified text-in-itself'.[88] Responding to Martindale's incisive discussion of the folly of this desired encounter with the 'holy of holies', a text whose meaning is 'placed beyond contingency', classical scholarship has embraced the importance of what people – writers, painters, dramatists, those responsible for the deployment of titles, translators, 'Englishers', and, above all, readers – *do* with texts. Martindale emphasises that the reader needs to be understood as always, in Roland Barthes' terms, 'transitive' rather than 'intransitive'– an active maker of meanings. In attempting to rescue the reader 'plunged into idleness' by the apprehension of the text as to be read not 'as it comes', or in the contexts of its publication, but to 'roll back the years' to find an imagined, original, 'gleaming, pristine purity'.[89] As Martindale and Philip Hardie note, Virgil's writings, the *Aeneid* especially and in a different way the *Eclogues*, are critical cases. When Hardie asserts that epic is a 'totalizing form' it is 'at the same time driven obsessively to repetition and reworking' he puts the agency of reinterpretation in the genre itself, but nevertheless conveys succinctly the sense of reworking, challenge and expansion of epic as a characteristic of Renaissance and classical approaches to epic.[90]

In a similar development scholars of the classical tradition in the Renaissance have revisited the assumed narrative of the Renaissance 'rediscovery' of the classics. As Craig Kallendorf emphasises in a summary of recent discussion, to simply accept the claim that the classics were 'reborn in the Renaissance' is to accept at face value the period's own mythmaking.[91] As Jean Seznec has shown, important as the classical tradition was for the Renaissance it was neither as fully distinguished from medieval materials as has sometimes been assumed (indeed it used those medieval materials) and, moreover, the compilers used late and early sources and often preferred more recent over ancient sources.[92] Malcolm Bull, again working primarily on images and objects of the Italian Renaissance has argued that – importantly – in the Renaissance, 'mythological imagery was not really in competition with Christian art' and that it was 'initially heavily concentrated in the decorative arts where no one took it seriously'.[93]

In putting together classical and other 'reception' this chapter has aimed to respond to Martindale's important insight that our very ability to read classical texts, on whatever terms, is built from 'the chain of receptions through which their continued readability has been effected' – there are many different kinds of use.[94] Specifically, that scholarship within reception studies, including the work of Liz Oakley-Brown and Siobhán McElduff, has begun to press 'reception' towards its logical areas of investigation – what might, by some standards, be called 'distant' reception enables us to sharpen our understanding of the materials under discussion in this chapter and facilitates understanding of the roles of classical reception in what follows.[95] Such work can be characterised as taking us to the borders of reception studies, potentially taking us away from 'high' culture and towards an investigation of what is more often understood as 'popular'.[96]

It is as in this grey area, this borderland of reception, that what follows in much of this study is best located. The findings of this chapter show metamorphosis rapidly absorbed into a receptive vernacular culture. As we will see in coming chapters, writers and thinkers reaching for their Ovid seem to be confident, not troubled. They are confident that readers will see why they use it, for example, to express enigmatic, tangled or disturbing problems – such as monstrosity. Therefore, in considering the uses to which Ovid's *Metamorphoses* found itself being put, I take my cue from Antonio Gramsci's discussion of the popular song as neither written for, nor by, 'the people' but 'which the people adopt because they conform to their way of thinking and feeling.' Gramsci argues that 'what distinguishes a popular song within the context of a nation and its culture is . . . the way in which it conceives the world and life'.[97] Evidently, classical tales of transformation find their way into a social and political world in a different way from popular songs in an age of mass production. Nevertheless, Gramsci's comment, like reception theory, invites us to consider how something is used and, above all, asks us to think about not only individual uses in a wide range of locations but also to ask whether they disclose dynamic connections amongst them – as a princess or a pauper might, differently, hum a popular tune or use a line from a popular song as a way to name and consider the world.[98] In terms of its location in culture, the classical metamorphoses investigated here are perhaps best understood as 'popular' or vernacular knowledge, in the sense discussed in the introduction as 'beliefs, literary and visual works, practices and festivities widely dispersed in society and in their appeal often . . . jumping barriers of birth'.[99]

Just as the texts discussed here suggest that the materials of the *Metamorphosis* existed and worked in vernacular culture in a range of both shallow and deep ways, deliberately used and unspokenly, perhaps sometimes unconsciously, it seems that Ovidian metamorphoses inhabited a range of cultural locations. Ovid might be used by elite humanists or by women embroidering. In embroidery, we find Ovidian material transferred from literary to visual form and so too in architectural ornament. Thus, in Haddon Hall in Debyshire we find above a fireplace a plaster relief, probably late sixteenth century, that places Orpheus not only amongst the heraldic emblems of the household (boars and peacocks) but in a wooded setting evocative of the castle itself, taming the beasts. Ovid, possibly through Golding, was lodged in the vernacular and the stories were, in this case at least, literally, built into the environment.

4 Plaster relief, Orpheus taming the beasts, Haddon Hall, Derbyshire (?late Tudor).

The case studies here have allowed us to consider the way in which classical texts can be seen at work in post-Reformation English culture, and crucially acknowledge the hybridised place of stories from Ovid. These developments invite us to acknowledge that there was indeed a highly hybridised reception of classical stories of transformation and so it makes sense to put together *The Blacke Dogge, Midsummer Night's Dream*, a fireplace depicting the taming of the animals by Orpheus. Following these cues, this chapter has attempted to both take the work done in vernacular texts by classical transformation as its main topic, and at the same time to suggest that we might find them in non-elite places, viewed and heard, if not commissioned and written, by servants as well as masters.

CHAPTER TWO

Sacred transformations: animal events

5 Cat, Edward Topsell, *Historie of Foure-Footed Beasts* (1607).

>looke upon these children, and sanctifie them with thy holy gost; that by this holesome laver of regeneration, whatsoever synne is in them may be washed cleane away[1]

With these words the minister implored God's regenerative and transforming grace for the new infant. In a ritual of separation and incorporation that started the life of each English Protestant, the infant was delivered by the father to the minister and passed on to the godparents who, as spiritual rather than corrupt and sexual agents, were to guide the child into education, community and full humanity. In this context transformation was something everyone in the sixteenth and seventeenth century had to consider; it was a foundation of their Christian life. As such, and as one of only two sacraments remaining from the pre-Reformation seven, baptism's power and importance can hardly be overstated. The infant's precarious hold on life, too, made baptism a matter of urgency.

Given the ceremony's importance why might a minister be suspected of jeopardising the ceremony by baptising a female infant 'in the church by the name of Fyndall'; why do the Sussex church archives reveal Peter Simons and Joan Goldyng being called to account for 'baptizing a catt'; why would a soldier in the Civil War be accused of urinating in a font? Such responses to baptism, and especially those using animals to replace or comment upon humans, are the subject of this chapter which asks what the reported events suggest about the transformative powers of baptism. That accusations of violation of the baptismal ceremony had a cultural life in seventeenth-century England is confirmed by Thomas Edwards' inclusion of it in his list of the errors of sectarian religion published in 1646. Error 104 reads: 'That Paedobaptisme is unlawfull and antichristian, and that it is as lawfull to baptize a cat or a Dog or a Chicken, as to baptize the infants of believers.'[2]

Baptism's huge claim was to enable the human to become fully Christian and that power was disputed. If the theologians controverted the nature of baptism, Laud's church courts sought out ministers who offended, and local civic and church authorities had possible animal rituals brought to their attention. We hear of many of the local objections via reports, courts and news and, although this is top down testimony, responses to baptism allow us to investigate not only the elite, but, to some extent, what people in different sectors of society thought happened, or should happen, at baptism. Baptism and its detractors, as well as those who protested against some other aspects of the church's rituals, were exploring how and what could change the human. Therefore, in asking what incidents of animal parody meant to contemporaries, this chapter starts from the assumption that such an event, especially one people troubled to perform or invent, report or record, might offer an index of fear or accusation, but might also articulate speculation and thought. Accordingly, what follows explores the role of representations of transformation and substitutions in debating the sacred, the Christian, and – perhaps, to a limited extent – the animal.

The kinds of metamorphosis involved include the changes claimed by baptism and other church ceremonies with the attendant question of how these change the individual. The place of the human in relation to these changes is addressed by the substitution of animals for humans. There is a great deal of evidence regarding such events. But what can such an actual or imagined substitution of animal for human imply? Let us start with a closer look at the ceremony of baptism before and after 1549.

I   1549: the beginning or the end of baptism?

Then let the Priest, loking upon the chyldren, say

> I commaunde thee, uncleane spirite, in the name of the father, of the sonne, and of the holy ghost, that thou come out, and departe from these infants, whom our Lord Jesus Christe hath vouchsaved to call to his holy Baptisme, to be made membres of his body, and of his holy congregacion. Therefore, thou cursed spirite, remember thy sentence, remember thy judgemente, remember the daye to be at hande wherin thou shalt burne in fyre everlasting, prepared for thee and thy Angels. And presume not hereafter to exercise any tyrannye towarde these infantes, whom Christ hath bought with his precious bloud, and by this his holy Baptisme calleth to be of his flocke.[3]

These words appear in the 1549 version of the ceremony of baptism. Just three years later they are gone and never return. Spoken by a minister in a ceremony that probably represents the most significant change in the life of the Christian, they closely echo the Roman rite and imply the devil's physical involvement in the infant body.[4] They seem to give an account of an unbaptised infant as actually evil rather than ready to be claimed for Christ. If exorcism was banished, a less violent language of transformation continues to inform the ceremony as resurrection is invoked; male infants were told God 'raised Lazarus from the tomb' and regeneration was a central concept in the new ceremony and in thinking on baptism.[5] Shifting towards Calvinist understandings of the sacrament as sign the baptismal liturgy in the Elizabethan form of 1559 lasted, with adaptations, until the *Directory of Worship* came into force, if not use, in January 1644–5 and it was the 1559 version that was reinstated, largely, in 1662.[6] The widest context for the changing liturgy, and for the texts and events questioning it, is the increased hermeneutical emphasis of the Renaissance and Reformation. However, the tensions and contradictions in 'reformation' were worked out at parish level. Baptism, both as acted in parish ceremonies and discussed throughout the church hierarchy, was a ceremony of transformation and promise, but also grubbily enmeshed in theological, social and political controversies.

The process of the reformation of baptism began with Thomas Cranmer's first, broadly Lutheran, *Book of Common Prayer* (published under Edward VI) which retained only two sacraments: the eucharist and baptism. Yet within the liturgy of baptism much of the Roman rite remained, including exorcism and the sign of the cross.[7] Baptism was deeply debated, but the Calvinist understanding of a sacrament as a sign only, not a mystery in which a physical state might be transformed, was influential and Cranmer moved towards this second understanding in his prayer book of 1552. Between 1553 and 1559 infants were again exorcised and dipped as at Edward's death the devotional heart of the Roman church was restored: the mass. Yet church lands were not returned, the Bible remained in English: language and economic base remained unmoved.[8] Anyone who had turned back to the old way of worship found that completely superseded by Elizabeth's prayer book of 1559, a modified version of the 1552 liturgy. James I brought in changes in 1604 and Charles's highly, perhaps, for him, fatally, controversial Scottish version appeared in 1637. The biggest change was marked by the *Directory of Worship*. Charles II's *Book of Common Prayer* stands as some kind of epilogue marking a gradual slide from the promise, or threat, of reform to an uneasy truce. The 1662 compromise emerged from a century of work to improve the intricate symbolic story implied and orchestrated in the Sarum Manual.

In the Sarum Manual an infant was 'passed from the profane world to the sacred through the hands of the many personnel involved', with each transfer happening at a 'ritually defined point'.[9] The coherence of the ceremony seems to have meshed with the world beyond for, among the Roman sacraments, baptism drew to itself a substantial number of extra beliefs and social functions. Customs and beliefs included that a child needed to be baptised to *survive*; that baptism might restore sight; that it should be done on particular days. More significantly, perhaps, under the Roman church the ceremony of baptism itself tended to slide into adjacent contexts. The caul with which the infant was born was baptised. Animals were regarded as benefiting from baptism. And women in labour were sometimes exorcised.[10] Under Catholicism, the seven sacraments had been supplemented and echoed by sacramentals – rites in which precious materials associated with sacred ritual functioned beyond the confines of the building, bringing good to the community.[11]

Under Protestant dispensations, as the emphasis shifted decisively to faith and word, such rites and practices were reframed as magic and superstition.[12] However, evidence suggests that elements of the associated customs survived locally. In the seventeenth century Robert Parker complained, 'Doe we not crie out upon the Doves let downe of old upon the baptized (one of which I saw at *Wickam* not abolisht some 25 yeeres past) for a signe of regeneration by the spirit?' He went on to argue that the sign of the cross made in baptism was as displaying 'a paire of Bulls hornes' as the 'signe of Christes death'.[13] Clearly, the appearance of liturgical stability given by baptism's continued presence as a sacrament is hugely qualified by internal changes which transformed what had actually happened and, as we shall see, by attendant controversy. It endured, but it did so as a focus for conflict.

Part of what left the question of the rite of baptism a live issue was that the Church kept two ceremonies – 'public' baptism in which the infant was brought to the church and baptised for all to see and 'private' baptism. If the church was not to allow infants to die unbaptised, private baptism, in which the child was hurriedly and privately baptised, was a necessary provision. However, private baptism seems to have been used for many reasons beyond the urgent need to baptise a fragile infant. People wondered what might have passed at such ceremonies where, at first, the women of the birthing room – the un-churched mother, the midwife – potentially have control over the administration of a sacrament. Perhaps some women, pushed, like poor Lady Frances Aburgauennie, to tell God: 'I feele thy promised punishment... iustlie pronounced against me, and the whole generation of Adam', had some clear incentives to turn again to the old ways.[14] James I put a stop to women baptising and the *Directory* affirmed that ministers alone could baptise and so, in an emergency, a minister had to be found.

However, it was not only the ceremony itself, or the way it might be done that was in question but also, for some, the very nature of the infant and his or her susceptibility to baptism. Taking the subject as its starting place, the debate on baptism canvassed the humanity of the infant in terms of discretion and rationality. Some of those who rejected infant baptism did so because if grace was determined by faith alone then baptism was an outward sign, rather than an agent, of change. For these people it would be superstition indeed to see the infant as having faith, whereas for others, baptism was the starting gun for education – only a baptised subject could reap the fullest benefits of literacy.[15] As Fudge notes, in her 'legacy', Dorothy Leigh insists that part of the duty of a godparent is 'to give you his faithfull word that the child shall be taught to read so soon as it can conveniently learne'.[16] Contrastingly, at the start of the century, though, Lady Margaret Hoby had doubts. After dinner:

talkinge with Mr Daunie, who inuited me to be a witness at his childes baptisinge, which I refused, in regard that my Conscience was not perswaded of the charge I was to undertake, nor Thoroughly taught touchinge the paruartinge [perverting] the end of witnesses from a christiane instetutione... siuell pollicie: but I will inquire more of this if I may, any friend such a Curtesie[17]

We don't know what Hoby decided at this point.

In sum, the sixteenth- and seventeenth-century changes to the ceremony of baptism chart its progress as a disputed ceremony in regard to its very power and efficacy; the form in which it should happen; the question of who is an appropriate subject to be baptised; the place it should occupy in religious but also social discourse. Underlying each precinct of dispute is the claim of baptism to change the creature into a potential Christian – a change repeatedly invoked, as we will see in the discussion of wild children. It was felt by some that baptism remained too close to the old ritual which itself was close to, or was, sorcery. Questions over the nature of private baptism were pressing. Most important, probably, was a growing debate about whether the infant was a suitable subject for baptism. To this we can add discontent with the officers of the church; anger at particular circumstances; jokes against people and ceremonies; nostalgia for the old ways – and fear of their return. It is not surprising, then, that a ceremony which cannot avoid making a huge claim in terms of changing the individual, in whatever terms that change is understood and which had theological, liturgical and concrete social and civic implications, should be a lightning rod for controversial events or ceremonies asking about the possibility that, indeed, the ceremony was not working.

The troubling question of whether, and how, the Christian was remade by baptism implied the opposite possibility that the creature might remain merely that, a beast, or, possibly, be damned as the presence of exorcism implied though subsequent teachings denied. It is clear that the possibility that Christians were making beasts of themselves, whether through misapplied ceremonies or over-zealous change, feeds into the use of animals in rituals parodying both baptism and other church ceremonies. Yet it may also be the case that the strong association of baptismal adjuncts with the fostering of animal well-being echo, also, in such ceremonies. Both, opposed, positions rely on the ready availability of animals and various forms of anthropomorphism. Some of these factors are present in Nehemiah Wallington's account of some drunks, 'inflamed with liqor', who 'would needs do something to be talkt on' in Eyam, Derbyshire:

the church dore being open, they drove a cowe into the church: and that which is appointed for churching a woman they read it for the cow and led her about the font: a wicked and horrible fact[18]

Wallington notes humour; the cow's milky association with maternity is assumed; the ceremony is travestied; the font is ridiculed. Maybe women are insulted, maybe, though, the ceremony of churching is mocked. For Wallington, writing in the 1630s, the point is that the drunkards who did this were punished by God. The point for the participants is more enigmatic.

Underlying this instance and the other animal events is the sense that, substituted for the human, the animal shows up something about ritual, or a person. Implicitly, these events can comment on the Book of Common Prayer, ceremonial practice and the nature of the human; they draw on a reservoir of understandings about the distinctions between animal and human and about the way those might be eroded. The participants may not be fully aware of the philosophical or natural philosophical investigations into animals and humans, but the consistent use of animal–human comparisons in these events suggest an anxiety concerning that border and the movement between animal and human – as evidenced in physical resemblance, quarrelling, speech and sound. Clearly, the animal–human distinction is contested and insisted upon as transformation generates both ritual and anxiety. In the early modern world such a ceremony can draw on daily and hourly, concrete, relations between human and non-human animals.[19]

In these ceremonies we can see analogy and anthropomorphism operating as ways of thinking that make the animal available in symbolic discourse. The old religion, the animal, sorcery jostle for our attention. The erasure of exorcism from the Protestant ceremony of baptism seems to have been an incomplete purge. It may have directly effected the bringing of disavowed animal rituals to roost in the church itself – that is a matter of speculation. Clearly enough, though, the eccentric pawprints of animal baptism take us rapidly to a politics of memory and forgetting central to Reformation cultural debates.

This section has taken time to outline the complex liturgical and social place of baptism as it was repeatedly redesigned after 1549. What follows examines the responses to the controversial claims of baptism to change the subject. Rather than surveying theological attitudes and doctrines, or attempting to dissect the precise meanings of the sacramental and liturgical language of early modern England, the rest of the chapter examines reactions and moments at which we can see that events apparently occurring or imagined at the margins of society are joined by strong threads to mainstream cultural changes. In taking texts as evidence of relationships amongst forms of representation often understood as distinct and analysed using distinct methods, the chapter canvasses events taken to be the domain of social historians and texts understood as the preserve of literary critics.[20] Seeking to understand specific ways in which sixteenth- and seventeenth-century people thought about sacred transformation by using animal substitutions, images and figures will lead us to wider questions of how controversy was articulated in distinct locations and levels of that society, and how far those ostensibly distinct locations were related. We can start with what seem to be the 'hot' moments and places of animal transformation in the first part of the seventeenth century – a largely, but not exclusively, Western adventure – and then consider the status of animal transformation in the courts, anecdotes and newspapers of the Civil War.

II Dogs for bishops

In 1599, newly appointed Bishop of Exeter, William Cotton found animal symbolism part of a vibrant scene:

> A dangerous increase of Papists about the coasts and country. Profane Atheists: A matter very common to dispute whether there be a God or not. A slender and loose observation of the Sabbath and holy days. Many hundred stand wilfully excommunicate, not caring for their absolution or for coming to church. There was ridiculous and profane marriage of a goose and a gander. A cat having an apron, and a partlet, brought to the church to be baptised. A horse head at Launceston lately lapped in a mantle and brought to the church for baptism, and afterwards the bell told and rung out for the death of this head. A dead horse brought to the communion table with its feet spread upon it, as being prepared to receive the Sacrament. A young youth of 16 years baptised by the name of Gurlypott, at which time the font was overthrown. Libels made upon every sermon almost in every town.

Nominated Bishop of Exeter in 1598, William Cotton had arrived there on 15 May 1599. On 31 January 1600 he wrote to Robert Cecil, complaining about the 'intolerable wildness and wickedness of the country' and enclosing this 'brief of some of the disorders'.[21] Under the headings of 'common disorders' (housing instances of the abuse of baptism), 'Abuse of the Ministers', 'Schism' and 'Disorderly behaviour', Cotton seeks to demonstrate immediate and troubling challenges to the church's authority.

Accordingly, he forwards a joke that asks why it is preferable to 'hang up' all ordained ministers than all dogs (answer: because the bishop always makes more prelates, whereas the supply of dogs might be exhausted). He says that 'many men' have 'three wives'. Deeper still into the presentation of Exeter as a world of criminal carnival reversal, Cotton asserts that a minister 'was made to kiss the bare hinder parts of a man'. There is bigamy, incest, and it is 'a common matter' to break into churches at night, and 'pull up pews to dig men out of their graves as if there were no law or government.' He concludes that 'these and many such abuses cannot be redressed by a due course of law' and begs to be sent 'an Ecclesiastical Commission'.[22]

Appointed bishop at the end of a decade of war and hardship Cotton saw himself as a new broom.[23] Hatred of foreigners, harvest failures, rising prices, diseases including plague had taken their toll on the social and political fabric already torn by Reformation conflict and resistance met with an insistence on state security as the authorities – Privy Councillors, Justices of the Peace and churchmen – worried intensely about populism, schism, social revolt.[24] Unsurprisingly, given his persona as an agent of liturgical but also social discipline, Cotton presented parodies of baptism as part of a challenge to the authority of the new church but also as part of 'common' issues of discipline. Like the Somerset Justice of the Peace who wrote to Cecil in September 1596, complaining of abuses which he cannot 'leave unadvertised, thowghe I should hazard my lyef by it', Cotton also seems to have been using his discovery to promote his own reputation.[25] Cotton's zeal seems to have backfired. When, in 1606, Cotton points out to Cecil his 'plain and fair proceeding' in a matter of 'escheated tobacco' he also writes that 'Sir William Stroud's canvass against the Ecclesiastical Commission in Devon ... and your favourable respect of him made me fear the loss of your favour' and goes on to emphasise his excellent progress against 'recusants' and the 'peevish'.[26] Cotton reminds Cecil that he would have 'reformed by the help of that commission many factious preachers, and reclaimed many papists'.[27] Evidently unwilling to drop a point when he feels his grudge to be justified, Cotton's texts demonstrate a tenacity of position. At a more general level, his case shows that in the 1590s concern about the rituals of baptism and their contestation linked the centres of church and state to the distant margins and parishes of the realm. The wider literary culture of the late sixteenth century, too, offers less immediate, yet relevant, contexts for animal sacraments.

Records of Cotton's career show him zealous against Catholics, self-interested, intemperate.[28] Keen to guard his own position and maximise his gains, Cotton was also keen to censure others. While anti-Catholicism supplied rhetoric and patterns of thought for such ends, it was far from a mere cover for self-interest. One effect of anti-Catholic commitment of the kind Cotton shows is engagement, under a negative sign, with Catholic belief and practices – themselves sometimes in the same frame as witchcraft. In this context an association between animals, particularly cats, and baptism has historical lineage reinforced by aural associations. The term 'Cathari' to describe witchcraft associated it with the worship of the devil in cat form, and witches were thought to kiss the devil in cat form under the tail. Of course, witches were also strongly associated with crimes against children, carrying them off, devouring them, and, as a special duty of Satan's servants, killing those who remained unbaptised.[29] Such associations between cats and heterodox religious practices found ambiguous and ambivalent but also formal, printed, fictionalised, expression in *A Marvelous Hystory intitulede, Beware the Cat*.[30] For sale 'at the North Door of Paul's' some seven years before Bishop Cotton was ordained, and appearing in a fresh version in 1584, this offers a sophisticated recital of humans learning animal language and becoming privy to sinister tales of cats with supernatural powers. A carefully framed and unreliable narrator, the cleric 'Streamer', tells stories proving 'cats do understand us and mark our secret doings'.[31] Playing on a symbolic association between cats and devils, the irresistible pun on cat and Catholic, and the place of cats in physical and emotional intimacy in the household, the cats in this text are both diabolic and moral agents. Specific as Cotton's circumstances are, we can see that his 'own' use of animals in his writing as an index of religious, social and political turmoil – quite regardless of whether the events took place – as the existence of *Beware the Cat* suggests, Cotton's concerns about the reach and stability of Protestantism were widely shared.

    Between the very specific and the national, animal theatre seems to have been a particularly live mode of expression in the West country. Cats, particularly, through their apparently punning names and perhaps enigmatic presence in human affairs, seem to have had an accepted, naturalised association with religious controversy, superstition, witchcraft. Just as Cotton finds cats prominent in the symbolic vocabulary of opposition to the church, so, in 1617, Francis Ashley, a Justice of the Peace in the South West, records an animal outrage. A lifelong practitioner in the Middle Temple and with some literary aspirations, Ashley's main labour was as a JP in Dorset, with responsibility to make initial investigations by interviewing suspects and witnesses, and then if appropriate sending them forward either to the Assizes or the Quarter Sessions. On 15 April 1617

Ashley's path was crossed by one 'Richard Chrismas of Sidling, gentleman' who he puts down for £20.[32] This was a day on which at least nine other men seem to have been fined for 'interrupting the preacher of west Lulworth' or, 'giving him foul language' but Chrismas, not a shoemaker or husbandman but a 'gentleman', went further:

> Also he prophaned Religion by setting a catt on a post in Siding, saying he would make her preache as good a sermon as some of them; took a text out of the Corinth., pincht the catt by the ear and made her crye, saying that was a sermon, and that if 500 were at a sermon 480 of them were whores and knaves.[33]

The event was sufficiently serious or contentious for Ashley to follow up. On 25 April he records the examination upon oath of Catherin Savage the fifteen-year-old daughter of Richard Savage 'of Sydling gentleman'.[34] She attests that Richard Chrismas 'about the beginning of September last... tooke up a cat in Sydling street and sit it on a post and said he would make the cat preach'. He 'pincht' the cat 'by the eares' and 'when the cat cryed he said it was as good a sermon as etc., but named no body'. This was all also witnessed by Chrismas's wife and one Jasper Devenish the latter of whom corroborates Savage's account. While the exact target of the parody disappears (perhaps because possibly Chrismas or, more likely poor Catherin, or even Ashley himself has a strategic lapse of memory?) it seems likely that the evidence presented here refers to an actual incident. The two accounts are slightly, but significantly, different; the first suggests the inefficacy of preaching, condemning preachers and congregations together. The second account fits closely to the concerns of reformers and Puritans with the need for an appropriately trained preaching ministry, but a hint about where Chrismas stood on these issues can be found in Ashley's book. On 24 May 1617 Richard Chrismas was before Ashley once again, having been involved in anti-Puritan scuffling on 7 November.[35] Perhaps Chrismas's cat ceremony was motivated by anti-Puritan feeling. Although the main concern of contemporaries with whether the incident happened or not cannot be ours, it seems clear, too, that perhaps unlike Bishop Cotton, Francis Ashley was at pains to make certain that something had happened and found the critical essence of the ceremony all too clearly critical of the preacher.

The dynamic amongst Chrismas, the cat, the village and the justice suggest the complex local dramas we might anticipate that might be thrown up by anxiety about religious change. However, at least two cases show town and village events precipitating national responses. Thus, soon after

Ashley was pursuing apparently parodic animal substitution in Sydling, a more obscure, perhaps darker, version of animal ceremony was at issue in Brixham in Devon. In March 1618 the High Sheriff of Devon received what seems to be a repeated request for the apprehension of John Prowse who, Lennard Trivillian (probably Trevellyan) complains, 'some fewe yeares since' committed 'a wicked and hainous impiety' in the parish church at Brixham. It seems that the authorities have requested his apprehension to no avail and locals are invited to bear in mind 'his Majesty's pleasure, who will not suffer so notable a prophanacion and impiety' to 'escape unpunished'.[36] Reported still at large on 14 April, on 29 April he is caught and, with his associates and brother-in-law sent up to London.[37]

On 5 May the 'hainous impiety' is revealed by Trevellyan:

> Petition of Leonard Trevellyan to the Council. Has long awaited the trial of John Prowse, committed at his complaint for riding on horseback into church, offering to have his horse christened, hanging up his dead grandmother's hair in the market place, as that of an old witch, &c.[38]

Prowse, 'cutting off the haire from his grandmothers head; being buryed longe before and hanging the same up ... saying there hangs the haire of an ould witch noe other greater'.[39] Those who may have been hiding Prowse are discharged but his case goes first to High Commission 'soe farre as belongs to the jurisdiction of the court' and 'afterwardes' on to Star Chamber where assembled to hear Trevellyan's petition against Prowse, yeoman, are: 'Lord Archbishop of Canterbury, Lord Chancelor, Lord Treasorer, Lord Privy Sealke, Lord Chamberlen, Lord Bishop of Elie, Lord Zouche, Mr Chancelor of the Exchequer, Master of the Rolles, Sir Edward Coke'.[40] Prowse's outrage, then, seems to set in motion a game of cat and mouse in which his kinsmen and associates eventually allow him to be taken by the perhaps not very zealous Devon authorities and shipped to London where this strange offence is subject to the force of High Commission and Star Chamber together. Admittedly, Prowse had dug up and cursed his grandmother; his crime was not merely against church ceremony and furnishings. Yet, even so, the question of what happened here shows national authorities entangled in sorting out the details of local attitudes to church ceremony and, perhaps, the changes in religion. By 1618 the preoccupation of the Church with the minutiae of parish behaviour was drawing together local and national in canvassing what happened in a ceremony or event in order to discriminate what was Catholic, what Protestant, what witchcraft, and above all what was punishable. Notably, stooping to examine a detail, church and state are hand in hand in this case.

This text, like the others we have examined, suggests that we need to locate animal incidents in relation to wider questions. If Prowse riding into the church is very clearly a challenge to authority, then the attack on his grandmother as a witch, particularly given the way in which witch prosecutions tended to take in families, seems to contains a strange undertow of self-accusation.[41] First, though, any reader must wonder who thinks the grandmother is an old witch – the accused is reported as thinking so, but what we actually have is the report of the accuser. Secondly, the two threats (to baptise the horse and to hang up his grandmother's hair) seem here to be connected by their suggestion of supernatural powers – the powers documented as historically associated with baptism and the conjuring of familiars and spirits by witchcraft.

Like Cotton's protest, Chrismas' ceremony and Justice Ashley's intervention, Prowse's profaning, too, directs us to the testing of official powers and the complex web of connections between the scene of protest or accusation and the powers, systems and theological and liturgical debates involved. The reports of Prowse and of Chrismas beg the question of whether and how such counter-ceremonies attempt to set limits to, or challenge official power, and what might be the reach of such challenges. It is sometimes possible to estimate whether the effects of such an event or accusation are limited to a parodic moment or whether the ripples of disturbance endure and disperse. We know that Chrismas, for example, was involved in another affray about 'Puritans' and it does seems that animal events addressing baptism specifically but also the ministry more generally were often bound to wider social and political movements. Although the information we have does not often very fully disclose underlying motivations, it is possible to trace key religious debates in the events.

An example of the interweaving of events and high politics is the case of Sarah Peck, the wife of a mariner, and the massively expanded Court of High Commission in the early 1630s. This densely documented story snowballed so that eventually it unites in conflict clerics, secular and sacred justice, the royal court, and, possibly, a dog. It seems that a long-running dispute between parishioners and minister in Harwich was first registered by the High Commissioners for Causes Ecclesiastical in 1629 when on 9 February when we have a draft 'Certificate of Inhabitants of Harwich' to go to the High Commissioners for causes Ecclesiastical. It seems that this is a defence of John Peck, junior, sometime churchwarden against whom the minister William Innes has brought a suit 'for removing the pulpit in the chapel there'.[42] Matters escalated and in 1631 Sarah Peck was apprehended for baptising a dog and appointing 'godgaffers'.[43] The Harwich minister was again, or still, at loggerheads with his parishoners. Sarah Peck was found guilty but the parishoners and townspeople petitioned the King who referred the matter to secular hearing with a court headed by Earl Rivers and including Sir Harbottle Grimston. Upon examining Innes this hearing found that 'there was not any such act done or committed' but it 'was a mere fiction [?raised] &c as may appear from the manner of Mr Innes his proofs'.[44] For Earl Rivers and others no dog was baptised. On January 20 1632 the Commissioners for Causes Ecclesiastical wrote to the Council that:

> If the writers had not seen the subscription of such worthy persons, they should by the sharpness of the style and the harsh passages against Mr Innes, have conceived the paper to have proceeded from angry adversaries, and not from indifferent commissioners. They condemn a judgement pronounced by the writers upon Sarah Peck for profane christening of a dog.

The 'strangeness, insolency, and ill consequence of this proceeding by private men against the highest ecclesiastical court in England' is reprimanded and 'Sir Harbottle Grimstone, Sir John Barker, and Sir Thomas Bowwes were this day sent for by warrant'.[45] Grimstone and Bowes were called before High Commission and told their judgement was in 'derogation of sentence', but, nevertheless, 'seemed in words' to defend their action.[46]

From the point of view of the meaning of baptism, this incident shows how deeply controversial that ceremony was in the English reformed church. Although the Harwich controversy touches many other things, the blame for 'profane' misuse of baptism is thrown back and forth as an effective smear. If Sarah Peck has not baptised a dog, but Innes has invented the accusation this matters because, of course, in that case it is he who becomes the criminal; he, the minister, who imagines a ceremony that parodies the transformation of the infant, acting out the critique of paedobaptism in images that he must have calculated to be recognised. If he did make up the accusation then it was cleverly designed to show Peck as an extreme Puritan and, potentially, as inappropriately facetious about the church. No wonder that the High Commission were furious to read that, yes indeed, the secular judges thought that this scene was the invention of none other than the Harwich minister.

More generally, as this incident suggests, conflicts over the interpretation of reformed religion involve personnel from the unidentified actors of Cotton's accusations to the justices and, ultimately, to Charles I and his commissioners. Clearly, animal ceremonies and particularly animal baptism come up at moments when the nature and personnel of church administration are being challenged and when the meaning of church ceremonies are woven into wider issues of religious, political and social authority.

In 1599 Bishop Cotton may well have been an unwelcome innovator in his diocese and his career may have foundered on his excessive interest in making money. He may also have had reason to insist on his Protestant credentials as at least some members of his family seem to have been Catholic.[47] However, whether they happened or he invented them, the incidents Cotton conjures up share with the parody of preaching recorded by Ashley the characteristic that the animal-ritual came up at a point of conflict over local circumstances and wider church priorities. In 1632 we can imagine the beliefs, behaviours and punishments of church offenders were intensely disputed aspects of Laudian versus Puritan ideology.

What frames of reference help us to read these kinds of writing? These texts are in part helpfully understood as part of the texture of parish and local life discussed by Christopher Haigh. As he notes, while some incidents suggest moments of intensity and rage in the ongoing struggle over what it was to be a Christian, others were clearly japes. In yet other cases the point was the victim – the human mocked – and the church ceremony was the means not the aim of mockery.[48] Haigh's pluralistic interpretation must be set against the more systematic accounts of the two main commentators on the question of animal ceremonies. First is Keith Thomas, in his compendious, sociologically informed, study of the transformation of 'magic' into 'religion'. Thomas notes that baptism like other sacraments 'generated a corpus of parasitic beliefs' unclaimed by the Roman church and concludes, 'some of the numerous cases recorded in the sixteenth and seventeenth centuries of attempts to baptise dogs, cats, sheep and horses may . . . have reflected the old superstition that the ritual had about it a physical efficacy which could be directed to any living creature'.[49] The most recent historian to touch this material, David Cressy, disagrees with Thomas, arguing that Thomas's arguments are 'more ingenious than persuasive; none of the evidence points in that direction'. He contends that, rather, first 'large animals were valuable properties . . . Cats, by contrast, were lowly beasts'; second, '[t]here is simply no trace of the supernatural in any of the mock baptisms we have covered, but abundant evidence that they had their origin in horseplay.' Finally, he argues 'Nor can it be argued that travesties of the sacrament were signs of a disorderly society, ready to break out in revolt... They were provocations to outrage and affronts to religious decorum, but hardly acts of resistance or incitements to riot.'[50] Thus, although he agrees that they profane the sacraments, rather than being linked to any deeper meanings, these events are best seen as 'festive misrule – skylarking' with a 'fundamental innocency'.[51] While this account has an intuitive rightness for some of the incidents – such as people caught making jokes about John the Baptist in Chipping Norton – its purchase on the overall phenomenon is problematic.[52] First, it does not clarify why the supposed authors of these dramas were reported to the authorities (and not, as we have seen, always to the same authorities). Second, it leaves unexamined what the symbolism suggests about what might be being represented. Third, it suggests that popular misrule be separated from more profound social concerns and, further, seems to see such misrule as the preserve of a particular stratum of society. Notably, while Thomas' thesis concerning religion and magic means that he follows this thread to all parts of culture, Cressy's use of the idea of 'popular culture' tends to see the popular as a sphere in itself, distant from elite concerns.

Given that people took time to write down these incidents, they are likely to contain some clues as to ways to read them, both individually and perhaps as a group. While such events may seem to us eccentric, the fact that whether they happened or not, they were recognised, reiterated, and at times prosecuted and punished, indicates clearly that contemporaries had frameworks within which to interpret them. The same is suggested by the location of the stories in reports, trials, and later, in printed news. Given this it is possible to read these texts not, as exactly 'isolated and unusual' but, for those who performed, witnessed or imagined and wrote them, related to the dominant culture or perhaps to points of pressure in that culture.[53]

The trajectory of baptism within, and outside, the emerging English Church traced in the first section of this chapter allows us to focus on the points of social and political pressure. As we saw, while remaining a ceremony of transformation, baptism changed in its meanings and practices as attempts at reformation continued and were resisted. The ceremonies for baptism were lodged in the *Book of Common Prayer* which (like the landscape and church architecture) was in repeated revision subject to the partial erasure of meanings. The results were a rededication and remaking of meanings marked also by what had gone.

The scholarly debate on the question needs to be situated in the context of a disputed sacrament reissued in three Tudor books of common prayer, amended by James VI and I, and completely re-ordered in the Directory of Worship. To return to the scholarly debate in this context we see that Cressy, while acknowledging the importance of Protestant debates, tends to over-emphasise the element of 'skylarking' (clearly sometimes present) without thinking about the religio-political contexts underpinning such fun with beasts. Thomas, on the other hand, tends to emphasise the significance of Catholicism in relation to animal events in terms solely of survival, rather than both survival and reaction. It may also be the case that Thomas' assumptions better fit the early part of the period, Cressy's the later, but that the full span is better understood as involving a deep and changing involvement with an increasingly distant world of Catholicism, on the one side, and on the other an increasingly riven Protestant present. Thomas' model tends, perhaps, to see the post-Reformation period as uniform whereas in fact, as the material discussed so far demonstrates, the debate about what was transformed at baptism, and how that might happen, developed and intensified. Most certainly, we can see that the Reformation debates over baptism are self-consciously addressed throughout the first half of the seventeenth century. And, as we see, these events as they are reported can also be linked to other issues fiercely debated in England from the Reformation on into the mid-seventeenth century, particularly the need for a preaching ministry and the Laudian reforms. Overall, we can see such animal events as addressing Reformation changes – though they don't necessarily do so from a single perspective, they do share a lexicon and an iconography that allowed contemporaries to interpret them.[54] Baptism offers a helpful point of focus because it was a sacrament and as such was the focus of attention in the sequence of new books of Common Prayer which appeared. Baptism brings up quite specific questions, some of which concern baptism, some of which concern human versus animal status, some of which concern the relationship between central and centralising agents and institutions of church and state versus local protest. The powers of the church, within that particularly the sacraments, and within that especially the power of baptism to transform the human, were addressed using ceremonies which invited the viewer to reconsider church practices. The Civil War brings a renewed focus on baptism and a spate of incidents using the vocabulary of animal parody that we have seen established. With the changes in circumstances the evidence is both juridical and, significantly, the swirling popular print of news and controversy.

III Error 104: Horse-baptism, news and Civil War

When the Earle of *Essex* was at *Lostithiell* in *Cornwall*, one of his Rebells brought a horse into that Church, led him up to the Font; made another hold him while himself took water and sprinkled it on the Horses head, and said *Charles I Baptize thee in the name of the Father, &c.* then Crossed his fore-head and said *I signe thee with the signe of the Crosse, in token thou shalt not be ashamed to fight against the Round-heads at London*; with a deale more such horrid blasphemy as no modest Christian is willing to repeat.[55]

So reports the royalist newsbook *Mercurius Aulicus* at the end of October, 1644. Aulicus emphasises that the event weaves together treason and blasphemy. Offending against the liturgy, the soldiers attack church and king. The accused is a parliamentary commander and, of course, a member of a famous and troubled dynasty. Aulicus takes analysis of the meanings of animal baptism to a limit in reminding readers that a challenge to the church's authority on the meaning of baptism is inseparable from a challenge to the state: one who substitutes an animal for an infant deliberately misconstrues and challenges true relationships of hierarchy, order and truth.

Aulicus' cue was the new parliamentary order concerning the ordination of Ministers, but he must also have had in mind parliament's intensifying campaign to transform the church interior. As Archbishop Laud languished in prison, parliament dismantled his vision of the architecture and furniture of the church. 'Popish' altars and altar rails went and, in August 1643, aspects of the by now traditional church environment were under attack. Communion tables were ordered to lose candles, basins and tapers; crucifixes, crosses and images were to be gone. In 1644 this disappearing magic extended to vestments, fonts and organs.[56] The soldiers in Aulicus' account don't attack the font itself – provokingly ornate and image-laden as it is. Instead, the story insists on the outrageous nature of this contestation of baptism.

As Aulicus' account suggests, the transformation offered by baptism became contentious in a new way in the mid-1640s. A contemporary diarist records that 25 December 1644, being a Wednesday, was kept as a fast day 'although it were Xmas day, by speciall order of parliament, and it was strictly observed' and on the 10 January 1645 'the Archbishop of Canterbury beheaded on Tower Hill'. Between the two events, on 3 January 1645, the *Book of Common Prayer* was prohibited for public use. John Greene, the diarist, does not mention this, but he does, later that year, attend a private baptism with godparents.[57] Scholarship on the 1640s strongly associates religious controversy and the sects, but, as we shall see, responses to the banning of the liturgy trouble that account while, at the same time, events are shaped by the growth of news, uncertainty concerning the source of authority, the strange conditions produced by the ejection of ministers in the early 1640s. While, in 1641 (and probably later, in London), the sectarian impulse is important in understanding developments, there is evidence that by 1643 parishes and individuals had responded negatively to the tough line on church furniture, the ousting of ministers, and the shock of losing the prayer book. John Morrill contrasts the alacrity with which the parliamentary instructions of 1641 were put into effect by churchwardens and parish officers, and the foot-dragging of 1643–4.[58] As he further notes, many more churches possessed the *Book of Common Prayer* with fewer than twenty-five per cent of church inventories recording purchase of the 1644 *Directory of Worship*.[59] By the autumn of 1645 the *Directory of Worship* had, officially, replaced the old liturgy even in private chapels. Three 'events' allow exploration of transformation in this new context – a trial, an exchange in which letters are transformed into print, and the newsbook controversy in which Aulicus' outraged repetition of 'horrid blasphemy as no modest Christian is willing to repeat' was the first salvo.

In June 1644, the summer before the events at Lostwithiel, we find John and Susan Platt, a poor London couple, bound to:

> appear att the next Sessions [or speake there?] to answere the complaint of William Ramsden of golding lane weaver and others for depraveing the two Sacraments of Baptisme and the Lords Supper especially the Sacrament of Baptisme (saying) that a catt or a dogg may be as well baptised as any child or children in their infancie.[60]

Soon, however, someone was called to the Sessions – for 'abusing John Platt and Susan his wife' and 'counselling the people to [?claw] her by the face & saying to the people yt she had christened a cat & other words whereby a mutiny was like to be raysed'.[61] The justices themselves were pulled into the medley of accusation and counter-accusation, as the original complainant, William Ramsden, was called for an outburst. Robert Dawlman, one of the justices accused him of saying, 'in my presence' that Dawlman 'would heare none but theefes, whores & Annabaptists'.[62] Soon the 'taking away' of Susan Platt's 'Holland apron' is in contention, it is asserted that the Platts 'did in a violent manner assault and wound the said Ramsden' – and accusations fly. If the originating event was probably less than the baptising of a cat, the incidents' implications were great enough to raise at least one 'tumult' as the nature of the sacraments were debated in local, religious and secular legal settings.[63] One upshot is clear: John and Susanna Platt spent time in the Counter for 'depraving the Sacrament of Baptisme' and saying scandalous words about it.[64] The cat, if such there was, seems to have walked free.

Once again, as with earlier cases, as we unplait the strands of the Platt case we find locality, theology and institutions twined together. The accusations against the Platts expose tensions amongst faith and liturgy (sacrament, prayer book); state; locality, status. Keith Lindley's research on the case demonstrates the poverty of John Platt and of some of the others who opposed him. Platt, a heelmaker, and two of the other side (a wiredrawer and a weaver) were assessed for subsidy at the low rate of 12d.[65] At the same time, as Lindley and Hughes note, the case leads us up the social scale through the way some of the justices and others were connected to the printer Thomas Paine, a radical, and to Independent congregations, such as that of Thomas Goodwin.[66] It would be only partially true to describe the events as those of low status, at street level, disciplined by those above them. Instead, we recognise a more complex dynamic pattern of accusation and counter-accusation linking the higher and lower parts of London society. Once again jumping barriers of birth and class, transformation, in this case animal transformation, clearly signifies across status-barriers. A distinctive feature is the tumult of the secular court process. While in some earlier 'cases' of parodic baptism the meaning of the offence was determined by the church authorities, as we have seen, the Platts are buffeted through the Sessions and on to the Counter.

In terms of reaction to the changes in liturgy in the 1640s, the specific circumstances of London seem to have made it a microclimate.[67] In London, parishes, churches, congregations, preachers, women preachers, lectures were densely packed together so that news, augmented by diurnals, could travel fast and newspapers could re-circulate gossip. Thomas Edwards, who published his list in which animal-baptism features as Error 104 in 1646, records many outrages from the streets around him, as well as taking letters from the provinces. Paul Hobson, one of the preachers with whom Thomas Edwards was obsessed, was said to have baptised a colt in London. When Edwards' *Gangræna* finally emerged in 1646, it contained a relation of the summer two years earlier – 1644 – when Hobson's associate, 'Captain Beaumont' was quartered with parliamentary troops at Yakesly, Huntingtonshire. There 'being a child in the Town to be baptized' the Lieutenant of the troop organised a detachment of soldiers to 'hinder it', and, 'guarding the Church', some of the 'souldiers got into the Church, pissed in the Font'. Worse, the soldiers fetched a horse to the piss-filled font – 'And there baptized it'. According to Edwards, the outraged townspeople sought to 'stirre up the Parish to complaine and prosecute' the perpetrators.[68] Edwards, because 'I well know that reports will flye variously' has acquired a 'certificate' of this 'prophanation and contempt of Gods Ordinance of Baptisme' should he ever be asked for it.[69] He prints a letter solicited in 1646, but describing early June, 1644, when Beaumont's soldiers:

> Fecht a bald horse out of Master *Finnamoores* stable . . . and in the Church at the font (having pissed in it) did sprinkle it on the horse and call him *Ball Esau* (because he was hairie) and crost him in the forehead: They had souldiers godfathers, and one *Widdow Shropshire*, a souldier so nick-named, was the Godmother.

'They all', the witnesses conclude, 'gloried in it' – and other souldiers later baptised 'a pigg'.[70] Colts, horses, pigs and soldiers are mixed in *Gangræna* as humans invoke contrasting authorities – army versus 'Parrish'. The object of the conflict, as well as its intensity, is marked as much, or more, by the piss as the horse. The baptism of an animal would have been disturbing to witnesses, but the replacement of the baptismal water, the only consecrated element in the baptismal ritual, by urine would perhaps have been even more troubling.

As Hughes points out, *Gangræna* was 'a Londoner's book'. Its reporting is informed by the agenda of the Assembly of divines seeking to replace the national church, and assumes the Church of England's defeat.[71] That Edwards, anxious that 'reports will fly variously', prints as evidence a letter attested by seven signatories, certificated by a 'godly Minister', and which he can produce as 'proof' suggests that, certain as he was of the right course, he recognised the power and complexity of people's responses to events, hearsay, law and print.[72] Edwards was aware of the power of fast-circulating news to stimulate scepticism, even frankly expressed disbelief, as well as confidence. Edwards' anxiety concerning how his audience might gauge the veracity of print was presumably stimulated by both the nature of the events he was purveying and by the nature of the medium. Certainly, if the Platt case shows the familiar contours of a mock baptism, then Edwards' discussion is aware that it takes place in the fast-moving, novel world of print. In the 1640s, during and after the first Civil War, struggles in parishes over the ejection of ministers and the nature of ritual and, as importantly, the movement of the parliamentarian army, brought out hot spots of ritual challenge.[73] Thus, in Radwinter in Essex the Laudian minister's insistence of making the sign of the cross in baptism, amongst other Laudian practices, led to scuffles and physical attacks in church.[74]

Back in 1644, when the events Edwards describes happened, animal baptism circulated in the intense heat of newspaper controversy, as indicated by the account of a baptism in Loswithiel with which this section opened. Aulicus, as always, generated a response from his pro-parliamentarian rival:

> I mislike it in nothing but in the circumstances of the manner of the action (in sprinkling water) and of the place (that it should be done at the Font) but as for the *signing* with the *sign of the Crosse*, I like the *mark* better upon a *horse* then a *Christian*, it being *the mark of the Beast*: This it is whereby the sottish, brutish Malignants desire to be distinguished from others in the use of *Baptisme*; and why do they not stickle for the other *Ceremonies* also, the superstitious *salt* and *Spittle* of their *Forefathers*? Why not for the other *reliques of Popery*, as well as this one? I think I must get some of our *Saviours* miraculous *eye salve* of *clay* and *spittle*, before I shall be able to cure these *wretches* of their *blindnesse*.[75]

In an explicit marginal gloss Britanicus writes, 'Why the Crosse is fitter for a Beast then a Christian.' For Britanicus, then, the sprinkling of water and the font are associated with popery in and of themselves; the Catholic signing is sorcery; building analogically, the sign of the cross is a sign of sorcery and – therefore – it is the mark of the beast (Satanic). There is a lurking implication that in some way *therefore* it is fitting for beasts and, he implies also, the royalists have abandoned their own human status in sinking back into irrational superstition. They have become 'brutish'. The whole event is a sign of the incredible ignorance of the royalists in holding out for baptism which is itself popish (and so more fittingly done as a parody using an animal). These assertions allow *Britanicus* to sponsor the position of a cat baptiser and condemn the others as Popish.

Here, at last, we seem to have in Marchmont Nedham a willing sponsor of animal baptism as preferable to human and, at first sight, someone willing to take a position. Not that Nedham, possible republican and agent of Cromwell's regime, did anything of the sort. In fact Nedham, like Edwards, spent time spying on the congregational churches though in Nedham's case he did it as a paid government agent. Nedham's complex relationship to authority notwithstanding, if the alternative is infant baptism he is prepared to sponsor animal baptism. If Aulicus makes clear the challenge to the king implied in challenge to the church, Nedham responds by attacking the mystifying properties of baptismal ritual, presenting magic, Catholicism and the ritual prescribed in the *Book of Common Prayer* as synonymous.

Nedham responds to Aulicus' attack by saying: no such event; Aulicus is a libeller; even if the event had happened then it was better than an infant being baptised. The first two of these moves seek to relocate the debate on print-culture terrain – who is libelling whom. The last – the sponsoring of animal baptism – can perhaps best be read as an attempt to scoop up animal ceremony and house it firmly within the confines of extreme but discursively bounded debate on baptismal theology. Nedham tries to take the scandal out of the incident by framing it as a comment on the nature of the soul and of baptism.

As Ann Hughes points out, the emergence of animal events in print does not help to quantify them or locate them with certainty in the real world.[76] It does not take an acute observer here to see that the story serves both sides and that, as newspaper proprietors, Britanicus and Aulicus are living off the same story. Animal baptism here takes on life as a 'print event', part of a populist debate on the nature and power of baptism circulated, and re-circulated, as 'news'. Two general effects of the shaping of the world as news can be the re-presentation to itself of a society's concerns heightened as sensation and melodrama and another is an emerging assumption that there is a social world, or at least a world of conversation and debate, into which this new news can insert itself. A specific condition of the re-circulation of cat baptism in print is that a representational vocabulary previously located in parish life is recycled and used as a vivid marker of controversy in national debates – as print events the animal transformations refer back to and use the animal lexicon we found earlier linking local and national conflict. Circulating in print these events constitute part of the way in which baptism is publicly debated.

Perhaps the very fact that Nedham addresses the scandal in detail, and with such strong accusations of Popery, suggests something else – at the very least the enigmatic power and importance of the sacraments that drew the debate towards them? If baptism itself is unclear in the reformed church, both a sign and something more mysterious, an initiating of the process of becoming Christian, the animal events we have been examining, for all that some of them (as they are told) seem to *seek* for clarity about who, and what, can be baptised, also address and partake of a situation in which the role of baptism is much canvassed but continues to be not completely clear. Indeed, as we find, although Nedham is happy to extrapolate a logic which tells us why it is better to baptise an animal than a human, even Nedham is unmistakably keen to remind us that no such event actually happened.

What, though, if we imagine it had happened? This is the scene all the accounts discussed invite their readers, observers, or imagined witnesses to conjure. Imagining the scene – in whatever terms that is understood – makes its scandal immediately vivid; for all the demystifying logic of

Nedham's answer, a cat being baptised suggests the power of baptism as a mystery and a sacrament and puts in play a vocabulary and iconography associated with magic and with the old religion of which the punning of 'cat' and 'catholic' are merely the most obvious associations.

IV Transformation, animals, humans

What do animal events suggest about the place of transformation in the writing of seventeenth-century England? If the place of metamorphosis in classical texts is much discussed by scholars, the material discussed in this chapter is rarely, if ever, considered in relation to transformation. However, the textual evidence discussed here suggests that, in a different way, these reports tell us much about understandings of change. The *Book of Common Prayer*, Francis Ashley's record book and *Mercurius Britanicus* offer a marked contrast with the literary material in the first chapter but each clearly addresses transformation, either as blending and change (in the prayer book) or in animal substitution.

Social historians have been the main group commenting on these materials, and they have tended to see these texts as 'popular beliefs' while understanding the popular as expressing a particular stratum of society. However, as I have argued, these textual representations suggest that events which happened in the parish context were at times understood as addressing theological and liturgical controversies. Reading these texts in juxtaposition with a body of literary material, like that addressed in Chapter 1, illuminates that, clearly, many of the texts imagining these events might be described as crafted. All share a symbolic vocabulary. Their relatively complex lexicon transports debate from the parish to the centre of power. Rather than it being a case of what happens in the parish stays in the parish, these 'events' invite a dynamic understanding of culture in which argument expressed symbolically links parish and the heart of government – even, at one point, the King. They invite, therefore, attentive reading – and consideration within the frame of change.

This chapter, therefore, offers both a test case and a fresh body of material for the discussion of vernacular metamorphosis. The material presented here reveals problems concerning change and transformation at the heart of the practice of reformed religion but also discloses something about assumptions regarding animals and animal–human relationships. Metamorphosis is at issue in each case, but in different ways. Baptism is subject to scrutiny because of questions concerning the nature and efficacy of a sacrament which bring to the fore the issue of how someone, particularly an infant, is changed by the ceremony. What we see, then, seems to be still smouldering textual embers of hot debate. Readers of the vernacular *Book of Common Prayer* asked how baptism produces the regenerate and redeemable Christian. What part works? Why? How? Old (Roman) and new theology offered troublingly different answers concerning what baptism did to the human.

That these transformations were part of a conversation, or, maybe, rowdy argument, concerning the power of sacraments does not mean that the force of the targeted ceremonies and furnishings was only diminished through such parody – obviously, each transgression was also a restatement. Even Nedham's insistence on justification through faith, was, in being elicited, an acknowledgement of the cultural power of the very sacrament in question.

The substitutions of animals for humans in parodic or critical events discloses something concerning human attitudes to animals and, therefore, to the human and, perhaps, potentially something about animals themselves. It is not surprising, perhaps, given the importance of the human in what is at stake, that insofar as these ceremonies attend to animals, they use them within broadly anthropomorphic comparative frames and exploit the representational value of animals' difference and similarity to the human. Thus, insofar as the animal can be isolated as a factor in these performances, the anthropocentric comparison of beast with human highlights the failings of specific humans or human systems. Yet, at the same time, the very symbolic presence of the animal suggests the crucial integration of animals, particularly cats, dogs and horses, into patterns of thought, representation and symbolisation, touch, looking and listening which are only partially recoverable in text, particularly text read in a sensory universe so distant from the animal-dense early modern world. Familiarity with the behaviour of animals, possibly individual animals, was pervasive but certainly that animals were symbolically bound to the web of Aesopian, Biblical and other lore concerning beasts was part of what made the ceremonies work. If we consider the events, momentarily, as equations then it is evident that the animals supply significant and probably only partially recoverable values within them.

However, notwithstanding that animals are, broadly, a given rather than a focus for participants, the choice and use of animals decisively shapes the nature of the critique by supplying a difference from the human. Thus, particular events draw on the animals in different ways: cocks, for example, lend themselves to being baptised as Peter; while the cry of a pinched cat sharply, savagely reiterates poor preaching, and there is also the association between cats and Catholics, also cats and devils.[77] Most obviously, the change of human ceremony to animal joltingly repositions the human. If the ceremony can be performed with an animal what does that suggest about the human role in the event? Whether it is a case of imagining or actually watching and hearing an animal participating in baptism, the de-familiarisation consequent on animal-substitution exposes the ceremony itself; all the strange and illogical aspects are suddenly and visibly accentuated.

The use of animals in such addresses to transformation discloses a little more about the animal when compared to other kinds of writing concerned with the relationship between animals and humans. Thus, in John Milton's *Maske Presented at Ludlow Castle* (performed in 1634, printed in 1637) those who drink the draught offered by Comus, son of Bacchus and Circe find it 'quite transforms' their 'visage' to 'the inglorious likenes of a beast'.[78] Milton's view clearly marks the drinkers' moral falling away, like Circe's prisoners, from human to bestial status. However, in the last edition of his book, in 1676, Izaak Walton writes that 'you may take notice, that as the *Carp* is accounted the *Water-Fox*, for his cunning; so the *Roach* is accounted the *Water-sheep*, for his simplicity or foolishness'.[79] Deeply concerned to articulate the virtues of angling and those of the *Book of Common Prayer*, Walton here uses the animal within a fabled mode to produce quite detailed implications. The qualities attributed to the animal draw on Aesopean and other habits of thought. Walton's messages are divided; he is interested in the *Book of Common Prayer* and its survival, but also deeply immersed in the streams and rivers he describes. Walton's writing makes the fish vivid because always, yet oscillatingly, like and unlike the human. Indeed, as Peter Harrison has pointed out, the animals were potentially better than people in fulfilling God's design for the creation. Though certainly Walton did not push his research this far, fishes had been singled out in patristic writing for following God's law while men do not.[80] To oversimplify, in *Comus*, Milton's semi-animals do one very clear job. They are metaphoric and allegorical of human falling away. Walton's writing is contrastingly analogical, similitudinous, impressionistic and evocative. Thus, while anthropomorphic and arktomorphic assumptions and practices are the foundation of both Walton and Milton's writing, there are differences. For Milton the moral axis is exclusive, for Walton, as for the observer of animal rituals, closer observation, and attentive interpretation, of animals is at play.

As Tom Tyler puts it, 'anthropocentrists, like Narcissus, have eyes only for themselves'; descriptions of the backsliding into beastliness of Comus' crew, or discussion of a fish in terms of human 'cunning' evidently rest on the assumption that the human is known, comes first and is an appropriate measure of the beast. The humans variously witnessing the written or actual events that we have explored here undoubtedly 'see a transmutation, a metamorphosis taking place' in which animal is 'cast in the image of man' – and vice versa.[81] The axiomatically lesser status of the animal (in theology, the Aristotelian hieracrchy, hunting) clearly governs the terms of human attention to the creatures rather than immediate detail or empathy with which they might be considered in particular situations. The clear articulation of a comparison between beast and human might co-exist with a knowledge of and attention to familiar animals. At the same time that these dramas enunciate the absolutely foundational place of the beast as not Christian or capable of salvation they work because the thinking on the Aristotelian tripartite soul (explored in the introduction) shaped the human as made up of the creature without humanity and salvation.

If the absolute contrast between human and horse made it ludicrous to baptise a horse, the shared animal status of horse and human operated in context to point up the question of how far an infant was in a state to realise the potential of the human soul, how far beastly in her, or his, grasp on world and heaven. There is, then, complexity in this entangling of human and creature at the base of the adventure towards human superiority, and this is used for the various audiences of these ceremonies. Change in its perhaps most deceivingly simple guise of substitution illuminates this.

The audiences of these ceremonies were diverse and, in some cases, powerful. Importantly, while the texts of animal baptism have been previously analysed as part of a particular sphere of culture, it should now be apparent that not only were they 'understood' as part of quite a rich and evocative symbolic vocabulary, but also that they addressed crucial issues at the heart of the Jacobean and Laudian churches.

Finally, the claim of baptism to transform, once it was in the vernacular, prompted canvassing in the use of animal ceremonies. Sometimes serious, sometimes playful these addressed transformation and used a different kind of transformation is the analogical use of animals. These ways of thinking were specific but also drew on patterns of thought found in many parts of seventeenth-century culture. In the next chapter we will explore the power of nature to change and generate marvels and we will be leaving behind, temporarily, this controversial world of animal transformation in order to explore myth and experiment. We will return to a world of integrated classical and sacred transformation with the werewolf, in Chapter 4.

However, rather than leave Walton and Milton as the last word on the use of animal symbolism, let us turn, instead, to another form of evidence – and one that suggests, perhaps, that traces of animal events have endured but not always as we find them in written evidence. In November 2011 improvements to a Pennine reservoir revealed a seventeenth-century cottage. Within the walls of the cottage was found the skeleton of a cat in a position more familiar from medieval buildings. If the unlucky seventeenth-century cat has been killed in a ceremony residual from medieval custom then, in the county of the Pendle witch trials, the cat's presence must also have had a meaning connected to the time of the event. My suggestion is that, in a world shaped by the complicated interactions of subject, practice and authority in Reformation England, there was, undoubtedly, a symbolic lexicon with which to read this cat.[82] The significance of this little cat is neither that it is from a world we know nor a world we have lost. Rather, its existence is a trace of a world that attention to animal transformations can help us to interpret more richly.

CHAPTER THREE

Transforming nature: strange fish and monsters

6 Cockatrice, Edward Topsell, *Historie of Serpents* (1608).

'What have we here, a man or a fish?' So asks Trinculo in *The Tempest* (1611) continuing, 'A strange fish! Were I in England now (as once I was) and had but this fish painted, not a holiday fool there but would give a piece of silver.' (2.2.24; 26–8).[1] Trinculo's attitude to Caliban is uncertain, inquisitive and acquisitive. Taking Trinculo's puzzlement as a starting point, this chapter asks what writing on the monster can tell us about seventeenth-century culture. In the sixteenth and seventeenth centuries a regular response to the question 'What have we here?' was to generate an image, list, catalogue, book or collection of anomalies. Wonders stimulated princes, merchants and intellectuals to build collections and writers to transmit and debate the thoughts of Aristotle on extraordinary things and transforming powers. These compendia, though they took distinct forms, expressed a curiosity about 'the secrets of nature' shared by the prince, surgeon and fairground customer – Trinculo's 'holiday fool'. Representation of the monster, in words as much as in images, gave it existence and it lived in published and unpublished writing as well as in images (usually circulated with texts), and collections. And, in a world both overwhelmingly generative and subject to God's laws, the monsters writers presented to their readers offered much to question.

While modern taxonomies, shaped by disciplines, usually define monsters as generated by opposed binaries – so either divine or human art; either 'natural' or 'artificial'; belonging to mythos or to logos; specimens of commerce or biology – the writing of sixteenth- and seventeenth-century England discloses quite other ways of thinking. Even the assumption that matter is divided into organic and inorganic, living and inanimate, made by nature or by art, does not hold good. And these differences from modern thinking remain, reconfigured, after Francis Bacon intervened in the tradition of, broadly, Aristotelian assumptions about matter, marvels and monsters. As the history of the modern disciplines made by the separation of 'science', 'philosophy', 'medicine', 'history' and that late-comer, 'literature', has itself become the object of study, the boundaries of genre have shifted. Given the diversity of sixteenth- and seventeenth-century people who were curious about the monster – theologians, surgeons, physicians, diarists, artists, pamphleteers – we need to emphasise factors linking texts as well as dividing them.

As the connections between 'scientific' and 'literary' texts have come more clearly into view for scholars, the critical field has been reshaped by both philosophical and historical interventions. Thus, the work of philosophers including Michel Serres has influenced critical analysis of the social, intellectual and political forces underpinning the formation of the Enlightenment disciplines and, increasingly, this has led to a reconsideration of the pre-disciplinary period.[2] Starting from the shared assumption that disciplinary categories are epochally bound rather than 'natural' or eternal, critics have investigated the place of wonder and wonders in Renaissance and early modern Europe. Mary Baine Campbell has provided a complex analysis of wonder and Katherine Park and Lorraine Daston have suggested a sense of the uneven, rather than developmental, shift in attitudes to prodigies.[3] The combination of theoretical questioning and scholarly archaeology applied to sixteenth- and seventeenth-century categories and habits of thought has enabled the renewed exploration of the pre-disciplinary shapes of monsters. Thus, the large literature of monstrosity – embracing the Bible, Ovid's *Metamorphoses*, medieval bestiaries, romance, pamphlets – is now regularly investigated by scholars. By contrast, however, the textual traces that mark the fascination with generation, and their links to the 'monster', have not yet been either extensively or deeply explored. Yet, as a brief survey of texts makes clear, monsters and generation are conceptual twins. Moreover, fascination with generation and marvels both marks vernacular texts and discloses social groupings that include collectors and travellers, but also theatre-goers and those attending London's displays, as participating in the discourse of marvels and generation.

Studies of literary language have much to gain from the repealing of the law of discipline which, for example, retrospectively allocated *The Tempest* to literary analysis and the widely read translation of Ambroise Paré's writing to the history of science. '[S]eemingly incommensurate sources', and people, have links – as Deborah Harkness notes.[4] In a similar pattern, the writers and readers discussed here read and consumed a range of texts and experiences. For all that Shakespeare and Paré have different aims, the audiences for *The Tempest* and Paré's *Works*, whether theatre-goers, readers or recipients of orally circulated tales and ideas, undoubtedly overlapped. If a wide range of texts besides the strictly 'literary' evoke transformation, this chapter explores how we might put those texts in the same frame. Accordingly, in response to the impact of the ideas and writing of the period, the ensuing analysis aims to track Trinculo's monster to the seeds of generation.

I Generating nature: the monster, the stone and the egg

Let us turn first to the arrival and circulation of wonders in vernacular writing. Obviously, the translation of a text into English indicates anticipated buyers and readers. Yet, far from isolated fragments, the monsters and marvels of published texts turn out to be connected to an understanding of the world as transformative – vibrating with life in its every fibre. In this network of meanings, distinct kinds of texts enabled English readers to see the monster alongside apparently more representative items, what we might consider things, such as eggs and stones. The web of writing that embraces monsters, stones and eggs has one origin in the writing of Aristotle, certainly, but its reception seems to have prioritised a discourse of evidence over detailed discussion of Aristotle.

Generating nature

Monsters came into the English vernacular in several ways. They lurked in the illustrations of bestiaries; were listed in surviving medieval catalogues and lived in translations, such as Stephen Bateman's translation of Lycostenes, as warnings of doom.[5] Edward Fenton's translation of Pierre Boaistuau's catalogue of monsters, *Histoires prodigeuses*, advertised itself as '[c]ertaine secrete wonders of nature' and these secrets were further, and differently, explored by Ambroise Paré, Edward Topsell, Francis Bacon, William Harvey.[6]

In 1569 Edward Fenton published a translation of Boaistuau's study of monsters. Far from positioning itself as a list of terrors or God's judgements, it claimed to facilitate productive discrimination between real wonders and deceitful abuse of 'our simplicitie' by spirits and illusions. Fenton, who went on to be a naval adventurer and so may already have had an investment in productive knowledge, locates his own wonders in nature because, he suggests, many things are 'called supernaturall bicause the reason is hidden from us'. Fenton's monsters are to be rescued from any 'twilight status' between natural and miraculous to be properly known.[7] He asserts that nature's secrets have been 'kept unknowne from us (as it should seeme of set purpose) to the end we might rather finde ourselves occupied in the search and knowledge of the same' and so his text is both 'plesant to read and necessary to know'.[8] Notwithstanding the text's claim to elucidate 'the generall causes of the generation of Monsters', to a late modern understanding Fenton's translation mixes monsters with wonders that seem to us to belong elsewhere, intermingling unusual lightning, comets, strange monsters generated by the sea, whales, mermaids, extraordinary cruelty.[9] From the perspective of post-disciplinary taxonomic laws such a catalogue lacks an adequate shaping principle. However, for Fenton and his contemporaries the wonders are implicitly linked by the earth's own astonishing, and metamorphic, generative potential. Although Fenton is only partly concerned, it seems, with the causes underpinning monsters it may be that underlying the grouping together of natural wonders and monsters rests on the assumption that there is a shaping power at work in nature.

As well as being an object of study in Aristotelian and post-Aristotelian natural philosophy, the wide literary and cultural purchase of the idea that nature itself was generative made it something that a vernacular reader might expect to encounter. This faculty was assumed to facilitate generation and in doing so give a form, or image, to matter (for example, it accounted for wonders we consider as fossils, or for rocks that look like animals). However, rather than aggregate the effects of Aristotelian thinking under the catch-all term 'vitalism', for the current discussion it is helpful to explore specific textual instances of the generative power of the earth. As the influential Antoine Goudin puts it, the earth has a 'certain force' which is 'similar to the maternal bosom from which animals arise' and so the earth comes to be understood as a female to the male virtue – and so not only gives rise to forms in the earth that are similar to living beings but also shapes a way of thinking about the world.[10] The rays of the stars, too, help to shape the masculine vital force in the 'womb' of the earth to generate spontaneous life forms.[11] So, if the monsters in Fenton's translation are wonders of extraordinary variety we can extrapolate from them an understanding of the processes of generation as extraordinary, transformative, gendered and pervasive in God's creation.

Fenton takes as his topic the natural world, but that natural world has different borders and properties from our own and spontaneous generation and the generation of prodigies were two effects explained by the actions of the world's vital forces. The generative world was shaped by Aristotle's opinion that, while menstrual blood had the full potential to form a complete human, that those cannot be brought to fruition without the semen which makes the promise actual and determines the end of the foetus – it is, in Aristotle's understanding, the formal and final cause.[12] Thus, female children occur when the movement of the male seed is weak and that of the menstrual blood is stronger. Monsters are generated when the weak movements of both seeds fail even to articulate a distinct human. As we find in Aristotle, '[e]verything produced naturally or by an art is produced by a thing actually out of what is potentially of that sort. Now the seed, and the movement and source which it contains, are such that as the movement ceases each part is produced having soul.'[13] Thus, in a strictly Aristotelian formulation, which as we will see was part of sixteenth-century thinking but by no means the whole, monsters were, simply, lacking in form and so mimic the animal.[14]

Within this pervasively generative world, monsters exemplify failures to achieve human shape. Such creatures, significantly for their consideration by contemporaries, are unique as records of usually reliable processes of reproduction gone awry. In this they can be compared with examples of successful generation – for instance, even spontaneously generated beings, arising from the naturally generative processes of the earth, take being as a genus – like the swarms of frogs, flies, mice and even serpents that were another kind of example of the wondrous generative quality of the earth. Spontaneous generation, while as wonderful as the generation of monsters, was a contrastingly reliable opposite effect to that of monstrosity. Fenton's translation, then, endorses Plutarch's opinion that, 'even as Honye flies are engendered of beasts, wasps of horses, & hornets of asses, so may it be, y^t of the marrow and carrion of men certain kind of Serpent are bred', moreover, he notes a serpent 'founde amongste a sorte of rockes or stones', a sepulchre, in a place closed by stone and with no air or space for a large serpent to pass through.[15]

Fenton's sense of a vital world need not have been derived purely from Aristotle. For Galen, also influential, generation was caused by the ejaculation of seminal fluids by man and woman into the uterus, and seventeenth-century commentary is often unclear, or unconcerned, about the distinction. More significant, as Justin Smith argues, is that these ways of thinking about the earth's fruitfulness – in terms of masculine and feminine – was pervasive from the writings of Marsilio Ficino to Henry More. Boaistuau, Fenton and their English readers, then, were likely to accept as natural a world animated by extraordinary life and vital spirit. Fenton's writing blends experience and animism, asking questions of a world in which matter melds and changes because of its vital properties and therefore lends the world a vital, procreating potential and tendency. The world itself, aided by the stars, generates life. Boaistuau's seventeenth-century English readers might have found similar assumptions elsewhere, including in more sceptical and practical sources – it was a part of what readers found in writing on the natural world.

One such sceptical and practical location of such thinking was the highly influential writing of Ambroise Paré, surgeon to a line of French kings. As early as 1629 a translation from Paré's French and Latin writings was registered for publication in England and in 1634, some forty years after Paré's death, the botanist Thomas Johnson published his vernacular edition.[16] Trained as a barber surgeon, Paré brought a combination of learning, skill and scepticism to his French and Latin writings, mediating amongst different kinds of evidence and authority as his own experience guided him. Paré, as translated in the twenty-fifth chapter of the English *Works*, is careful to distinguish monsters as contravening the 'common decree and order of nature' – so 'wee term that infant monstrous' born without an arm or with an extra head. He reserved the term 'Prodigies' for happenings 'contrary to the whole course of nature.' Paré's discussion of monsters is logically organised in relation to the causes that shape these alarming deviations from species. As 'causes' of monsters Paré offers 'the glory of God' made manifest to the ignorant; punishments and portents from God; 'an abundance of seed and overflowing matter' or a deficit in adequacy and amount of seed; the 'force and efficacy of the imagination'; sexual intercourse 'without law or measure' (or 'luxuriously and beastly' coupling); several distinct physical aspects of the womb; a fall or blow; 'hereditary disease'; 'confusion and mixing together of the seed'; the 'craft' of the devil.[17]

Although Paré's sharp demarcation of the realm of the natural monster excludes the prodigies that jostle against monsters and bodies in Fenton, Fenton and Paré share assumptions concerning the generative power of the world. So, we know that Paré's work is unparalleled in its influence, many readers tracked many instances linking particular phenomena to likely causes. And almost every page of his discussion of monsters demonstrated to readers the astonishing ability of the natural world to generate extraordinary forms through a diversity of causes. Paré both uses and challenges the other catalogues of monsters, and treats classical authorities in the same way while privileging the apparently first-hand accounts of contemporaries. Thus, using Aristotle amongst other authorities, it is not clear whether in his discussion of 'seed' Paré intends a careful Aristotelian discrimination between the soul-engendering male and the female or whether he is working with a looser understanding. Certainly, for Paré, Aristotle's authority is to be set against other evidence and particularly his own experience and that of his contemporaries.

Stones, often discussed by Paré, illustrate some of the differences between our own sense of the natural world (with its modern divisions into organic and inorganic, living and dead) and the powerfully transforming world of Paré and his readers. Turning to 'the wonderful originall, or breeding of some creatures', Paré recounts reading 'in Boistey' of a serpent found in an opened 'leaden coffin' but argues 'the originall of this creature is not as prodigious as he supposeth' – the breeding of serpents in any putrefying carcass being 'usuall'. However, not merely the rotting human form but rocks themselves generate life:

> *Baptista Leo* writes, that in the time of Pope *Martin* the fift, there was a live serpent found enclosed in a vaste, but solid Marble, no chinke appearing in such dense solidity, whereby this living creature might breath.
>
> Whilst at my vine-yard, that is at *Meudon*, I caused certain huge stones to be broken to pieces, a Toad was found in the midst of one of them.

Having seen this with his own eyes, 'much admired', checked with the authorities and, having it confirmed by the stonecutter as 'a common thing... he saw it almost every day', Paré concludes in Aristotelian vein, 'the celestiall heat mixing and diffusing it selfe over the whole masse of the world, the matter may be animated for the generation of these creatures'.[18] Spontaneous generation, an extraordinary and fascinating manifestation of the earth's power, produces creatures distinct from the monsters Paré lists in being within the forms of species. Monsters shed light on the process of generation as exceptions – but that very status is an indication of the over- or under-transformative action of generation. The creatures of spontaneous generation cannot be predicted but are consistent with species reproduction – and enquiry into the generation of species underpins the listing of unique exceptions. The monster was catalogued as an example of a malfunction.

Evidently, if stones can generate toads, Paré's world offered him a very different ordering system from the modern taxonomy of organic and inorganic. Translating Boaistuau, Fenton had described the 'propertie and procreation of stones' – particularly precious stones and 'other straunge things, breedying in the bowels of the earth'.[19] Stones, in Fenton's translation, generate in the earth and many bring with them powerful properties. A 'cause of wonder' in excess of all, and 'meritorious of philosophicall contemplation', is the 'excellent propertie of precious stones, who being once drawne out of the intrailes of the womb of theyr mother and nurse the earth' are more than striking to both vision and reason. Fenton notes, 'most Greek and Roman writers agree' that not only do stones:

> engender, but also do suffer diseases, old Age and Death. And touching the procreation, they are of diverse opinions. For some say, they engender betweene rocks, when the sappe of juyce of other stones distilles within the crevices or hollow places of the same.

However, others think 'they grow in the earth, as knots in wood', and yet others, citing the 'Adamant', insist that they 'have sense & motion'. Further examples include rocks that move, 'being made of an humor very subtil which may be converted into vapour by the force of wine' added to it – and so is a 'cause of wonder' to those who 'see it stirre' without 'understanding the reason'.[20]

The provenances, powers and life histories of what Paré and Fenton both called stones take us to the heart of some of the concepts underpinning expectations of transformation. A 'stone' was a term embracing hard objects found inside animals or humans and materials mined in the earth; the two categories were distinct in some circumstances, similar in others. The human body, as Paré's contemporary, Michel de Montaigne, knew all too well from his own physical trials, generated stones. Under the heading of 'strange or monstrous accidents in diseases' Paré turns to the question of stones generated within the body. He includes in his list an incident from 1566 wherein a confectioner, 'called commonly *Tire*-vit' because he was so troubled that he 'continually scratched his yard', eventually had removed three stones, each 'as big as a Hen's egge'. Weighing twelve ounces these prodigious specimens were extracted and presented to King Charles who, ordering one to be broken with a hammer, and found inside another, 'of a chestnut colour, otherwise much like a peach stone'. These were presented to Paré and he evidently kept them in his collection.[21] 'Certainly', Paré commented, 'there is no part of the body wherein stones may not breed and grow'. And, in dissecting the dead, he encountered many stones 'of various forms and figures, as of pigges, whelpes, and the like'.[22]

In comparison to the restricted life of modern stone, doomed at best to mere decay and chemical reaction, the Renaissance and early modern stone participated in an animated natural dance. Distillation, petrification, engendering and the possession of special powers were all potentially within its sphere. Yet, as Paré's procedure when he found the toad indicates, that framework did not at all forestall investigation and one of Paré's most famous experiments concerns the bezoar stone, a 'stone' made in the guts of an animal, most often a goat, and considered to be an antidote to all poisons. Paré, challenging the French king's belief in the stone, experimented on a prisoner doomed to die. As the story goes, a condemned felon from the King's dungeon was invited to take poison and antidote but, as Paré had expected, antidote notwithstanding, he died a slow and agonising death.[23]

Petrification, whereby matter becomes 'stone', intrigued sixteenth- and seventeenth-century writers and put before them in an explicit form, the question of changes of state from animal to vegetable. Stones presented a mystery perhaps even greater than their powers over humans in terms of their ability to imitate the forms of 'natural' and 'artificial' life. In a fascinating discussion of the Jesuit Father Athanasius Kircher's interpretation of the subterranean world and, above all, of the 'stone' forms that in various ways are evidence of or evoke the forms taken by living matter, Stephen Jay Gould teases out some of the issues generated by a broadly Aristotelian approach to stones as 'form' and 'matter'.[24] In attempting to understand the range of intellectual tools with which Kircher approached what we now know to be the fossil record, Gould's discussion also helpfully explores how the armoury of the modern scholar itself makes it hard to recognise Renaissance taxonomies as logical.

As Gould notes, what we consider to be fossils for Kircher generated several categories, two of which were, on the one hand, materials that had once been organisms and which were preserved by petrification and, on the other, materials which, while not falling into this category, had been acted on to resemble organisms or the 'products of human activity'. Many writers of the sixteenth and seventeenth centuries shared Kircher's fascination with this enigmatic category, and his work was fairly widely read.[25] Casts, like the moulds of fossilised fish, are one example of the phenomenon of stone taking the form of life, but grouped with them are the examples, much more enigmatic, of materials which seemed to be marked with shapes from the world of nature or culture – such as eggs, on which, apparently, images or forms taken from the world of natural or created life had been mysteriously imprinted.[26] While Kircher is specifically investigating the world below the ground, the question of the impression of images and even words on natural objects such as stones and eggs provoked curiosity and speculation amongst many of his peers and the next generation.

For many, including Paré, the human and the stone could be considered together. In a bizarre combination of generative power and decay, he and others noted that the human body itself could generate stone infants. As Paré, following others, records, in mid sixteenth-century Sens, near Paris, Mme Colombe Chatri became pregnant, went into labour, but delivered no child. Left gravely ill she nevertheless lived on. At her death, gossip and curiosity concerning the child that never arrived was still sufficiently strong for her to be opened and, sure enough, a petrified babe at full term was found in her abdomen. Mislocated, transformed into stone, the infant seemed to contemporaries to have undergone a reverse metamorphosis from that of generation. The process whereby, hidden inside a womans's body, a baby gradually turned to stone provided a fascinating and repeatedly retold anecdote. As Helen King notes, from 1597 accounts of this wonder were sometimes accompanied by a Latin verse:

> Pinxit Deucalion saxis pot terga repulsis
> Ex duro nostrum marmore molle genus:
> Qui fit ut infantis, mutate sorte, tenellum
> Nunc corpus saxis proxima membra great![27]

Ovid's creation story in *Metamorphosis*, when Deucalion and Pyrrha scattered behind them stones which shaped themselves into humans, is reversed in the petrification of an embryo. The shock of petrification occurring in the very seat of generation is registered in the comparison with Deucalion (mentioned alone here, in contrast to the mother of the stone child), who creates life from stone. Although Deucalion is an instance of life-giving metamorphosis, of course, the deathly inflection of transformation pervades Ovid's poem in its stories of human dissolution into or capture by the animal and human world – as his flying nymphs, weeping mothers, desperate grievers are partly absorbed, partly enduring of their integration into a sub-human world. For all the vital life of stones, obviously the baby becoming its own stone funeral effigy implies only a sinister, deathly, metamorphic power of the womb. Fascinated, contemporaries drew the child in its mother's body.[28]

Troubling and startling as it is, the Lithopodion offers evidence that chimes with a wider view of the world and which links stones and humans in life. The stone baby, long-concealed in the body of a woman, was produced from the body of its mother to be displayed and drawn, studied by many including Paré. Although omitted in Paré's English *Works*, the story persisted well into the eighteenth century, and James Duplessis included the story of 'A Child Petrified in Mother's Womb' as an 'Uncommon a Sport of Nature' in his manuscript history of prodigies and monsters.[29] The infant itself was transferred to the realms of representation. The petrified body was transported to a collection where the gradual decaying of its features and limbs is recorded in images even as its extraordinary story continued to fascinate readers.[30] Arrested mid-transformation, preserved statically within a living body and then collected, drawn, described and circulated, the lithopodion was evidence of a world that, like Ovid's, was both transformative and fixed.

The stone child was evidence of transformation effected; it was subject to decay but not further extraordinary movement and so provides a polar opposite for the mysteries of the generative body – imaginatively located in the egg. The egg, felt to hold, and therefore potentially to show, the hidden processes of successful and unsuccessful generation, became increasingly the focus of enquiry in natural philosophy. In the sixteenth and mid seventeenth centuries, the egg, with its implicit potential to disclose, was the focus of attention of midwives and surgeons as much as philosophers and collectors. On its external surface, an egg might bear extraordinary marks that fascinated collectors. To what extent might external marks be indices of activity within, of God's purpose, of the process of generation?

The Expert Midwife, circulating in seventeenth-century England, translated Jacob Rueff's guide for midwives. It begins discussion of human procreation by making an analogy between the world and the human, asserting that

> [w]e observe the naturall Procreation of man, to be altogether such as we perceive the generation & beginning of Plants or Herbs, of every kind to be. For they, every one of them, from the seede of his kinde, cast into the wombe of earth, do bud or increase, and doe naturally grow into the perfect term of his proper Nature.[31]

12 *The expert Midwife.* Lib. 1.

The seede congealed and curded together like a tender Egge.

Therefore both seeds mingled, blended together and received into the womb, are eft soone compassed, and inclosed about, with a certain little coat or caule, ingendred by the heate of the Matrix, and are congealed and curded together, after the manner of a tender Egge, which is compassed about with a most thinne rinde, or little skin, as the figure annexed doth demonstrate and explaine.

Chap. III.

Of the three Coates, wherewith the Feature is invironed, defended and covered.

THe little roome, or coffin being ingendred after the conception; the vitall Spirit inclosed in the same, rouseth and putteth forth it selfe, and then the defences or caules are

7 Jacob Rueff, *The Expert Midwife* (1637).

This process is extraordinary and ordinary in its everyday mysteries, and Rueff visualises it as in process inside an egg. As the lavishly imagined broiling matter clouding it indicates, the egg held the hidden secrets of conception and generation, so that what is authenticated in the image is the location of the mysterious process. For writers and collectors the egg, with its curtained inner world, seems to have epitomised the extraordinary potential of generation. And, as eggs (unlike dragons) were relatively directly part of the lives of many cultural agents, they were discussed in a range of texts touching on the nature of conception, generation and the potential for reproduction in single creatures and the earth itself. For example, the idea that external events can affect gestation inhabits the practical discourses on poultry breeding. A late sixteenth-century poultry manual suggests that human control can affect the colour of chickens. In order to 'make white byrdes come of anye egges', the breeder must:

> Take your egges of what byrd ye wil, and lay them two dayes long in honye and then put them agayn in the neast, and let them be sat on, and ye shall have them whyte.

To select any colour is simple – the instructions are to take the eggs of a 'broode henne' 'colour them' as desired. The hen then hatches the egg and, according to this writer, in due course you 'see the Chickens to be of the same colour ye coloured the egges'.[32] As a statement of the idea of influence of external events on the process of generation, the very practical (though impracticable) nature of this advice suggests the wide currency of such ideas.

At the other end of the social spectrum, both the fact that marked eggs featured in major collections and that visitors singled them out for comment indicate fascination and speculation. Accompanying the naturalist John Ray on a tour of the collections of sixteenth-century Europe, the civil war combatant Philip Skippon visited Modena, where a 'letter from Zennon the Bolognese apothecary' gained them admission to the Duke's museum, and among the treasures saw 'a hen's egg having on one side the signature of the sun imprest, which the father said he saw laid'.[33] Thomas Browne, too, had a special egg and wrote of 'This egge you sent with this notable signature of a duck soe fully detail'd as to the body, head, eye & bill somewhat opene'd from the shell', as 'a point greatly remarkable & one, not made out by phancy butt apprehended by every eye'. It was 'a present greatly remarkable', the like of which he has never seen though he has 'very intentively looked upon the gosse egge in Aldrovandus'.[34] If poultry farmers might want to influence, for example, the colour of birds, the egg is of interest to Browne and others as the earliest material and visible evidence of any transformation beyond, or deviating from, accepted transformation. What could attentive gazing disclose concerning the amazing processes of species formation within? As we see, Ambroise Paré was far from alone in hoping that an egg might display the early stages of the growth of a monster or carry the marks of the forces that influenced it. Recording the 'shape of a monster found in an egge' he describes a creature echoing Medusa 'the face of a man, but haires yeelding a horrid representation of snakes' and, sure enough, a cat that ate the white of the egg died (see Fig. 8).[35] While collectors certainly gathered all manner of wonders, it seems that, in keeping eggs with extraordinary and evocative marks on them, collectors anthropomorphised or described these marks in ways that suggest they were perceived as potentially giving evidence of the generative process at work – a distinguishing feature of eggs to which we will return.

In sum, vernacular writing of the sixteenth and seventeenth centuries characterises the world that appears to us as primarily, though not exclusively, material, as part of a living process. Partially, eccentrically or attenuatedly Aristotelian as the vernacular writing is, classical, Biblical, folkloric and observational details are also important as writers and readers witness the enigmatic traces of transformation. Turning from the stone and the egg to the promised creatures of classical literature and scripture – the hydra, the dragon and the basilisk (and its fellow-creature, the cockatrice) – we can explore some of these complex issues in the writing of transformation and generation.

II Writing, collecting and making: dragon, basilisk and hydra

If tales of stones, eggs, monstrous births came to their readers with complex claims to originate in the world, then the dragon, basilisk and hydra had long-lived but extremely fraught histories. Monstrous creatures raise all the same questions about the nature of generation as do stones and eggs – and many more besides. Extraordinary creatures invited contemporaries to consider nature and art; the machine and the living being; the nature of transformable entities. As we shall see, writing on them also suggests that the strange and dubious nature of the creatures also sometimes put into question the identity of the reader and viewer – like Trinculo, they both questioned and wondered at the evidence of their senses.

'[N]ot long as a Hens Egge but round and orbicular: sometimes of a dusty, sometimes of a boxy, sometimes of a yellowish muddy colour'. So Edward Topsell describes the cock's egg that 'bringeth forth the

966   *Of Monsters and Prodigies.*   Lib. 25.

The shape of a monster found in an egge.

The monster you see here delineated, was found in the middle and innermost part of an egge, with the face of a man, but haires yeelding a horrid representation of snakes; the chinne had three other snakes stretched forth like a beard. It was first seene at *Autun*, at the house of one *Buncheron* a Lawyer, a maide breaking many eggs to butter: the white of this egge given a Cat, presently killed her. Lastly, this monster comming to the hands of the Baron *Senecy*, was brought to King *Charles* the ninth being then at *Metz*.

The effigies of a monstrous childe, having two heads, two armes & foure legs.

Arist. in problem.

In the yeere 1546. a woman at *Paris* in her sixt moneth of her account, brought forth a childe having two heads, two armes and foure legges: I dissecting the body of it, found but one heart, by which one may know it was but one infant. For you may know this from *Aristotle*, whether the monstrous birth bee one or more joined together, by the principall part: for if the body have but one heart, it is but one, if two, it is double by the joyning together in the conception.

The

8 Ambroise Paré, *Works* (1634).

Cockatrice'.[36] In his early seventeenth-century study of serpents, Topsell drew on a rich but potentially contradictory textual, visual and anecdotal inheritance to explore the basilisk, hydra, dragon. When Topsell came to publish his analysis of the creatures the serpent was already the subject of a manuscript treatise by the famous sixteenth-century collector, Aldrovandi, but this was not published until 1639 and did not reach the vernacular English reader directly.[37] Topsell, working from and supplementing Conrad Gesner, presented a taxonomy of serpents ranging across our current distinctions to include snakes, worms, bees, tortoises, the boas and dragons.[38] Topsell's general introduction to his *Historie of Serpents* shows that they bring up some of the key problems of generation, but also of identity and identification – and, therefore, representation and 'counterfeiting'.

Dragons, hydras and basilisks seemed to have been promised by the Bible and by classical texts but, as Topsell recognised, were found more often in representation than in the world. Topsell's introductory discussion uses Genesis 1.24 and 3.1 to ground these '"creeping things"', though '"more subtile than all of the Beasts of the field"', as God's own and, notes that the Prophet David's exhortation to the animals to praise their maker names 'Dragons, which are the greatest kinde of Serpents' (Psalm 148.7).[39] However, even as 'it is most plain in Genesis' that the earth produced creeping things at God's command and so even the dragon, existing by Biblical authority, is to be numbered amongst God's creatures, 'since that time' serpents 'have engendered both naturally and also prodigiously'.[40] So, at the root of the serpent's cultural ambiguity is a doubt about generation. Discussing true and fabulous accounts of the generation of serpents, Topsell, inevitably perhaps, turns to Ovid, quoting Golding's account of the serpent generated by 'the putrid back-bone in the grave rack'd, / Or marrow chang'd, the shape of Snake to take'.[41] And Ovid describes the 'drops of bloud' which 'do distil from Gorgons'. Taking these morbid appearances as an example of spontaneous generation, he brings in Arabic influences on the Renaissance in reminding readers that '[i]n Egypt as Frogs and Mice are engendered by showres of rain, so also are serpents: and Avicen saith, that the longest hairs of women are easily turned into Serpents.'[42] Strangest of all are stories of human–serpent generation, such as the tale of a woman who 'brought forth a living Serpent in stead of a childe'.[43] Finally, Topsell's sources also reveal the serpent's troubled relationship to humans and creatures, for '[e]ver since the Devil entered into the Serpent', it has been 'hateful to all'. Topsell explores the snake's association with cats and foxes, two other animals understood to have complex and potentially antagonistic, though less malign, relationships with humans. Throughout his discussions, however, the possibility of the spontaneous generation of snakes is a given, and he is able to refer quite casually to snakes 'thought to be engendered of the earth'.[44]

For Topsell, serpents can vary in size from twice the height of a horse to the small snakes in fishponds; they can be dragons; they can be grouped with bees or tortoises; they can appear from or in rocks and from the bodies of men; they are the 'creeping things' of the Bible, both God's creatures and the Devil's.[45] In all their aspects serpents are figures of transformation and in their creation and generation – as God's and the Devil's creatures, certainly, but with that as part of their character as they appear in the natural world, too. Serpents are examples of the world's ability to generate creatures – a process of natural metamorphosis in their case strongly morally inflected.

Serpents, then, lived an uncertain life between the natural and supernatural realms and were supreme instances of generational transformation. The king of the species, 'called by the Grecians, Basilisoes, and the Latines Regulus, because he seemeth to be the King of Serpents' crystallises problems of generation within and beyond nature that were more loosely associated with all serpents. The creature is not particularly big, and his defining attribute is not his 'uncurable' 'poyson', but his fearsome hissing. The creature 'goeth half upright, for which occasion all other serpents avoid his sight', as well they might. As for humans, they perish soonest by proximity to the cockatrice because, 'with his sight he killeth him, because the beams of the Cockatrices eyes do corrupt the visible spirit of a man', causing death.[46]

The serpent is extraordinary in its ability to raise its head, in its crown and in its powers. But its natural history is disputed:

> There is some question amongst Writers, about the generation of this Serpent: for some (and those very many and learned) affirm him to be brought forth of a Cocks Egge. For they say that when a Cock groweth old, he layeth a certain Egge without any shell, in stead whereof it is covered with a very thick skin, which is able to withstand the greatest force of an easie blow or fall. They say moreover, that this Egge is laid only in the Summer time, about the beginning of the Dog-days, being not long as a Hens Egge but round and orbicular: sometimes of a dusty, sometimes of a boxy, sometimes of a yellowish muddy colour, which Egge is generated of the putrified seed of the Cock, and afterward set upon by a Snake or a Toad, bringeth forth the Cockatrice, being half a foot in length, the hinder part like a Snake, the former part like a Cocke, because of a treble combe on his fore-head.[47]

While citing other writers on 'the hidden miracles of nature' Topsell is himself uncertain whether 'a Cock can conceive an Egge', but persuades himself that such a phenomenon is indeed possible, when a cock 'groweth old' and 'ceaseth to tread his female' so that 'a certain concretion bred within him by the putrefied heat of his body, through the staying of his seed generative, which hardeneth into an egg'. This, hatched by the cock or another beast, duly 'bringeth forth the worm' which is, either by sight or venom, so deadly to man. He thinks the hatching and 'nourishing' can be by the cock itself or another beast, but what hatches is 'a venomous Worm, such as are bred in the bodies of men, or as Wasps, Horse-flies, and Caterpillars engendered of Horse-dung, or other putrified humors of the earth'.[48]

Located in the realms of the marvellous and the natural simultaneously, the generation of the basilisk suggests that underpinning the interrogation of monsters ('man or a fish?') lies the deeper question of generation. How do beings reproduce? Topsell, for all his attention to the life of the animal in the world is attentive to the more extraordinary processes of generation from the half-formed status of the bear-cub as it comes into the world, to the extraordinary genesis of the basilisk. If the mating of stones in the crevices of rocks deep underground brings about the generation of marvellous and precious gems, then the generation of the poisonous creature makes the reader consider monogenesis, age and gender in the process of creation. Rocks have a place in the catalogue of monsters, as does the basilisk – and both show thinking both on the generative power of matter in relatively populist discourse as opposed to the learned tomes that historians of science stack up as 'modern' and scholastic and point back to the strange process of generation.

In the basilisk's case, the question of generation, if taken in the sense of where the basilisk might come from, leads to the question of representation and counterfeiting. The listing of names for creatures from several sacred and secular languages is a repeated feature of Topsell's descriptive technique, and in the case of the cockatrice it seems that the listing of names indeed stabilises a potentially highly diverse creature found in African, Egyptian, European and domestic narratives and traditions – as well as Greek and Hebrew. Especially as there was cultural diversity in what was found to be a cockatrice, perhaps such a richness of versions destabilised as well as confirming its status. Thus, the King James Bible Isaiah 59.5 suggests, 'They hatch cockatrice' eggs and weave the spider's web: he that eateth of their eggs dieth, and that which is crushed breaketh out into a viper'. However, as Thomas Browne rightly noted, there was

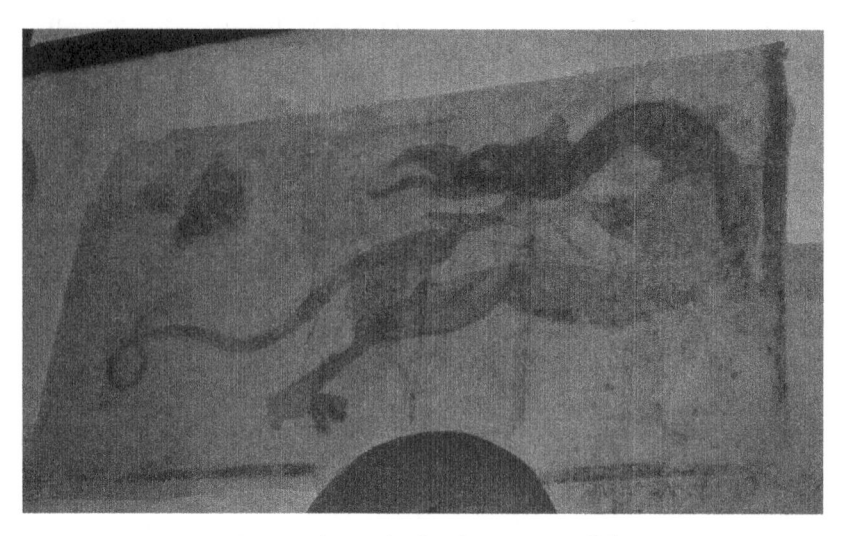

9 Dragon, St Mary's Church, Wiston, Suffolk.

'a misapprehension' in scripture, as to whether cockatrice or adder was intended. Thus, by the time Topsell explored the creature it came with fearsome, but also slightly compromised, classical, and above all Biblical, authority.[49]

The Biblical presence of dragons and basilisks gave it an identity, not an earthly form. It was representation in word and image, often working together, that gave them life. These creatures have a vivid and established representational life with a deep written history, iconography and vernacular narrative associations – more established, perhaps, than that of the near mythical rhinoceros. As pre-Reformation wall paintings suggest, dragons and beasts were readily recognised by congregations where, arguably, they offered representational evidence that returned viewers to the Bible stories they knew equipped with iconographic and interpretational tools.

Discussing the basilisk, Thomas Browne cites Scaliger's authority that 'men commonly counterfeit the form of a Basilisk with another like a Cock, and with two feet; whereas they differ not from other Serpents, but in a white speck upon their Crown.'[50] Writing in the mid seventeenth century, Browne goes back to Scaliger as an authority enabling discrimination between a truly and falsely represented basilisk (in Browne's designation Topsell's representation was close to correct). There is, perhaps, ambiguity in Browne's use of the term 'counterfeit' as both imitation and pictorial or literary representation. A 'counterfeit' dragon, basilisk or hydra seems to imply the existence of a real one. To 'counterfeit' such creatures might be to draw them, or, perhaps, to use human skill to make them in other ways. Thus, when Leonardo da Vinci came to draw a dragon, for him, 'one of your imaginary animals', he proposed that the head be an assemblage including the head of a mastiff, a greyhound's nose, a cock's temples and the neck of a 'water tortoise'.[51]

Da Vinci's dragon recipe suggests some of the distinctions between modern and Renaissance perceptions of the relationship between nature and art. Where, if at all, should we see a break between creation by nature and by human art during this period and, specifically, later in seventeenth-century English writing? Famously, Francis Bacon's analysis of the world conjoined nature and art, with art as nature forced.[52] He noted that 'nature, like *Proteus*, is forced by art to do what would not have been done without it; and it does not matter whether you call this forcing and enchaining, or assisting and perfecting'.[53] Usually cited as part of the debate on whether Bacon incites the 'torture' of nature, this passage is also a summary of Bacon's understanding of nature in its different manifestations.

Bacon's modelling of nature brings into play another set of ideas about the world's transformability. As Sophie Weeks notes (and as discussed in the introduction), for Bacon 'nature' can be unbound (free and unshaped by humans), bound (shaped by humans), or manifest in phenomena that could not have come into existence without human art. Weeks discusses the examples of a rainbow; a humanly manufactured rainbow; things which would not '"exist except by the hand of man"'.[54] Weeks argues that this understanding of nature is itself derived from Bacon's hyper-materialist view of the atom being the origin of all – no mere thing but the very cause of nature's many manifestations.[55] The nature of Bacon's understanding of matter, and therefore of the natural world (discussed in the introduction), is important within the history of science but in its specificity is adjacent to this discussion of the wider vernacular. However, a key motivation for Bacon's interest in matter is the question of metamorphosis. One of Bacon's driving motivations, based on the understanding of matter as protean and so found either free or in the shapes of Protean energy (bound), is the question of whether – given that within that scheme marvels can occur – human intervention could not only mix or combine elements of nature, but could effect transformation of matter at the deepest level.[56] In *The Wisdom of the Ancients* (1609), the fable of Proteus is important to Bacon because he wonders whether humans might be able to alter the very atoms of nature. Given nature occurs unbound and bound, and that monsters and marvels (in his opinion) bear witness to extraordinary and apparently unique changes to the very atoms that are nature's building blocks, man might be able to make Protean, struggling nature take wholly new shapes in the same way nature itself does so. Such would indeed be an effective capture of Proteus, wrestled back into his own shape yet under human power.

Bacon, therefore, seeks to intervene at a 'deep' level to effect metamorphosis just as monsters are metamorphoses of nature's more usual procedures. For some vernacular writers, therefore, although originating very differently, Bacon's ideas did not seem to be highly distinct from the Aristotelian potential for metamorphic change. However, it did mean that Bacon was interested in trumpery and the fakery of such effects. Accordingly, Salomon's House, he is at pains to indicate, will discriminate amongst nature, art and fraud. In a perverse collection there will be, "'houses of deceits of the senses; where we represent all manner of feats of juggling, false apparitions, impostures, and illusions; and their fallacies'", whereas no one is to "'shew any natural work or thing, adorned or swelling; but only pure as it is, and without all affectation of strangeness.'"[57] The closer attention to the atomic level is, apparently, suggested in the prescription, for the College to interest itself in '[v]ersions of bodies into other bodies' – metamorphoses, though not necessarily of human or animal 'bodies', but substances.[58] Clearly, then, Bacon saw marvels as clues to knowledge of and so, potentially, human manipulation of, the world; hence his disapproval of confusions.

Thus, just as vernacular writing (in part and distantly derived from Aristotle) suggests any retrospective deployment of assumptions concerning organic and inorganic would be problematic, so too would any definitive understanding of 'art' and 'nature' as simply opposed – and here, for writers aware of them, Aristotelian and Baconian concepts can coincide. There is enough information to speculate a little on habits of thought and assumptions that might have impacted on thinking about wonders. For collectors, as for Bacon, the impetus seems to have been to reconstruct a history of how the world comes to be as it is – a story of transformations. The key activities of vernacular engagement with transformation involve circulated knowledge: visitors to collections followed in one another's footsteps, viewing and reviewing key objects of curiosity; descriptions in letters and notebooks multiply, challenge and cross-reference exhibits and interpretations; printed texts and images proliferate representations and narratives as do craft books; representation is particularly foregrounded as techniques of telling and display facilitate the exchange and prototypic use of images.

That strange creatures and monsters inhabited the world was attested by Pliny, the Bible, Ovid, and, in the evidence of their existence, like the unicorn's horn found in collections, juxtaposed wonder and evidentiary status. If the Bible and other texts were to be worked into the fabric of living, then to imagine the world one had not seen from what one had before one, was almost necessary. Such extrapolation is implied in da Vinci's dragon and he clearly saw the potential of the actual world to yield such known of, but not yet found creatures in material as well as pictorial form. Belon's *L'histoire naturelle des estranges poisons marins* (Paris, 1551) thus states that what the Greeks called the sea dragon was, as anyone knows, no dragon but invented from disguised rays to look like a flying serpent.[59] Indeed, if we return to Paré we find him noting that when Gessner recorded a sea monster he 'had the figure thereof from a Painter, who tooke it from the very fish, which hee saw at *Antwerpe*' and again Gessner claimed to have received from Cardano 'this monster, having the head of a Beare, the feet and hands of an Ape'.[60] While collectors seem to have accepted fake monsters as guarantors of true, there was also a persistent ambiguity about their representation, description and counterfeiting. The desire to authenticate, which might appear to force a distinction between 'natural' and 'made' monsters, seems in fact to co-exist with an ambiguous willingness to leave doubt unresolved and to allow verbal and visual representation to take priority over any desire to definitively assess authenticity. The ambiguity of the monster in terms of art and nature is registered in da Vinci's comments on the painting of dragons indicating that they might be natural, might be made, but that they continue as creatures of metamorphosis at the border between natural and supernatural.

As we see, the visual aspect of creatures such as basilisks and hydras is as important in accounts of them and in reports in printed texts. Some creatures, like the dragons in Aldrovandi's collection, were seen again and again by different generations of visitors and circulated for many years.

Commenting on the centrality of circulated images, Paula Findlen notes that each becomes a prototype for manufacture. As she puts it, 'the process of inventing nature fascinated early modern naturalists' and early seventeenth-century English engagements with dragons, basilisks and hydras suggests pleasure as well as fear – naturalists 'wanted to know how they were made while avoiding the question of whether they existed'.[61] Moreover, these creatures, reproduced in word, image and object, ensured their continued consideration. Certainly, scripture and other texts underline the possibility that such creatures are part of the great scheme of things, even if (as with the hydra) they are at present known only in versions that might be manufactured. It seems that like images and stories, specimens, even if understood as in some way only representations

108 Transforming nature

444   Vlyssis Aldrouandi
                Draco effictus ex Raia.

uianus & Rondelet. quoq. oftenderunt; legendumq pro βάτος βάτραχος, ideft, Rana, nimirū marina fiue pifcatrix, quæ quemadmodum, & Squatina, quamuis pifces fit cartilaginei, & plani, tamen pinnas habent ad natandum, nec folùm fua latitudine natant, vt ipfe Ariftot. docuit his verbis: οἱ δὲ βάτοι καὶ τὰ τοιαῦτα ἀντιτῶν πτερυγίοις τῷ ἐπιάτῳ πλάτει νέουσι: ἠδὲ νάρκη καὶ βάτραχος τὰ ἐν τῷ πρατεῖ κάτω (ἴχυσι) διὰ τὸ πλάτος τῶν ἄνω, ideft, Raiæ & fimiles pro pinnis extrema fui corporis latitudine natant. Torpedo verò, & Rana pinnas lateribus accómodatas, infra gerūt propter amplitudinē partis fuperioris. Cęterū & ifte locus mēdo nō caret, nā pro ᾗ δέ νάρκη legi debet

10 Dragon made from ray, Ulisse Aldrovandi, *De piscibus* (Bologna, 1613).

of the deferred, though promised, object, are as likely to stimulate as jade observers' appetites. The emergence of these creatures in partly acknowledged, partly disavowed adumbrations of other animals, besides inviting reflection on the relationship between nature and manufacture, also invites us to consider the places they were housed within the culture that created them – their homes in collections, printed books and, sometimes, theatrical performance.

Scholars now agree that rather than being random assemblies, European museums or collections provoked questions about art and nature, at least in the minds of informed observers.[62] Anthony Grafton reviews the presentation of the natural world in the collection set out in Francis Bacon's Salomon's House. Nuancing and challenging Horst Bredekamp's sense that Bacon saw no opposition between 'natural and artistic form' Grafton argues that 'artists and collectors came to see nature as changeable and human effort as a force constantly acting on it' and therefore, in Grafton's analysis, Renaissance art practice was at least in part in competition with nature.[63] Grafton illustrates his thesis that humans sought to compete with nature by citing Julius Caesar Scaliger's view that art can create a beauty so close to perfection that it suggests the world before the fall – a formulation which allows art to contest, and exceed, fallen nature.[64]

Certainly Francis Bacon explicitly sought to control and manipulate nature in order to create similar effects. However, Grafton's assertion is only loosely applicable to most collectors. Thus, museum-makers were aware that the demand for rarities generated their production, and they knew that commerce and the investigation of the natural world overlapped. At the same time as being aware of fraud as a possibility, and sometimes having to reconsider designations, the marvels of the bestiaries nevertheless drew collectors to buy from merchants trading in exotic remedies who had commerce with distant lands, and they bought, too, on the street or in the square.[65] Mark A. Meadow points to the Kunstkammer as a copious environment, a treasure house conveying a sense of plenitude and display, within which operate 'multiple, simultaneous, and dynamic systems of value'.[66] Amongst the numerous values were commercial, aesthetic and investigative concerns – as Meadow reminds us, Samuel Quiccheberg's *Inscriptiones* (1565), the first guide to museum display, was itself a job application.[67]

Hydras and basilisks were mobile signifiers in the collections' ambiguous systems of value. Ostensibly objects of great fear, as in Topsell's description of the gaze of the basilisk, basilisks and hydras appear tamed in European museums. For example, the hydra apparently in the possession of the French king (the hydra being associated with the French monarchy) appears in Conrad Gessner's *Nomenclator aquatilium animatium* (1560) and reappears in Topsell's *Serpents* with the same illustration. Starting from the myth of Hercules, Topsell tells his readers of 'some ignorant men of late days in Venice' who 'did Picture this Hydra with wonderfull Art' and displayed it 'as though it had been a true carkase'.[68] Giving Gessner's illustration, Topsell describes the monster given to the French king:

> The head, ears, tongue, nose and face of this Monster, do altogether degenerate from all kindes of Serpents, which is not usual in Monsters, but the fore-parts do at most times resemble the kinde to which it belongeth; and therefore if it had not been an unskilfull Painters device, he might have framed it in a better fashion, and more credible to the world.

For all that he, too, reproduces the image of the hydra, Topsell thinks others 'ought to have enquired about the truth of this Picture, whether it were sincere or counterfeit'. He has heard, though, that a seven-headed serpent resides also in the Duke's 'treasury' in Venice – which, 'if it be true', suggest that the Poets were 'not altogether deceived', and concludes, 'and thus much for the Hydra, whether it be true or fabulous'.[69] Topsell's dubious, even scoffing, approach to the hydra contrasts with his respectful ambivalence concerning the life-cycle of the basilisk, and it also contrasts with Gessner's evasion of the question of veracity.[70]

The basilisk unites concerns about generation, monsters and manufacture and where a reader or spectator who encountered it would shape their reaction. This may well have been true for other metamorphic creatures which seem to have evoked pleasure as much as fear for all their mythic importance. So, one answer to Trinculo's question about the monster – 'What have we here, a man or a fish?' – is that it depends on where he encounters it. In the stories of generation the monster might be a product of natural or supernatural transformation. In stories, the basilisk might evoke terror. But if it were Sir Thomas Browne's own basilisk, the answer would be: fish. He would explain that, using Aldrovandi's account of invention as a recipe for a basilisk as 'commonly contrived out of the skins of Thornbacks, Scaits, or Maids' he had 'for satisfaction of my own curiosity ... caused some to be thus contrived out of the same fishes.'[71] Just as Trinculo encounters the monster of his travels, so did many other Europeans. John Evelyn met a manufactured hydra in Rome in 1645:

> Passing the Ludovisia Villa, where the petrified human figure lies ... I measured the hydra and found it not a foot long; the three necks and 15 heads seeme to be patch'd up with several pieces of serpents skins[72]

Where Evelyn is partly interested in the manufacture of the hydra and singles out its specific measurements, part of the impact of such creatures seems to have been to do with their display and location. The accounts of visitors make clear the importance of trust, representation and context in shaping, perhaps governing, seventeenth-century responses to 'marvels'. In the mid seventeenth century Philip Skippon, travelling with John Ray, visited many collections and in Venice, he writes:

> We visited one Rosachio, a reputed astrologer, who was a mountebank that sold medicaments in the piazza of St. Mark. He shew'd us his collection of rarities, which were kept in pretty good order . . . We observed the tail of the Pastimaca piscis; maxillae piscis Lamiae, [an shark?] serpens volans, which had a long furrow on either side, in which were cartilaginous parts (he said) when it was alive, that served for wings; a Pyraustes or salamander, shaped like a lizard, but broader and flatter and bigger than a rat.[73]

Skippon's description of a basilisk pays as much attention to its proprietor Rosachio – astrologer, mountebank, collector and potentially fraudster – as to the creature. Skippon's travelling companion, John Ray, had a great influence on the representation of animals in histories of nature in vowing to eschew 'Fables, Presages, or ought else appertaining to Divinity, Ethics, Grammar or any sort of Humane Learning' in the description of animals.[74] In his *Observations* (1673) Ray records a visit to the Duke's palace at Modena:

> What we most minded was the Cabinet or musaeum, furnished with choice of natural Rarities, Jewels, ancient and modern Coins and Medals, ancient and modern Entaglia's, curious turn'd Works, dried Plants pasted upon smooth boards whitened with ceruss, which may be put in frames and hung about a room like pictures; and a great collection of designs of the best Painters. Among other things we took notice of a humane head petrified, a hens egg having on one side the signature of the Sun, which I the rather noted, because some years before Sir Thomas Brown of Norwich sent me the picture of one having the perfect signature of a Duck swimming upon it, which he assured me was natural. Moss included in a piece of Crystal, silver in another. A fly plainly discernable in a piece of Amber. A Chinese calendar written on wooden leaves.[75]

Clearly, Ray's reaction suggests a desire to test each thing against his own experience, to pick up tips for the collection and display of natural objects. Yet, if Ray's attitude is different from others he still registers the copious nature of the experience and picks out similar objects indicating, amongst other interests, the enduring fascination of the egg as the seat of generation. However, if his correspondent, Thomas Browne, is less consistently empirical and modern, Ray's comments show some of the limits of believing that nature exists in a way that can be apprehended by humans without the shaping of learning. Earlier, Ray had visited the collection of '[o]ne Jan vander Mere an Apothecary in this Town, with a Musaeum well stored with natural and artificial rarities', including 'Dens Hippopotami, as he pretended, though it be a Question whether or no there be any such Animal as the Hippopotamus.' He also observed without demur 'a Giant's tooth . . . the Head of a Horned Hare. A Chamaeleon. A Soland-Goose out of Greenland'.[76] The collection went on stimulating wonder, scepticism and fascination even in those who, like Ray, saw themselves as challenging the older logic of exotic accumulation. And this was in part because of the ability of the collection to yield up both much represented categories (the egg) and to create a dynamic of display that gave a context to the materials shown.

In the second half of the seventeenth century Ray sought explicitly to improve on Aldrovandi's conception of his collection as a theatre of nature.[77] However, for all their assertions, even writers associated with the Royal Society, striving to establish synchronic taxonomies of nature and histories of the interweaving of humans and the natural world, could not see everything with their own eyes. There certainly was a Baconian discrimination of nature, with a greater investment in the identification of what nature is doing in making marvels and with a greater emphasis on the unmasking of fakes which interfere in the scientist's plan to shape nature by harnessing its very, Protean, essence. Yet, earlier knowledge and its forms shaped their activity – Ray sees a giant's tooth and questions the existence of a hippopotamus. The Florentine displays of Francesco Redi, who in a courtly theatre of disenchantment, conducted experiments to prove, for example, that a Brazilian fish had no special powers against profuse bleeding. Of course, Redi's negative proofs drew their dramatic effects from the very superstition they exposed.[78] Ray relied on the knowledge of others – from his patron Francis Willughby whose work he used, to the studies of Aldrovandi and Gesner whose methods and conceptual frameworks he questioned, and brought his 'knowledge' to what he saw.[79] His contemporaries, too, were engaged with past texts so, perhaps inevitably, we also find him corresponding on the subject of unicorn fossils.[80]

Scholars have rightly emphasised the networks of knowledge and exchange which saw wonders made, amassed and exchanged but just as important were the inherited materials – objects, texts, ideas – of the generation we are examining. Less, perhaps, has been made of the ways in which materials were passed on, inherited or simply remained in place. Thus, the library of Joseph Banks, the naturalist, housed some of the volumes discussed in this chapter. Aldrovandi's collection was viewed by several generations, and his writings were printed and circulated long after he wrote. Just as the endurance of the objects and texts associated with collections was long, so versions of the collection spread Europe-wide. To return to England, although the most-researched collections are those of the second half of the seventeenth century, others existed. Certainly, reliance on the collecting of others was part of the enterprise for the Tradescants. The Tradescants, according to Arthur MacGregor, amassed rarities as a by-product of their avid botanical collecting. While the Tradescant collections follow a well-trodden path in being understood as botanical and medicinal, Tradescant may also have been familiar with a collector from a generation earlier. Sir Walter Cope died in poverty in 1614, but he had been a wealthy collector and friend of the first Earl of Salisbury – Tradescant's patron.[81]

However, as well as being shaped and reshaped by succeeding generations of collectors, the appeal of wonders crossed barriers of status, collections having popular as well as elite appeal. Henry Peacham wrote in his panegyric prefatory verse for *Coryat's Crudities* – 'Why does the rude vulgar so hastily post in a madnesse / To gaze on trifles, and toyes not worthy the viewing?'[82] Amongst the remains of kings we find 'the Fleet-streete Mandrakes', a 'horne of Windsor (of an Unicorne very likely)', the 'cave of Merlin', a 'live-caught Dog-fish', 'Harry the Lyon' and 'Hunks of the Beare-Garden'. For Peacham, in ironic mode, these wonders were as nothing in comparison to Coryat's footwear, the homely 'shoes of Odcombe', preserved even to the present hour. By 1611 the case of Coryat shows a discourse of travel elaborated to a point of highly self-conscious and celebratory irony, such that Peacham can assume his readers will recognise the interplay of cynicism and wonder drawn from travel writing in his exoticisation of London's curiosities. If some of Coryat's writings from his European tour of 1608 were helped into print by Prince Henry, the Palace at Whitehall was itself an object of tourism, with both Peacham and Thomas Platter admiring the 'immense whale rib' in Whitehall Palace.[83] The wonders brought the world to London and the experiences of distant and extraordinary scenes were evoked by the materials they left behind.

Thomas Platter records his stay in London in terms of visits and experiences, detailing the palace at Whitehall, the bear garden, the playhouse, the cockfighting and alehouses – where tobacco is taken. Fascinated by tobacco, Platter describes its pleasures, noting '[t]he herb is imported from the Indies in great quantities', and was first learned of as a 'medicine from the Indians, as Mr. Cope a citizen of London who has spent much time in the Indies informed me; I visited his collection with Herr Lobelus, a London physician'.[84] Platter segues from the cockpit to the alehouse, which makes him think of smoking, and from there moves seamlessly to recount discussions with the proprietor of a collection of wonders which he goes on to list. Platter's account is discursively unified by the discourse of curiosity and, perhaps, the emergent discourse of tourism. Particular objects or experiences are found in diverse cultural locations but when displayed elicit from Platter a dual focus on the circumstances of viewing and on the objects. Platter obviously recognises the differences between visiting Whitehall palace and smoking tobacco at an alehouse, but he also recognises linking elements of display, exoticism and wonder. Once the subject becomes Cope's collection, however, he adopts the discursive method we see so often in the response to wonders and makes a numbered list, including the following objects:

1   An African charm made of teeth.
2   Many weapons, arrows and other things made of fishbone.
3   Beautiful Indian plumes, ornaments and clothes from China.

. . .

8   An Indian stone axe, like a thunder-bolt.

. . .

10 A string instrument with but one string.
11 Another string instrument from Arabia.
12 The horn and tail of a rhinoceros, is a large animal like an elephant.

. . .

16 A round horn which had grown on an English woman's forehead.
17 An embalmed child (Mumia).
18 Leathern weapons.
19 The bauble and bells of Henry VIII's fool.
20 A unicorn's tail.

. . .

23 a thunder-bolt dug out of a mast which was hit at sea during a storm; resembles the Judas-stone.
24 a stone against spleen disorders.

. . .

27 Flying rhinoceros.

. . .

29 Flies which glow at night in Virginia instead of lights, since there is often no day there for over a month.

. . .

35 Many holy relics from a Spanish ship which he helped to capture.

40 A pelican's beak, the Egyptian bird that kills its young, and afterwards tears open its breast and bathes them in its own blood, until they have come to life.
41 A mirror which both reflects and multiplies objects.

...

43 Heathen idols.

...

47 A sea-mouse.
48 Numerous bone instruments.
49 Reed pipes like those played by Pan.
50 A long narrow Indian canoe, with the oars and sliding plans hung from the ceiling of this room.

Besides these Platter sees here 'all kinds of corals and sea plants in abundance'.[85] Like the European collections that contained basilisks and dragons, Cope's collection mixes natural and crafted objects, apprehending the world ethnographically, perhaps, rather than in a way that seeks to find the boundaries between nature and art. Henry Peacham and Thomas Platter engage the discourse of curiosity distinctly, but share the assumption that the objects are unified by the processes of display and observation; by the dynamics at work in their accommodation as objects of wonder. What has this investigation of seventeenth-century writing on stones, eggs and promised creatures, such as the basilisk, suggested? Rather than disclosing the nature of 'the monster', the evidence suggests that the monster is bound into complex, suggestive rather than always systematic, ways of thinking. Most significantly, it indicates that conceptions of living versus dead matter; nature, art and machine – and the relationships amongst them, worked differently for seventeenth-century writers than in our own time.

III *The Tempest*

A sea-mouse, a flying rhinoceros, a thunderbolt; such objects embodied questions about the world. 'What have we here?' Sixteenth- and seventeenth-century Londoners were eager to show and see the more extraordinary products of the earth and their own encounters – and acquisitions. As the play's most recent editors suggest, *The Tempest* shares the qualities of a cabinet stocked with ethnographic, natural and metamorphic marvels. The curious nature of what is shown and the dynamic of spectatorship links exhibited rarities to question-provoking displays of theatre.[86]

116   Transforming nature

The Tempest is chock full of marvels and metamorphoses. More significantly, the play's meditations on the cultural meanings of transformation and belief, scepticism, magic and illusion echo the concerns of those found in the compendia of monsters but in a reflexive and developed mode. Thus, addressing metamorphosis under the sign of generation, the play poses the conundrum of the monster alongside the magical resolution of the problem of inheritance in the main plot, strongly linking the two through Caliban's past attempt to 'people the isle' with his own progeny and his mother's flight to the island. Caliban is, for Prospero, a 'born devil' – both human, a product of generation, and devilish. For himself, he is either subject to Prospero's magic in a way that torments him or, perhaps, alienated from 'his' island by Prospero's 'humane' European knowledge and magic. Caliban has inherited the island from his mother; two pairs of brothers are divided and one plans to murder another; Prospero's explanation to Miranda foregrounds the biological aspects of inheritance, causing her momentarily to doubt that her grandmother was chaste who could bear two such contrary sons. Describing political crisis and usurpation, Prospero tells Miranda his brother 'new created / The creatures that were mine, I say, or chang'd 'em, / Or else new formed 'em' (1.1.81–3) and so, '[l]ike a good parent', trusting Prospero 'did beget of him' a 'falsehood' (1.1.94). Prospero's description of the past, and his political and familial relations are framed in a mode cognate with the island's breeding of strange and extraordinary creatures, and with his concern to reintegrate political power and family ties in the next generation. Through his language the problem of monstrous inheritances shadows the dynastic plotting.

The generation and uses of monsters, and the possible interpretation of experiences, can be explored in Trinculo's discovery of Caliban (2.2); the masque (4.1); the epilogue. These scenes, while performing much other work in a complex text, put before the audience the question of the 'monstrous' in a way that leads directly to questions of transformation and generation.

Shipwrecked and stranded, Trinculo, like Caliban, suffers from the island. He expects another storm and knows 'not where to hide my head' (2.2.22). Turning his eyes from sky to earth brings his gaze to – what?

TRINCULO: What have we here, a man or a fish? Dead or alive? A fish: he smells like a fish, a very ancient and fish-like smell, a kind of – not of the newest poor-John. A strange fish! Were I in England now (as once I was) and had but this fish painted, not a holiday fool there but would give a piece of silver. There would this monster make a man; any strange beast there makes a man. When they will not give a doit to relieve a lame beggar, they will lay out ten to see a dead Indian. Legged like a man and his fins like arms! Warm, o'my troth! I do now let loose my opinion, hold it no longer: this is no fish, but an islander that hath lately suffered by a thunderbolt. (2.2.24–36)

The evidence of his senses enables Trinculo to recognise Caliban – smell, sight and finally touch gradually reassure him that Caliban is a stunned islander rather than an extraordinary fish. Yet this discovery in itself does not invalidate his earlier scheme for display – if he can be deceived into understanding Caliban as a monster then, surely, it would be equally possible, indeed, to make his fortune with a real or fake monster, dead or living 'Indian'. Trinculo's valuation of Caliban is, notably, as an import to London and he foregrounds the creature's status as extraordinary, displayed, potentially, like the basilisk, assembled.

The commercial possibilities of wonders, Trinculo's speech suggests, inhere in their contextual signification. Caliban, flat on the ground and covered, looks to Trinculo like a monster show in England – which, of course, it is – Caliban is an actor whose role is to perform the border between the human and the monstrous. As Alden T. Vaughan and Virginia Mason Vaughan note, the text and the 1623 folio indicate that Caliban is to be understood as human. He is, the folio tells us, 'a salvage and deformed slave', but, like Trinculo, critics have been uncertain about whether or not Caliban is to be considered truly human. Caliban tells us:

> PROSPERO: ... Then was this Island
> (Save for the Son that [s]he did littour here,
> A frekelld whelpe, hag-borne) not honour'd with
> A humane shape.[87]

As Vaughan and Vaughan note, the final lines are often mis-punctuated, or wrenched from sense, to indicate that Caliban is not human, whereas, they argue convincingly, the syntax is accurately understood as above – with the implication that humans came to the island with Sycorax. However, the fact that there can be confusion about Caliban's human or monstrous status amongst editors as well as within the play indicates that his figure indeed foregrounds the border between human and monster. Certainly, the tradition of emphasising this question in literary texts had a theatrical correlative in masques and plays where figures such as the wild man posed this problem for the audience. The intense fascination sparked by such figures is suggested by a horrible incident at the Court of Charles VI in the late fourteenth century when actors who 'seemed lyke wylde wodehouses' were so fascinating that their costumes were set on fire by the torches of spectators curious to examine their faces.[88] That Caliban, though human and played by an actor, continues to be a problem of generation and social monstrosity is, of course, strongly felt by his 'parent' who sees him as inadmissible into culture because he fails to achieve humanity by being 'A devil, a born devil, on whose nature / Nurture can never stick; on whom my pains / Humanely taken – all, all lost quite lost' (4.1.188–90).

On stage Caliban, then, poses the problem of the border of the human, and, like Trinculo, critics of *The Tempest* have sought to solve it. As Vaughan and Vaughan are aware, the resolving of the question of Caliban's humanity on the terrain of the text, although accurate in itself, is a distinct question from the play's emphatically repeated presentation of Caliban as a problem of classification. For example, no sooner has Trinculo climbed under Caliban's covering than the drunken Stephano stumbles upon them – 'some monster of the isle, with four legs', shivering from 'an ague' but, alarmingly, speaking 'our language' (2.2.64–6). Like Trinculo, Stephano sees a commercial opportunity: 'If I can recover him and keep him tame, and get to Naples with him, he's a present for any emperor that ever trod on neat's leather' (2.2.67–9).

Caliban, in this scene and those each side of it, as elsewhere in the play, poses some of the problems and potentials of the monster as a border between the human and other categories. Is he natural or supernatural? If a monster, is he an exotic creature or a lame beggar? If a human, what is his parental political relationship to the island? These questions compound Caliban into a metaphor for the conundrum of the island, conjoining in his stage appearance the problems of generation and monstrosity. Trinculo's is, perhaps, the most literal attempt to place Caliban in the world. Himself displaced, Prospero too struggles more intensely with his relationship to his monstrous progeny.

However, Trinculo's exploration of the monster is only one part of a pattern of investigations. In a play deeply concerned with generation and inheritance, we find the question of generation and transformation approached in several distinct ways. The scene in which a masque is conjured by Prospero to divert Ferdinand and Miranda takes us to a quite distinct set of debates on *The Tempest* (4.1). Clearly, as critics note, familiar to audiences from Jacobean courtly entertainments, the scene may also participate in the theatrical mode of interpolating 'other kinds of drama' within the diegesis – as in the players' dumb-show in *Hamlet*. In the masque scene the thematic of generation and the question 'what have we here' are split, with the masque's framing as an aid to chaste courtship and its classical thematics emphasising generation, while its actors pose a problem of choice between or acceptance of the overlapping of the categories of actors; spirits and illusions. The masque links *The Tempest* to the English court's central interest in metamorphoses, registered in its employment of wonder and the exotic, and its mechanical and human marvels. Certainly, abstracted from their shows, the masque's black princesses, giants, machines and living landscapes are a collection of wonders and problems.[89]

The masque fashions the question of sexual love in classical discourse, and is used as an entertaining lesson in chastity for the young lovers. Yet the impact of the masque, not key to plot, is not dominantly diegetic but in terms of the nature of its illusion. The scene's distinction in mode from the overall text, inviting some editors to focus on it as an interpolation, a scene incorporated for a special event or simply written by someone else, badly, and stuffed into the play, might more helpfully invite discussion of spirits, illusions and transformation in a distinct mode.[90] Trinculo is disappointed in his monster for display, but Prospero and Ariel shape a strange show on the topic of appropriate generation. Thematically circling sexuality and generation, the mode of the masque forms and invites questions about illusion. The scene is 'magicked' by Ariel in a matter of seconds. Immediately, Iris appears and introduces Juno:

> IRIS: ... the queen o'th'sky,
>   Whose watery arch and messenger am I,
>   Bids thee leave these, and with her sovereign grace,
>   JUNO *descends*]
>   Here on this grass-plot, in this very place,
>   To come and sport. Her peacocks fly amain.
>   Approach, rich Ceres, her to entertain.   (4.1.70–5)

Summoned from her banks to this spot, Ceres is to meet Juno and seems to enter while Juno, it seems, may descend as 'her peacocks fly amain' (4.1.74). If Juno descends, the trick is performed by stage machine. However, she is not the only mystery in *The Tempest* – a banquet vanishes in what Alan Dessen reminds us is a trick of evanescence, but one which fits the desiring figures' longing for power. Leaving and vanishing are key in many ways to how magic and theatre work in the play and exist as both moments of transformation – for example when Ariel becomes invisible or the banquet vanishes – and also, possibly, moments of disruption.[91]

As many critics note, John Dee dates his reputation for conjuring not from his practices as a conjuror, but from an experiment in classical theatrical illusion. When an under-Reader in Greek in Cambridge, in 1547, he participated in a staging of Aristophanes' *Pax*. Dee created a dung beetle which flew up to Jupiter bearing a basket of food – 'the Scarabeus his flying up to Jupiter's palace, with a man and his basket of victuals on her back; whereat was great wondering, and many vaine reports spread abroad of the meanes how that was effected'.[92] The beetle caused huge outcry as the stage-machine appeared to be an insect resurrected and endowed with movement. What have we here? For the audience the question was how far Dee had transgressed – had he resurrected and re-animated an animal?

If Dee's beetle rose, alarmingly animated, to Jupiter, Shakespeare's Juno 'descends'. The dominant critical frameworks within which *The Tempest*'s marvels and miracles have been considered has been magic and colonialism, but these two approaches to the play have been substantially separate. From Walter Clyde Curry to Frank Kermode's influential edition, investigation of magic in *The Tempest* has focused on the nature and extent of Prospero's magic.[93] Barbara A Mowat stands out in this debate in her suggestion that the figure of Prospero is the product of 'several magic traditions', and acknowledges that 'Prospero's magic powers slide into fakery'.[94] Critical acknowledgement that *The Tempest*'s exploration of magic involves mixed sources – Hermetic, Cabalistic; classical myth; the idea of the wizard and popular entertainment suggest that, just as with colonial exploration, immediate contexts might shape the approach of play and audience.[95] From the vantage point of transformation, discovery and colonial desire and magic have vivid lives outside, as well as inside, *The Tempest* – staged at the heart of the city where mathematical instruments found direct application in economic exploration of new worlds. *The Tempest*'s marvels are theatrical examples of the intimacy between mechanical marvels and magical practices – a border not always clearly foregrounded even in mathematical writing. As J. Peter Zetterburg has argued, investments in status and in the recreational potential of mathematics tended to preserve the mystery by minimising, or eschewing, mechanical explanation and – in any case – although mathematics and magic were mainly separable, mathematicians like Dee were also conjurors and mathematical magic did, itself, exist. The border was blurred not only by vulgar misunderstanding but by the intimacy of the two subjects; the similarity between metamorphosis (with its diabolical implications of resurrection) and mechanical animation, conspired with the actual confluence of practices, to maintain ambiguity.[96] As discussed earlier, Francis Bacon did not distinguish art and nature but saw art as nature forced. Where *The Tempest* has been approached as a play exploring the *opposition* of art and nature, the idea of those two terms as opposed, as well as the content of the terms (as we have seen, the vital, 'Aristotelian', natural world had quite different borders from our own) renders such an approach highly problematic. In the light of the evidence accumulated so far it is possible to productively reframe *The Tempest* as exploring an important set of 'mysteries' under active investigation in the culture it addresses and represents. The questions: man or fish? Spirit or illusion? Devil or machine? Mechanics or magic? – these are all key to *The Tempest*, but not as questions it proposes to answer. These are not matters *The Tempest* wants, entirely, to decide but the nexus of ideas it explores and exercises.

The evidence of the play, and of the epilogue spoken by Prospero, suggest that the audience were expected to leave the theatre in a state of some speculation about what they have seen both intra-diegetically (are they spirits, devices, illusions?) and in terms of theatrical practice:

> Now my charms are all o'erthrown,
> And what strength I have's mine own . . .
> . . .
> . . .   Now I want
> Spirits to enforce, art to enchant;
> And my ending is despair,
> Unless it be relieved by prayer,
> Which pierces so that it assaults
> Mercy itself, and frees all faults.
>   As you from crimes would pardoned be,
>   Let your indulgence set me free.
>   ('Epilogue' 'spoken by Prospero')

While epilogues function by splitting and re-joining diegesis, this epilogue suggests that the relationship between a story of illusions and the theatrical manufacture of them has been at the core of the audience's experience. Alan Dessen, in his foray into the reconstruction of theatrical practice from texts, understands the epilogue as posing choices for actor and audience, arguing that '[t]he speaker in this Epilogue asks the playgoer to make a choice with significant implications for Prospero and for the actor playing Prospero'. For Dessen, we, and the actors, must 'choose between the verisimilar and the imaginative–conventional options' and this choice is 'a choice or problem at the heart of this romance. What do the onstage figures see? What do the playgoers see? What emerges from the conjunction or disparity between the two?'[97] Dessen wonderfully frames what a modern audience, indeed, may well be educated to experience as a *choice* between verisimilitude and stage machines; perhaps between a magus and a hocus pocus. Yet, as we find with Dee's beetle, the stone, mathematics, the basilisk, it might not be that this was a choice facing the early modern audience. If the world, in the form of vernacular texts and vernacular 'knowledge', allows the machine and the vital to coexist, even to slide into one another, how much more might the theatre live in the mode of in-between or, the undecided, or, most precisely offer the audience the pleasure of both/and.

However, as the epilogue itself permits, and as the two other scenes examined distinctly foreground, the main question – 'what have we here?' is asked and the play responds to it, but it does not require, and is not interadiegetically or (in terms of the theme of Prospero's magic), given a *single* answer. Machines, metamorphosis and making blend in *The Tempest*. If we begin from an assumption that 'nature' and 'art' are opposites then, truly, monsters and marvels in the play demand to be classified as one or the other. However, as we have seen, rather than being consistently opposed these might blend, coexist, or turn into one another; writing and thinking did not necessarily pose them as opposites. Spectacle, sight and observation in the play show nature and art as mistakable one for the other and, at other times, ambiguous.

The reactions of contemporaries to theatre, mathematics and to creatures promised by the Bible but yet undelivered as well as Bacon's discussions of 'nature' suggest that in some circumstances machines and monsters could be intimately related. Witnesses might not distinguish one from the other, or might ask whether one can become another. There seems to be a contingent rather than consistent boundary between machine and creature. We can also distinguish between an Aristotelian sense of the possibility of a falling away of creature-status, towards monstrosity and, potentially, an even lower order of being, and a Baconian sense that the world is, indeed, Protean but that very quality is a cue to humans to capture, manipulate and control – to force the natural world to work human will.

To go back to Trinculo's question, then, although he does resolve his doubt about Caliban's humanity that that doubt is so often replayed in approaches to the text alerts us to an implication of the shift in the nature of the natural world as it is modernised by discipline. The response to Trinculo's question, just like that to Dessen's, need not be that of choice but can, indeed, be that of degree – 'to what extent'. Thus, as Bacon's intimate linking of nature and art asserts, maths might become magic; a beetle might be nature resurrected and re-animated. 'Magic' named an extreme metamorphosis between machine and nature, but that one might *see* metamorphosis, transformation of shapes, was a lively possibility. And several explanations for the experience were available. Not choice but the disturbing possibilities of both/and thinking animated the moment of vernacular mixture and metamorphosis: Caliban might be human or monster; actors might play clockwork or spirits; the masque might use spirits or illusions. Thus, when strange shapes bring a banquet to the exhausted Alonso, Sebastian and Antonio they elicit the response:

> SEBASTIAN A living drollery! Now I will believe
>   That there are unicorns; that in Arabia
>   There is one tree, the phoenix' throne, one phoenix
>   At this hour reigning there. (3.3.21–4)

Antonio, too, marvels in explicitly sceptical terms rejoining,

> I'll believe both;
> And what else does want credit, come to me
> And I'll be sworn 'tis true – Travellers ne'er did lie,
> Though fools at home condemn 'em.' (3.3.24–7)

As we have seen, machines could be recognised as generating magical metamorphoses; stones might spawn serpents; words conjure basilisks and dragons into actual existence. The borders of the human, the natural, the supernatural and the mechanical were, indeed, not where we know them. However, significantly – as we have seen, although sharply defined theologically (resurrection, for example, is forbidden), the categories themselves are not altogether constituted as in a modern world – they are clearly not wholly distinct or bordered categories in the vernacular or even 'scientific' imagination. And we can see that the very forbidding of resurrection suggests that it is, after all, a possibility. *The Tempest* shows the island as repeatedly producing problems of knowledge and wonders – but rather than deciding it shows Trinculo resolving doubts, Sebastian and Antonio abandoning scepticism.

The small-scale question of what might be implied by Trinculo's discovery of Caliban, and the way he discusses him, has led to much wider questions of culture. What we would see as machine versus metamorphosis; nature versus art, for Trinculo, and for early modern vernacular interpreters more generally, presented a much more ambiguous and potentially undecided range of possibilities. In attempting to put apparently distinct kinds of writing into discussion with one another it has emerged that, at least in the uncontrolled experiment that was seventeenth-century London, marvellous nature and art was the preserve of science, collecting, spectating, and, above all, was explored rather than answered – in writing. Furthermore, the intertwined meanings of metamorphosis and generation, crystallised in the problem of the monster, were canvassed in collections, geometrics, compendia and theatres all at once. In terms of transformation and metamorphosis, this short study of generation and monstrosity suggests that the living and the inert were not always foundational categories in seventeenth-century thinking, but they might also be an ambiguous and vibrant interplay of the two. Texts repeatedly put before audiences the enigmatic question of how generation happened. We have been looking at an epoch of metamorphosis, a particular time when transformation was in the minds of writers and mathematicians, nature and art were intimately linked and the egg was a house of mystery that might disclose a chicken or a flying serpent – a basilisk.

There are evidently strong relationships between generation and transformation in sixteenth- and seventeenth-century writing; the two are linked by the evidence of human and animal reproduction, and, by understandings of the nature of the world itself. The very process of the generation of beings could be called metamorphic in either Aristotelian or Baconian formations. Such intertwining of generation, change and life instantiate a long-held moment in which a flying beetle might be mechanical, magical or an aspect of the earth's extraordinary generative power. But is it possible to identify more precisely patterns of expression and thought that are linked to the specific underpinnings in Aristotelian and Baconian thinking rather than being aspects of imagination and textuality, speculation? More specifically, we can ask how enduring was the mode of 'both and' that characterises the writing we have been exploring, and what does its status tell us about the culture that produced it? In order to explore the cultural place of the way of thinking we have been looking at, let us turn to the more limited field of the writing of generation and transformation, and to the relationships between experiential science and textual imagination, in the second half of the seventeenth century. After the Civil War, in theory at least, the new world of science was beginning to bloom and flourish – so what does vernacular writing suggest about the place of transformation in scientific and wider thinking on doubt, experiment, experience, texts, objects and animals.

IV Generation disenchanted? Egg, lobster, dragon

> From Words, which are but Pictures of the Thought,
> (Though we our Thoughts from them perversely draw)
> To Things, the Minds right Object, be it bought[98]

So wrote Abraham Cowley in his poem prefacing Thomas Sprat's history of the Royal Society, published in 1667. It is perhaps paradoxical that poetry is used to offer a tendentious assertion that the metaphorical, figurative and

Generation disenchanted? 125

linguistic is to be removed and replaced by an uninterrupted encounter with 'Things'. By the time John Locke came to write about monsters, they had a different cultural valency. The Royal Society reinforced the claim of the vernacular to describe the natural world. But does this imply a thorough disenchantment of the world in which metamorphosis is newly, but solely, the magic of the closely observed transformation of insects?

Responding to that question, this section explores some of the themes and creatures we have encountered – eggs, dragons and made creatures – in the later seventeenth century. Cowley's announcement notwithstanding, writers continued to wonder about the source and causes of unusual forms. How is a creature made, shaped and misshapen? Exploration of the slightly later writings of the period of the Royal Society clarifies a little the specific ways in which that discussion changed. In the later seventeenth century, figures such as Francesco Redi in Florence and William Harvey, John Ray and Edward Tyson in England justly claimed to re-examine the natural world systematically and to implement versions of Baconian, and, at times Cartesian, understandings.

As we saw in the Introduction, this moment is widely understood as involving the loss of an 'enchanted' view of nature. Historians of science both question the status of that disenchantment and trace the status of competition, collaboration, networks amongst participants. Thus, as a recent discussion of the importance of the 'scientific revolution' puts it, though the claims to revolution have been overstated, even taking into account 'continuity with the past, it seems undeniable that some things did change'.[99] In the long term these shifts do mark epochal change and lead to disciplinary development; in the short term, writers and readers were aware of immediate writings but also the huge body of past writings, a small section of which we have explored. Taking as a small sample the writings of Edward Tyson (an innovative anatomist); the compilation of a non-scientific figure, James Duplessis; William Harvey's discussion of the egg; and finally a story of the Oxford Physic Garden allow us to examine the rhetoric, argumentation and figurative language with which the writings of this period register and engage with transformation and generation.

Let us turn to anatomy, one of the key projects of the Royal Society, and to the writing of Edward Tyson. The 'Preliminary Discourse' to his printed account of the dissection of a 'porpess' advertises Edward Tyson's claims to innovation and a serious, critical engagement with past writings. For Tyson, not even 'the discoveries of the *Indies*' have 'more enriched the world of old, than those of *anatomy* now have improved both *Natural* and *Medical* Science'.[100] He finds 'Nature's *Synthetic* Method' best described by this '*Analytic*' method of taking apart 'this *Automaton*' and 'viewing asunder the several Parts, Wheels and Springs that give it life and motion'. Interrogation of animal bodies (zootomy), he finds, can 'extort a Confession of its admirable contrivance and workmanship. In every animal there is a world of wonders; each is a Microcosme or a world in itself'.[101] In this passage we might find Tyson a mechanist in his commitment to anatomy, Baconian in his ready plan to force nature to 'confess' and reaching for the evocative old language of microcosm to describe the 'wonder' of animals as miniature worlds. That the wonder of anatomy embodies a divinely sanctioned curiosity is reinforced on the title page, where Tyson quotes Sir Thomas Browne's insistence that the 'world was made to be inhabited by Beasts, but studied and contemplated by Man: 'tis the Debt of Reason we owe unto God, and the Homage we pay him for not being Beasts'.[102] The term 'contemplation' binds together meditation and reason, hinting at prayer. Yet this defence is more specific than Fenton's reminder that God left the world unknown that we might discover it, in that Tyson, the anatomist, focuses on the simultaneous availability and wonder of the animals. These have a place in the world on their own terms, but also for man who, in the very act of contemplating them, proves himself above them. In this short extract from a longer passage dealing with the need for man to repay God's labour in the creation by investigating the world, Browne offers Tyson an energetic coupling of the use and wonder of animals.

Tyson's 'Preliminary Discourse' deploys a rhetoric of enthusiastic innovation, proposing, as if on the spur of the moment 'a rude Draught or Sciaography of a *Natural History of Animals*', and one focused initially on British, not exotic, creatures.[103] The schema he proposes embraces '*Physiological*', '*Anatomical*' and '*Medical*' evidence. Physiology will include the places animals are bred; their food and lifespan. But it will also include 'Names' and '[a]ny remarkable Observations relating to their sagacity, *&c.*'[104] So, the history of an animal, or a species, is to be understood using very much the same evidence that Topsell had used at the start of the seventeenth century; both history in culture and environment are foregrounded. This is to be combined with Tyson's innovation in anatomy and an 'accurate Dissection and Description of all the *solid* Parts', with 'figures' where necessary and, particularly 'Lastly, *Embryotomia* and the History of *Generation*' with an amorous description of naked nature:

> Nature viewed in her naked form, in the first organization of Animal Bodies, before she hath drawn over the veil of flesh and obscured her first lines by the succeeding varnish of her last hand, more freely displays herself, and suffers us to behold the disjointed Parts of this admirable Machine, and how it is that in time she puts them all together.

Finally, the medical account is to establish a 'history of Cures performed on Brutes'. Backed up by an innovatively 'realist' rhetoric of dissection, this amounts to both innovation and, once again, advertisement. Animals themselves, in Tyson's account were miracles of detail and, potentially, system; he observed, had drawn and collected and stored tissue and whole beasts.

Above all, Tyson insists, the study should work from the small to the bigger picture – '*Malphigi* in his Silk-worm hath done more, than *Jonston* in his whole book of Insects'.[105] Malphighi here stands wonderfully well for starting small and building up, for besides many other discoveries, Malphigi's use of the microscope in insect anatomy made crucial discoveries in their respiratory systems. Tyson's innovations here are in harmony with, not contradistinction to, earlier approaches. 'Zootomy' is a key innovation, grounded in systematically rigorous attention to detail, but this sits easily beside other investigations conceptualised in ways profoundly contiguous with the past and – in moving to zootomy – there is no doubt that Tyson's interest in generation follows naturally from writers such as Paré. The rhetoric of innovation and renovation of the discipline of natural history, or, rather the rhetoric of its inauguration, is powerful and, certainly, claims novelty. Assertions of innovation are forcefully articulated in Sprat's *History* of the Royal Society. Sprat here makes explicit the bracketing from discussion of 'two Subjects, *God*, and the *Soul*', leaving '*Men's bodies*', 'the *Arts of Men's* Hands' and '*works of Nature*' as the proper objects of inquiry by the '*Fundamental Law*' that wherever possible '*Experiment*' by members themselves was the preferred method.[106]

Tyson was undoubtedly keen to pursue the agenda of the Royal Society but even as he termed his zootomic subjects 'automata' he found a world within each one. Like Paré, Tyson was interested by resemblances between animals and humans and his consideration of the anthropomorphic pig of Weeford is suggestive. In 1699, soon after he published his dissection of an Orang-Utang, which in the prefatory essay used myths of fairies and the wild man of the woods to trace out possible relationships with the human, Tyson sponsored a paper read at the Royal Society and subsequently published in the *Transactions*: 'A Relation of Two Monstrous Pigs With the Resemblance of Humane Faces. The paper was by Sir John Floyer, the longtime physician of Lichfield, a man who occupied an intermediate position in communication with his patients, strange pigs, local knowledge on the one hand and, on the other, with the Royal Society where his findings were '[c]ommunicated by Dr. Edward Tyson'.[107] The intention, to describe 'Monsters' in order to 'prove that the Distortion of the parts of a *Fetus*, may occasion it to represent the Figure of different Animals without any real Coition betwixt the two Species', fits Tyson's zootomical agenda:

> In *May* 1699. There was shewed to me a Pig, at *Weeford* in *Staffordshire*, with a Face something representing that of a Man's; the Chin was very like that of a Humane *Fetus*, and the roundness of the Head, and flatness of the Ears, surprized all Persons, and they did usually apprehend it to be a Humane face, produced by the Copulation of two Species.

But after looking at it for a long while the author notices 'a depression of the bones of the Nose in that place which was betwixt the Eyes; in which the Pig's face seem'd to me to be broken', and concludes that the monstrosity derives not 'from the Conjunction of both Kinds' but was caused by 'compression of the womb'.[108] This conclusion is reinforced by a consideration of the pig's imaginative faculties, concluding that '[i]t is not to be thought that the Imagination of the Sow could be so violent as to distort the bones without injuring the rest of the Pigs, which appeared all sound.'

Considering further what might have caused the deformity, he considers 'the figure of a Mule, that being an Animal produced by the Copulation of an Ass and a Mare, the extremities of the body (feet, tail etc.) resemble an ass'. He argues that 'by this we can observe that the Female contains in her Eggs the first Rudiments of the animal of her own Species, and that the impregnation only changes some of the extremities into resemblance of the Male', so the egg, it seems, literally rules the core of the animal.[109]

Floyer goes on to compare this natural monster with one 'born at *Brussels Anno* 1564' described by Paraeus as sporting 'a Humane Head, Face and fore Feet like Hands and Shoulders; but the rest of the Body like another Pig'. This example is crucially different from the pig in question which 'had no Hands, neither any part truly Human'. At the same time, though, its existence (at least in writing) allows us to examine the terms on which Floyer engages with writing on monsters. He notes that:

> *Licetus de Monstris*, gives many odd Stories of the mixture of many Animals, of Pigs with a Man's Head, and Pigs with Dogs Heads; and a Monster half Man, and the lower parts like a Dog, and this both *Cardano* and *Paraeus* describe. This seems to contradict our new Discoveries; for if the Male supplies the *Animalcula*, the *Fetus* must always be of the same Species as the Male, if the Female supplies it of her Kind, but this Monster must be by a mixture of Species.[110]

Under the heading of monsters caused '*by the confusion of seed of divers kinds*', in Paré's English *Works* the half man half dog and pig with man's head are duly illustrated.[III] Floyer's engagement with earlier authorities is far from dismissive. It carefully tests the monsters of earlier literature against the new assumption of the offspring of species mixture. In Paré's case, particularly, the report goes to the trouble of finding a similar monster in his text, but, more significantly, Paré's understanding of confusion of different kinds of seed as the cause is accepted within the narrative and, while the actual monsters in his work are questioned, the diagnosis of cause is shared and more intensively discussed. Thus, the paper qualifiedly accepts that species mixture can happen, and when it does can cause particular and specific mutations not found when the cause is an event during gestation. Rather than rejecting the evidence of earlier authorities this is reinterpreted to indicate that while some monsters were created by accidents, other, human monsters occur through imagination, yet others through species interbreeding. For all that the paper ends on a sceptical note, asserting 'I believe either Fiction, or want of Observation has made more Monsters than Nature ever produced', it in fact offers three possibilities for the formation of monsters: physical deformity; imagination and species mixture – in this case, clearly, bestiality.

Rhetorically this text is engaged in re-evaluation, comparison and contrast and is clearly both drawing on earlier writings and understandings and excluding certain previously implicitly permissible components in the discussions of monsters (such as interventions and punishments by the divine or extraordinary marvels – issues which in other writings continued to be invoked). It offers a re-evaluation and refreshing of the hierarchy of likely generational causes of monstrous transformations. Within that reorganisation the significant shifts include a reinterpretation of the value of imagination which is shifted in being re-allocated from the influential dreams of the mother in shaping the foetus and in the critical approach to the anthropomorphising eyes of beholders and pens of writers – busy making monsters. The claim that 'Fiction, or want of Observation' make, proportionally, most monsters decisively shifts responsibility for monstrosity to storytellers and audiences. And, in pushing for decisive and precise definition based on observation, the paper presses towards natural causes. However, at the same time, the question of species mixture is isolated as a key cause.

As the causes of monsters are narrowed, and certain things are dropped or more thoroughly excluded from 'scientific' analysis (so God's judgements and diabolic intercourse, for example, are unmentioned) the question increasingly comes to focus on the mysterious process of generation, particularly the large or limited properties of the male and female seed and organs of generation. And, as the egg comes to be shared amongst all creatures, the monster seems indeed to come closer to home, while remaining just as intensely associated with transformation as in earlier texts. When species mixture was one cause amongst many of the creation of monsters, bestiality was an accepted explanation but not a pressing one. When the possibilities for the generation of monstrosity are restricted, though, sex between species, and so between beast and man, being physiological, come to the fore. For example, in the Floyer and Tyson piece where just three possibilities are in play – the imagination; physical accident in the womb affecting the process of generation; species mixture creating mule-like but, presumably in more distantly related creatures, unviable monsters – sex between man and beast becomes a major explanatory force. Monsters come close to home, then, being produced by intra-human sex and by sex with animals. It is a matter for speculation whether this characterisation of extraordinary unions and amazing, or maimed, offspring is disenchanted or, more precisely, a further and more systematic location of the transformational mysteries of generation in the realms of the natural.

While Floyer's and Tyson's accounts emphasise the place of anatomy in understanding the animal, and so monstrosity, they do so on the terrain that remained so important in the discussion of monsters – the question of the relationship between the self and the monster. Monsters, as Floyer's paper indicates as clearly as Paré's writing, attract thoughts and dreams not only because they present an object potentially distinct from the self but one which also promises, or threatens, similarity to the subject. At the same time as hinting at a metamorphic potential between reading subject and shocking object, the object hints at a greater ambiguity of matter, inviting the subject to ask not only about his own, but about the world's ability to transform and generate startling new exceptions.

Clearly, the safety and nature of the self had always been at stake in writing and reading about monsters. Thus, Caliban is troubling because he is, if compromisedly, human. Paré notes the plight of surviving monsters – who 'doe not love themselves, by reason they are made a scorne to others' and live 'a hated life'. Explicitly investigating the self, Michel de Montaigne wrote on many of the same 'monsters' as Paré.[112] Arguably, in its narrowing down of the possible causes of monsters, Floyer's paper, endorsed by Tyson, intensifies and in its concentration on sexual reproduction and species makes specific and bounded – limited, but at the same time more intense – the bond between the subject and the naturalised monster.

We can compare such texts with the testimony of an eighteenth-century amateur in James Duplessis' manuscript, 'A Short History of Human

Prodigies and Monstrous Births'. Duplessis, writing more than half a century after Cowley's assertion of the encounter with the 'Thing' as the basis of a new philosophy, binds the reader into a web of story, exoticism, testimony, popular culture and hand-coloured illustration. A wide range of extraordinary humans, culled from a number of sources, gambol and bump through Duplessis' pages, many carefully illustrated. He lists the phenomena of travel literature ('A Spotted Negro Prince' is carefully illuminated); a hermaphrodite's genitals are revealed by a flap. We find monsters likely to imply mixtures of seed, but quite extraordinary, such as 'a child born of a sheep in France'.[113] Unsurprisingly, then, the Lithopodion of Sens is lodged, petrified, amongst the other exhibits.[114] At the same time, though, he illustrates a detail that links him closely to the catalogue. Offering the reader an image of a 'lobster', potentially a child in the form of lobster, he notes that this particular 'Monster' was 'born' to his own mother in law.[115] Given the conclusions of Paré and others that species mixture was a likely cause of such births, we can see why Duplessis would take notice of a lobster-birth. We can speculate that his motive in advertising rather than concealing such a fishy happening might be related to his insistent exoticisation of wonders. Certainly, in the world of Duplessis' miscellany, bad luck can simply strike – he may be related to a lobster but we need only pause to see that many have suffered worse, implicitly arbitrary, fates. Like the lithopodion, perhaps, the lobster is an 'Uncommon', and implicitly undeserved, 'Sport of Nature'. Many of the various approaches to the monster and contextual frames flourished for a very long time in popular vernacular representations. In texts like Duplessis' writing on the world and his family, as in the case of the much reprinted *Aristotle's Masterpiece*, the interchange between what readers bring to texts and the importance of cheap print in creating what Mary Fissell calls 'vernacular epistemology' within which ideas of the influence of maternal imagination, the power of external experience to influence the foetus (for example), co-existed with other causes.[116]

While this evidence suggests that it is Quixotic to put a terminus to the metamorphic beliefs and texts within the seventeenth century, it is also clear that in formal, as opposed to vernacular, knowledge metamorphosis in generation was being naturalised and reframed. In this context, the egg was a favourite focus of experimental attention and occupied an increasingly important role in theorising the transformative magic of generation. Intense debate over the role and significance of the seed and the egg was developing.[117] Just as monsters remained the starting place for investigation and speculation on metamorphosis and the human and animal, the egg remained at the heart of the mystery of generation and transformation. Given that he did focus on the egg, we might expect that the disenchantment of metamorphic generation, an enchantment sustained in different ways in Aristotelian and Baconian writing and thought, would come from a figure largely absent in this debate: René Decartes, with his emphasis on experimental observation and the testing of hypotheses. However, although as Vincent Aucante discusses, Descartes' work suggests three distinct phases attempting a complete understanding of the workings of the human body (an investigation into the nature of seed; experiments on eggs; a return to the question starting with the role of the blood mixed in circulation with the seed) his work was far from making the running on generation.[118] Starting from an insistence on material causes, Descartes does indeed reject the idea of the earth itself playing a vital, generative role. He argues against Aristotle that there is female seed. Clearly trying to reach inside the egg to observe the 'why' and 'how' of the process of generation, Descartes followed the lead of Fabricius d'Aquapendente who, like Aldrovandi had experimented with eggs by charting the growth of a foetus day by day.[119] In this experiment eggs hatched at the same time were allowed to grow, one being broken each day in order to chart the growth of the chick.[120] However, this did not yield Descartes fresh insights. The egg, as for Rueff, still screened the mystery of creation from prying eyes. Even when Descartes returned to the question of generation, basing his thinking on the action of the blood, his findings remained inconclusive – so much so, indeed, that as Aucante points out many have regarded his work in this area as juvenile fragments.[121]

In terms of transformation and generation, then, Descartes' work might represent a new approach but the transformative process whereby seed changed to yield up a creature both like and unlike its parents remained a mystery. Descartes' insistence that heat and motion were at the heart of physiological processes did not solve the mystery of generation. Indeed, while spontaneous generation, whether taking Aristotelian form or partaking of the Paracelsian emphasis on putrefaction, was not compatible with Cartesian materialism, Descartes was far from triumphant. His use of the laws of motion as an approach to generation was inconclusive and, as importantly, failed to find support. In fact, John Farley argues, the problem of apparent spontaneous generation was challenged by the argument that the 'germ of preformed parts is not produced by the parent, rather it is created by God'.[122] If belief in spontaneous generation is enchantment then the magic was banished at the end not of the seventeenth, but of the nineteenth, century.[123] Moreover, more significant than Descartes in

English thinking on the embryo was Sir Kenelm Digby in his work on bodies in *Two Treatises* (1644). Influenced by Descartes, but critical of the philosopher in some ways, Digby saw and trusted in his own experiments, finding with Aristotle the animal embryo formed in a gradual process, epigenesis.[124]

Much more influential than Descartes in its consideration of the egg, William Harvey's *Anatomical Exercitations*, translated in 1653, foregrounds both the miraculous and precise nature of the egg. Yet it was prefaced by a poem which offers, perhaps, a closer view of vernacular reaction to any disenchantment of the egg – a satirical, Ovidian expostulation at the equalisation of animal and human in the egg. The editor's prefatory poem describes Harvey's discovery that 'Castor and Pollux were an *Egge*' through his investigation of beasts '[i]nnobled by the *cunning* of thy *Knife*', falling '*sacrifice* to th'Publick Good'. This is brought to the politics of family relations. The translator concludes, 'both *Hen* and *Housewife* are so matcht, / That her son *Born*, is only her Son *Hatch*' – ending 'If thou cans't scape the *Women*! There's the Art' Harvey's own writing is contrastingly reverent, affectionate, metaphorical and filled to the brim with wonder. Eggs, locating themselves within the body, move – they can claim life much more credibly than stones. The egg's vegetative soul is rhapsodised, 'An innate spirit feeds, an Infus'd Soul / Into each part'.[125]

We have raised the question of when the way metamorphosis signified changed and that is taken up again in Chapter 5 and in the Coda. For the present, the epoch of transformation in generation can be illustrated by the tales of two dragons. A dragon was discovered outside Bologna on 17 May 1572. Appearing on the day of Gregory XIII's investiture the dragon was captured and sent to the 'museum' of Ulisse Aldrovandi, where the dragon was an object of curiosity and, very soon, the subject of a treatise on dragons and serpents. Housed in the museum, the dragon is located ideologically, too, as Paula Findlen suggests, becoming a curiosity rather than a portent, firmly located in the realms of patronage and dynamically mobile in its ability to signify nature and art, a vital or a made world.[126] More than a century later another dragon was found, examined, exhibited. It was found in the Oxford Physick Garden by the director, Jacob Bobart. This English dragon is said to have been celebrated by the Oxford academy. It was examined. Descriptions circulated amongst the cognoscenti. Verses were composed upon it. During its incorporation into 'learned' circles an accurate description was sent to the bibliomaniacal Antonio Magliabecchi, librarian to the Grand Duke of Tuscany.

Yet, at length, Bobart confessed the dragon was his own work. He had, he revealed, found a dead rat in the Garden, dried it hard with a stick through the middle to shape the skin into wings and altering its head and tale. Not a portent, not a natural wonder, this dragonlet was a small joke – an aside from a practising botanist perhaps pointing at the credulous susceptibility of an engagement with the natural world founded on myth. At this point, though, its remains were preserved, we are told, as an example of 'art' in the 'museum or anatomy school' at Oxford.[127] If Aldrovandi's dragon took pride of place in a collection and secured its discoverer's social standing, Jacob Bobart's dragon seems to mark a turning point – its purpose to expose the pitfalls of fantasy and fable as a guide to planet earth. In such a role Bobart's dragon is said to have made an appearance in Samuel Butler's *Hudibras*.[128] Yet, once again, novelty itself proves a kind of dream, as the (presumably miniature) dragon was apparently preserved in the Oxford Anatomy Theatre.

Let us return, one last time, to Trinculo's question, 'What have we here?' When Georges Canghuilhem responds by describing Renaissance monsters as 'a game in which tools and even machines were treated as organs', with, at times, 'no demarcation between organisms and utensils', his powerful sense that there should be discrimination between these two shows him a modern.[129] So foundational is the division between living and inanimate in modernity, and so tightly bound to claims to accuracy, even truth, that, in shaping assumptions about the location and nature of borders between animate and inanimate matter, it is operationally true. Thus, one answer to the question of how we can mark an end to the time of metamorphic generation of monsters had traditionally been that, in the long run, the rational disciplinary protocols of 'science' brought about a victory for naturalisation.[130] That we see monsters and generation differently in modernity is perhaps evidence of the epochal difference between modern assumptions about the world and those of the earlier period. Indeed, Descartes' dissection of eggs; Cowley's 'Thing'; John Ray's 'real' – these acts, words and ideas are clearly themselves deeply in thrall to the magic of the very, infinitely receding, 'real' as much as the banishing of shadows and metaphors.

Vernacular writing on monsters and generation drew audiences from throughout seventeenth-century English society to offer forms of knowledge and pleasure to a wide audience. The evidence suggests that entwined with the sometimes specific and recondite, sometimes populist, debates of surgeons and natural philosophers on monsters, generation, the vital world, there was an audience for representations – plays, collections, shows, even medical texts – presenting the enigmas of the metamorphic universe. Yet, in the long-enduring narrative of the history of science, at the same time as readers and audiences, Platter, perhaps Shakespeare himself, the 'holiday fools' flocked, fascinated, to collections, shows and words that invited them to consider the world as a vital and transforming entity, the enchanting vital dance was winding to its end. In the ancient pattern, then, an increasingly empirical analysis of the world – as, we are told, found in the writing of Ambroise Paré, Francis Bacon and much more intensely in that of John Ray, William Harvey, Edward Tyson – breaks the charm which made a moving, metaphoric world. The time of vernacular writing and metamorphic thinking, then, is also the time of its challenge and, in defeat, its reconfiguration. The English writing of metamorphosis engages with a subject at the heart of that culture's ability to question itself – animal generation – in a century which, we are told, saw the understanding of that process transformed. Yet, perhaps the fact that they were translated into the vernacular suggests that the impact of texts such as Paré's *Works* or Harvey's *Excercitations* on generation substantially, deliberately, exceeds any narrow 'scientific' readership.

The vernacular writing of seventeenth-century England suggests that an understanding of a process of metamorphosis was at the heart of assumptions on generation and culturally pervasive in a way that for us would embrace relatively disparate concepts including hybridity, inheritance; vitalism, identification, environment. If the basic quality of generation was expressed in the world's vital spirit generating beings – spontaneous generation, as we think of it, then, clearly, as this pattern echoes in the rest of nature, metamorphosis is integrated into, not apart from, generation. *The Tempest*'s reflexive qualities remind us that the fascinating qualities of monsters and wonders were far from those of post-disciplinary separation and recombination. Rather than being a game of selection and combination that chooses to over-ride the border between living and material, as Canguilhem sees Renaissance monsters, the texts considered here suggest that the game of imagining monsters was not one of choice between 'real' and 'unreal' but, in the mode of thinking increasingly confined to 'vernacular epistemology', allowed the co-existence of possibilities that modernity was to reframe as opposites. Trinculo, of course, does decide that Caliban is an islander but even as the play knows Caliban as a subject he is also a monster, Prospero's dream progeny and a stage assemblage of displayed parts. The other shows and transformations in the play, too, may live as visions and illusions; myths and machines; nature and art.

At the other end of the century, William Harvey, with his gaze narrowed on an object – the egg – saw not the Thing that Abraham Cowley prophesied but an extraordinary mystery and an invitation to enquire within. Harvey's response to the egg shows a continued ambiguity of organic and inorganic, art and nature at 'work'. The patterns of thinking and writing that ambiguously compound generation and making (here copulation and conception); mechanical and vital; organic and inorganic are here knitted together. Harvey's egg is a metamorphic process, a metaphor and a riddle – full of promise, play and philosophy:

> The *Egge* seems to be a kinde of *Medium*, not only as it is the *Principium* and the *Finis*, but as it is the Common work or production of both sexes, and compounded by both; which containing in itself the *Matter*, and the *Efficient* or Operative *Faculty*, it hath the power of both, by which he produceth a *Foetus* like to One, or the Other. It is also a *Medium*, or thing between an *Animate* and an *Inanimate* creature; being neither absolutely impowered with life, nor absolutely without it. It is a Mid-way or Passage between the *Parents* and the *Children*; between those that were, and those that are to come, and the very Hinge and Center about which the Generation of all the Race and Family of *Cocks* and *Hennes*... for it is hard to say, Whether the *Egge* be made for the *Chickens* sake, or the *Chicken* for the Eggs.[131]

CHAPTER FOUR

Metamorphosis and civility: werewolves in politics, print and parish

11 Wolf, Edward Topsell, *Historie of Foure-Footed Beasts* (1607).

'Who, then, can doubt but that these wolves were Lycanthropes?' So Henri Boguet concludes a list of men 'changed into beasts' from Ovid's Lycaon to a wolf who recently killed thirty people in Geneva.[1] Boguet's treatise, published in French in 1590, was influential and his rhetorical question introduces us to a debate which makes the werewolf a key case in vernacular representations of metamorphosis. Could there be animal–human transformation in God's creation? Taking up Boguet's question, this chapter examines the case of the werewolf in the oral and written culture of sixteenth- and seventeenth-century England and Scotland. In pursuing the question of how becoming a werewolf transformed the human the chapter returns to the terrain familiar from the discussion of baptism, but we will also look back to Golding's Ovid.

In 1597, seven years after Boguet's suggestion that history, classical precedent and common sense tell us that men could become wolves, James King of Scotland and future King of England used the dialogue form to explore lycanthropy:

> PHILOMATHES: And are not our war-woolfes one sort of these spirits also, that hauntes and troubles some houses or dwelling places?
>
> EPISTEMON: There hath bene an old opinion of such like things, For by the Greeks they were called *lykanthropoi* which signifieth men-woolfes... suppose I that [melancholy] hath so viciat the imagination and memorie of some, that they have thought themselves verrie Woolfes indeede... and so to become beasts by a strong apprehension as Nebucad-netzer was seven years. But as to their having and hyding of their hard & schellie sloughes, I take that to be but eiked, by uncertaine report, the author of all lyes.[2]

James' Epistemon assumes the orthodox position that such are the creatures of illusion and devilish fantasy. Immediately afterwards, however, Epistemon refers to 'our war-woolfes' who are found 'preassing to devour women and barnes, fighting and snatching with all the towne dogges'. As we see, James was writing in Scotland where there were, indeed, wolves and so even as he disavows transformation his text appears to register a social world in which men experience wolf-transformation.

The debate played out here about whether or not the werewolf's actual body was transformed, or whether some other effect made that appear to be the case to both the wolf and witnesses, was an old one. In the late twelfth century Gervase of Tilbury noted the 'often raised' question 'as to whether Nebuchadnezzer was really changed into an ox by divine power'. Gervase continues, '[o]ne thing I know to be of daily occurrence among the people of our country: the course of human destiny is such that certain men change into wolves according to the cycle of the moon'.[3] Gervase of Tilbury's discussion draws on the foundational position on divine power in the creation. The medieval *Canon Episcopi* provided the official position that the devil could not encroach upon God's power. As the English Protestant John Cotta wrote, '[n]ature is nothing else but the ordinary power of God in all things created, among which the Divell being a creature, is contained, and therefore subject to that universall power'.[4]

However, that even in the twelfth century the church did not have the final say on the cultural meaning of wolf-transformation is indicated by Gervase of Tilbury's example of lycanthropy. He describes Raimbaud de Pouget, a French knight, who was cast out by the structure of vassalage. He:

became a vagabond and a fugitive upon the earth. One night when he was wandering alone like a wild beast through unfrequented woodlands, deranged by extreme fear, he lost his reason and turned into a wolf. He then wreaked such great havoc upon his country that he drove many of the inhabitants to abandon their homes.[5]

Thus, Gervase finds men transformed, but while his assertion concerns the physical body, the experience of social and political exclusion and fear seems to be an important focus here. This story of lycanthropy suggests a state generated by the collapse of a social order as manifest in individual political and psychic pain.

The orthodox position on werewolves co-existed with much apparently or actually contradictory testimony by victims, witnesses and participants, both in trials and in stories. The werewolf was further complicated by the strong association between wolves and political crisis. This political dimension of the werewolf is hinted at in Gervase of Tilbury's account and in Boguet's. Thus, in some werewolf writings God's relationship to human–animal metamorphosis is not the sole or main focus.[6] Let us turn to what these stories do tell us about the wolf, the human and their English context. The basic constituents of this context are that there are no wolves, there are witch-trials, and there is an active, indeed burgeoning, oral-literate sphere of storytelling and debate.

I Wolves

Let us turn to the wolf itself. In 1577 Sir Philip Sidney dined with Philip Camerarius in Nuremberg. Camerarius records the conversation which turned to the reason for the absence of wolves in England. Sidney was asked '*Whether it was true* (as the ancients say and the Moderns believe) *that England cannot endure wolves, either bred in the country, or brought thither out of other places*'. England's antipathy to wolves was '*a mere tale* (said Sidney)'. Rather than '*some natural and knowne propertie*' liquidating all lupines, in truth wolves did live in England – as exotic status symbols. In '*divers places of the country*' wolves were to be seen '*in parks of great lords, who send for them out of Ireland and other places to make a shew of them as of some rare beast: but it is forbidden, upon grievous penalties, to let them escape out of their enclosure*.'[7]

The curiosity of the Nuremberg humanists about the absence of wolves from England was matched, Sidney suggests, by the curiosity of the English nobility about wolves. This picture is reinforced by Edward Topsell's description of wolves 'kept at the Tower of London to be seene by the Prince and people, brought out of other countries'.

We will return to Sidney's conversation about wolves in England. For the present, we can draw from his comments some sense of the comparative nature of wolf presence and absence. As Topsell says when he mentions the magical properties of the 'partes of wolves', 'heads, teeth, eares, tails & privy parts', there is no point in him giving details, 'because I cannot tel what benefit shal come to the knowledge of them by the English Reader'.[8] The body of a wolf, natural or supernatural, is not something Topsell's readers were likely to lay hands on. Topsell's discussion of the wolf dates from 1606 and his writing partially follows Conrad Gesner. Although he does describe the bodies of the beasts Topsell does not exactly supply his readers with anatomical detail. Rather, as William Ashworth puts it, he lodges his animals in 'that complex web of associations' that links animals with 'history, mythology, etymology'.[9] As Ashworth implies, Topsell is a helpful guide to how the wolf was lodged in the thinking of early seventeenth-century England and, on the subject of the wolf, his text mediates the animal for the English reader.

The Anglophone pleasure in wolves as exotic creatures, registered in the accounts of both Sidney and Topsell, contrasts with the threatening presence of wolves in Europe. The actual presence of wolves seems to be registered, for example, in the witchcraft trials of Lorraine where, from 110 records of the trials of individuals between 1580 and 1630, 36 (33 per cent) mention wolves – against 34 cats, 16 dogs (31 per cent and 15 per cent, respectively) and the wolf beats any other wild animal with a score of two mentions each of bears and birds (at 1.8 per cent).[10] We will return to the contrast between the wolf natural and phantasmagoric, a familiar object of terror in the life of the peasant and the display of the English country house is extremely marked, and offers a distinguishing context for the circulation of werewolf stories.

Representations of wolves in early modern England draw on a rich and partially contradictory, imagistic vocabulary. Thus, in Topsell's account, the wolf is not exactly the opposite of the human but represents an animality so extreme that human society cannot mix with it. Moreover, besides being irredeemably antipathetic to the human, the wolf does display some of the characteristics which, in seventeenth-century thought, undermine human status, particularly a willingness to mix species by breeding with other kinds including with other species understood as having abilities peculiarly hostile to humanity, such as the hyena who could kill a man by merely lying on him.[11] The wolf stands in a contradictory relation to the rules of civilised human behaviour. He is understood as refusing all forms of reciprocity, amity or brotherhood, yet simultaneously, as the following chapter explores, humans are represented as strengthened (though also in some narratives subject to the degeneration associated with species-mixture) if they are able to draw on the qualities of wolves.[12]

Discussions of early modern wolves put them in a literal but also a figurative relationship to wildness. Accordingly, tracing the associations and significances of the wolf with a view to their symbolic significance rather than consistency, Topsell repeatedly distinguishes the power of the wolf from that of the lion, and reminds us that the wolf is not only savage and ravening but 'it cannot be safe for strangers to live with them in any league or amity, seeing that in their extremity they devour one another' (though, characteristically, he nonetheless gives narrative examples of such leagues).[13] Having no claim to be human, such creatures are not actually degenerate, for this is a human quality. Rather, in discussions of their collective personality, they are nevertheless perceived as sharing some of the characteristics of the degenerate and reprobate. And, of course, figuratively wolves consistently represent those who had fallen so far from God that it was safe to assume that they were damned. As this suggests, the place of the wolf in the wild co-exists with a highly developed mythic dimension of wolf-lore and, as might be expected, the werewolf, though definitely not a 'wild' creature, is referred to this material.

The 'wild', even more than the wolf, functions as a mythic category. As Hayden White puts it, '[t]he notion of wildness (or its Latinate form, 'savagery') belongs to a set of culturally self-authenticating devices... used... to confirm the value of their dialectical antitheses'. White, locating 'civilisation' as the mythic and dialectical opposite of 'wildness', goes on to discuss a specific form of degenerate wildness in which humans have fallen below the level of the human (or the differently set standard for the animals). He gives as an example those who have confused species by copulating with animals as prohibited in Leviticus 18.23–30.[14]

The status of the werewolf becomes a little clearer, then, when compared to its truly wild cousin, the wolf. The werewolf, drawing on but transforming the qualities of the wolf, embodies tension between early modern apprehension of the wild as a category completely other than the social and a sense that the werewolf is wild in a way much closer to home.[15] The werewolf can tell us something about the soul, certainly, but also about the civic and psychosocial world of post-Reformation England.

II Human in wolf likeness? Wolf-shapes in narrative

Two separate printed English narratives of the German werewolf 'Stubbe Peeter' differently indicate the need to resolve the question of the soul, exploring wolf-transformation as an index of the presence of the human.

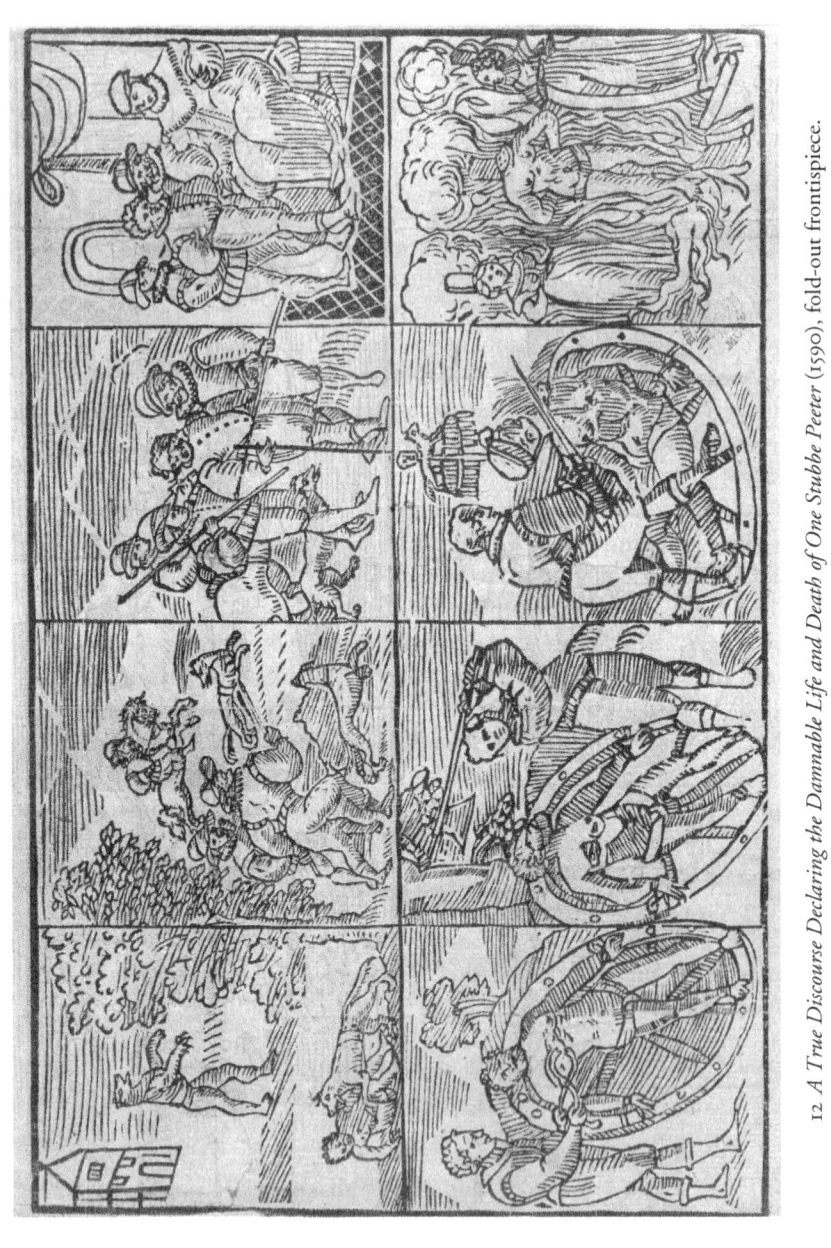

12. *A True Discourse Declaring the Damnable Life and Death of One Stubbe Peeter* (1590), fold-out frontispiece.

They also register the association between the werewolf and civic discontent. The first narrative, an English pamphlet, analyses the question of the wild and the civil, of what might be met in the fields, and the question of in what way a man might 'become' a beast:

> The Devill... gave unto him a girdle which, being put about him, he was straight transfourmed into the likenes of a greedy devouring Wolf, strong and mighty, with eyes great and large, which in the night sparkled like brandes of fire, a mouth great and wide, with most sharpe and cruell teeth, A huge body, and mightye pawes: And no sooner should he put off the same girdle, but presently he should appeare in his former shape, according to the proportion of a man, as if he had never beene changed.[16]

Stubbe Peeter's Faustian compact with the devil means that he, 'a most wicked Sorcerer', is given twenty-five years to pursue the 'divelish practice' of werewolf transformation. Having a 'tirannous hart, and a most cruell bloody minde' he becomes a werewolf of his own volition: as one who had 'followed the imagination of his own harte' without thought of redemption, because the 'shape fitted his fancye'.[17] No sooner would someone he hated or desired 'walke abroad in the feeldes or about the Cittie, but in the shape of a Wolfe he would presently encounter them, and never rest till he had pluckt out their throates'.[18] So he continues, 'sometime in the habit of a man, sometime in the Townes and Citties, and sometimes in the woods and thickettes to them adjoyning'; sometimes human and sometimes in the 'likeness of a greedy devouring Wolf' he rages in the fields outside the city.[19]

The narrative enlarges Stubbe Peeter's doings beyond the most energetic criminal career. The authenticating signatures of four named witnesses and 'divers others that have seen the same' are scarcely sufficient to retain these extraordinary and exciting events within the boundaries of the criminal yarn or trial narrative.[20] When he found 'a Maide, Wife or childe' that he lusted after 'if he could by any meanes get them alone, he would in the feeldes ravishe them, and after in his Wolvish likenes cruelly murder them'.[21] While in wolf-form he is presented as having a complex relationship to sexuality and to children (he had 'murdered thirteene young children') mutilating his victims with an epicurean savagery. He killed 'two goodly young women bigge with Child, tearing the Children out of their wombes, in most bloody and savedge sorte, and after eate their hartes panting hotte and rawe, which he accounted dainty morsells and best agreeing to his Appetite'.[22] In his human guise he has sex with his daughter (though the narrative notes that merely fornication, unrepented, is enough to warrant damnation), corrupts a previously upstanding woman to become his concubine and finally he needs a 'she-Devil' – a fully supernatural and diabolic figure – to serve his lust.[23]

As the narrative emphasises, he remained throughout at home in the city, rubbing neighbourly shoulders with those who were to fuel his solitary cannibal feasts: 'sundry times he would go through the streetes of *Collin*, *Bedbur*, and *Cperadt*, in comely habit, and very civilly as one well known to all the inhabitants therabout, & oftentimes was he saluted of those whose freendes and children he had buchered, though nothing suspected for the same'.[24] Inviting the reader to imagine fantastic danger ready to erupt in the heart of the civic order, the narrative is also careful to lodge moral responsibility firmly in Stubbe Peeter himself. In this narrative the decision to change shape remains one of will. That the human underlies the wolf is made absolutely clear in the denouement which, even as it re-stages a scene of magic transformation in Stubbe Peeter's return to human form, insists on the human agency of the wolf.[25] Men hunting 'espye him in his wolvishe likenes' and attack him so severely that:

> presently he slipt his girdle from about hym, whereby the shape of a Wolfe cleane avoided, and he appeared presently in his true shape & likenes, having in his hand a staff as one walking toward the Cittie; but the hunters, whose eyes was stedfastly bent upon the beast, and seeing him in the same place metamorphosed contrary to their expectation: it wrought a wonderfull amazement in their mindes, and had it not beene that they knew the man so soone as they saw him, they had surely taken the same to have been some Devill in a mans likenes, but for as much as they knewe him to be an aunceint dweller in the Towne, they came unto him and talking with him they brought him by communication home to his owne house [.][26]

The metamorphosis to human form indicates an 'underlying' humanity throughout his wolf behaviour and shape.

What happens to Stubbe Peeter, and what is it that the text asks us to believe? The cartoon accompanying the text picks him out in his true and false shapes – an upright wolf wearing the girdle and then a man broken on the wheel (see fig. 11). Stubbe Peeter may look like a wolf but never completely sheds his humanity, signalled by his girdle and upright posture. Moreover, as Erica Fudge has observed, Stubbe Peeter's crimes committed in wolf form are darkly human – deceit, incest, rape, violent and potentially sexual assault on children. To eat human flesh is natural for wolves, cannibal for humans and Stubbe Peeter's activities are those of a depraved or degenerate human.[27] In this telling of his story the border between the wolf and Peeter, that between animal and human, remains and, it seems, being a werewolf names the desire and imagination to become not a wolf but a werewolf so, in a different register, transformation such that he appears 'like' a wolf (possibly in different ways in the text and the illustration) while 'being' human. Ultimately, this crisis of the coincidence of the natural and the human is resolved with Stubbe Peeter located in the human and species difference – which the text strives to maintain – is reconfirmed. We are not required to believe that Stubbe Peeter became a wolf, only that he took on the likeness of a wolf for, in the various incidents of the text, the putting on of the girdle remains an act of will. Stubbe Peeter has the likeness of a wolf, but becoming a werewolf does not, in this story, involve the magical dissolution of the border between man and animal but rather suggests the co-existence of the wolf's likeness with the soul and reason of the man. Before we begin to think of this werewolf as hardly distinguishable from an Ovidian metamorphosis the text's ending reminds us of the hierarchy of species and the supernatural implications of transformation. In the monument to the events erected by the authorities, we are told, the wheel on which he was broken is set on a pole, above that 'the likeness of a wolf was framed in wood, to show to all men the shape wherein he executed those cruelties' and 'on the top of the stake the sorcerer's head it selfe was set up'.[28] The head, although in a traditional position for a trophy or transgressor, also perhaps speaks of Stubbe Peeter's consciousness, set over all and determining all his actions. In his decision to metamorphose he has decided to betray political and social contracts and to abandon his privileged human form.

In another, summary, version of the story the Roman Catholic and compiler of ancient lore, Richard Verstegan, is contrastingly careful to elucidate the implications of werewolf transformation for human status. Verstegan raises the question of human responsibility for wolf actions, asserting that '*were-wolves* are certain sorcerers' who:

> having annoynted their bodyes, with an oyntment which they make by the instinct of the devil; and putting on a certaine inchanted girdel, do not only unto the view of others seeme as wolves, but to their own thinking have both the shape and nature of wolves, so long as they wear the said girdel. And they do dispose th'selves as very wolves, in wurrying and killing, and moste of humaine creatures.
>
> Of such sundry have bin taken and executed in sundry parts of *Germanie*, and the *Netherlands*. One Peeter Stump for being a *were-wolf*, and having killed thirteen children, two women, and one man; was at *Bedbur* not far from *Cullen* in the yeare 1589 put into a very terrible death. The flesh of divers partes of his body was pulled out with hot iron tongs, his armes thighs & legges broke on a wheel, & his body lastly burnt. He dyed with very great

remorce, desiring that his body might not be spared from any torment, so his soul might be saved. The *were-wolf* (so called in Germanie) is in *France*, called *Loupgarou*.[29]

Verstegan's synopsis condenses and interprets the earlier, more discursive, narrative to offer the official position about the illusory nature of werewolf transformation. Verstegan pinpoints the question of animal–human transformation in terms of body and soul, and in so doing the meaning of transformation is oriented definitively towards the question of salvation. While in the earlier text we are told he confessed because of 'fearing the torture', here the question of soul–body relations and repentance are used to moralise (and justify, or explain) the violence and 'terrible death' to which he was subject. Verstegan's highly condensed interpretation restricts its interest in the narrative of killings to numbers ('thirteen children, two women, and one man') and privileges the means and meanings of werewolf transformation and its effects on the being of the transformed, who – in his slightly ambiguous phrase – 'to their own thinking' (is this wolf or human thought? human, presumably) 'have both the shape and nature of wolves, so long as they wear the said girdle'.[30]

In Verstegan's tangled apprehension of werewolf transformation and werewolf consciousness, Stubbe Peeter seems not to be *wholly* responsible once transformed. Although he enters into hallucinatory wolvishness voluntarily, the resultant wildness combines human agency and animal compulsion: the wolf shape compromises the human status of the shape-changer so that it is only after his return to human form that he can recognise and repent of the atrocities he committed. The synopsis has a religious emphasis absent in the first version and so illuminates the other text's hollowing out of what perhaps 'should' have been a theological core. By comparison earlier text has taken the debate quite a long way from any theological ground. In the two versions we have attention to 'shape' and 'likeness' on the one hand, and on the other to soul, blame, repentance. The two tales contrast in the power they give wolfishness, with Verstegan understanding it as a power in itself which takes over once the act of transformation is initiated. Each text analyses the point at which human becomes animal but they resolve that distinction differently. Both narratives, though, belong to a rich seam of printed witchcraft stories in which the theologically determined status of the soul of the perpetrator is not the sole, or even main, focus. In the attention to the final punishment, however, in each case, the narratives make the body witness to the soul. Such tales, meditating in religious, political and social ways on wolvishness, though theologically dubious, form a significant part of the werewolf corpus.

As Robin Briggs points out, the intense imaginative power of the idea of witchcraft was bound up with its 'ambiguities, even... inner tensions'.[31] One of the founding tensions in interpretation was that, as discussed in the Introduction, since the publication of the Latin treatise on witchcraft, *Malleus Maleficarum* (1487), the church itself began to be divided about the possibility of human–animal transformation. Trials and folklore continuously produced testimony, including that of those claiming or confessing to have been metamorphosed, and demonological treatises used such accounts and stories.[32] The werewolf presents a particular example of these tensions because of the tension between the official stance, that werewolf transformation must be considered an illusion, and the experience of wolves and werewolves in Europe and in Scotland.

The narratives of Stubbe Peeter are not unusual in having several explanatory frameworks in operation. The presence of contradictions, often inhabiting popular stories and titillating treatises without resolution, mean that often the werewolf represents a metamorphosis between human and animal in process, unresolved or multiply resolved. The werewolf is, then, potentially an impasse in identity and, to an extent, therefore in terms of what it represents. The ambiguity and the marketability of demon narratives of all kinds also mean that the figure calls up discourses of myth and folklore. Bearing in mind the multiple significations of the figure we can look next at the diseased lycanthrope.

III Hairy on the inside: the wolf within?

As the treatment given to the werewolf in the two accounts of Stubbe Peeter might suggest, demonologically speaking, lycanthropy is a borderline case and it is worth investigating the interrelationship of natural and supernatural transformation a little further. We have seen that much theoretical material (though, as we have seen, with significant exceptions) asserts that actual human–animal transformation is impossible. When theologians and demonologists asked themselves whether the devil is able to transform the human shape they almost all answered 'no', though with qualification. In *The Discoverie of Witchcraft* (1584) Reginald Scot comments ironically on acceptance of shape-changing: 'I mervell, whether the divell createth himselfe, when he appeareth in the likenesse of a man; or whether God createth him, when the divell wisheth it' and he found 'beastlie' the idea that 'a man, whom God hath made according to his owne similitude and likeness, should be by a witch turned into a beast'.[33] Or as John Cotta put it, although the devil could override 'some particular natures' he cannot 'command over general Nature' – although 'the Devill as a Spirit doth many things, which in respect of our nature are supernaturall, yet in respect of the power of Nature in universall, they are but naturall unto himselfe and other Spirites, who are also a kind of Creature contained within the generall nature of things created: . . . against or above the generall power of Nature, hee can do nothing.'[34] Unable to alter the natural world, the devil makes 'seeming and juggling transformations'. The devil's inability to create fresh forms means that lycanthropy is understood in other, more ambiguous, terms and generated 'a gamut of explanatory languages'.[35] Explanations include that transformation is suggested to the lycanthrope by the devil inducing hallucination ('glamour'); that the devil (taking advantage of dream-states induced by unguents applied to the body) superimposed hallucinated shapes on the lycanthrope's body to deceive the victim and observers.[36] Thus, in witchcraft texts the focus of discussion is often on the nature of metamorphosis as true or illusory, and what is much canvassed is how the illusions are produced, and where the devil is in that process.[37]

Such discussions of illusion and hallucination have a focus on what *is* human and what is not, what is and is not transformed in the werewolf, which is shared between theological and other werewolf texts. The debate was unresolved, but heated, and facilitated the circulation of European werewolf stories for English readers. However, the ambiguous theological status of werewolf transformation meant that to consider the werewolf was to speculate about state of mind as well as soul, and led towards the humoural vision of lycanthropy as melancholy, mania, frenzy. Thus, in the case of lycanthropy, rather than possession, as Stuart Clark indicates, psycho-physiological and social meanings are important on the one hand, and on the other, demonological debate is connected to 'scientific' testing.[38]

Related to theological debate, but not wholly inside it, lycanthropy reaches its English audience in many-layered vocabularies and meanings. Ambiguously like possession without being possession, the idea and stories of werewolves concretised issues of wider purchase than the narrowly defined theological. One such text is John Webster's *The Duchess of Malfi* (performed 1613/14, printed 1623), which explores the melancholic werewolf. For all that the representation of lycanthropy in this text is medically inflected and put before the audience in scenes of doctor–patient dialogue, and that the play is probably the literary text which is best known for an exploration of the diseased, hallucinatory dimensions of lycanthropy, it also, crucially, binds the question of hallucinatory consciousness to the civic and even political implications of metamorphosis. *The Duchess of Malfi* foregrounds the social and psychic dimensions of wolf-transformation which are implicit in the Stubbe Peeter narratives. But here lycanthropy is also framed by two other strains of language – the first the discourse of animal annihilation (in which, for example, the gender-shifting hyena figures as a woman who can, merely by lying on a man, draw all the breath out of his and the other the opposition between transformation and fixity in which geometry and mathematics are opposed to other malleable textures – most particularly femininity. And like the question of animal significances, metamorphosis permeates the text.[39]

Bosola, whose malcontent alignment with Ferdinand is the product of compromise following partial release from slavery, uses the language of animal–human relations in order to illuminate human monstrosity:

> But in our own flesh, though we bear diseases
> Which have their true names only ta'en from beasts –
> As the most ulcerous wolf and swinish measle –
> Though we are eaten up of lice and worms,
> And though continually we bear about us
> A rotten and dead body, we delight
> To hide it in rich tissue. All our fear,
> Nay all our terror, is lest our physician
> Should put us in the ground to be made sweet.
> (2.1. 58–66)

Voicing anxiety about inevitable physical decay, Bosola's language draws its force from the moral connotations it carries. The animal, here, articulates a moral and potentially religious as much as a physical deterioration. Truly animal in being both of the body and lowering, the animal-diseases here are shown as feeding off the human which they also replace. Thus, the disease of the ulcerous wolf ambiguously combines the wolf as preying upon human flesh and as a characteristic of human degeneracy, rotting from within and exposing raw, diseased, flesh.

Bosola's animated clichés connect human and animal under the sign of dizzying decay. Besides this Ferdinand's developing lycanthropy, in which, in the early part of the play, he projects wolvishness and then, in the second part, identifies with it, makes the connection between human and wolf more firmly because he makes it psychic or conscious as well as physical and moral. Ferdinand sees wolves everywhere, saying of his sister's language, 'the howling of a wolf / Is music, [compared] to thee' (3.2.97–8), her children are 'young wolves' (4.2). Visiting his sister in prison he asks 'where are your cubs?' (4.1.32) and in the next scene, seeing them strangled, comments that 'the death / Of young wolves is never to be pitied' (4.2.247). It is in his ascription of wolvishness to others that Duke Ferdinand comes initially to appear lupine to the audience. At the death of the duchess Ferdinand's perception of his deeds is transformed, and, perhaps, realigned with that of the audience. As he claims 'She and I were twins, / And should I die this instant, I had lived / Her time to a minute' (4.2.257–9). Thus, at this point, his language shifts to become perversely identificatory, climaxing: 'The wolf shall find her grave, and scrape it up – / Not to devour the corpse, but to discover / The horrid murder.' (2.2.297–9) And this, it seems, is what Ferdinand, as the lycanthrope, does.

Having established Ferdinand as a lycanthrope, the play canvasses and exploits that category's meanings. Taking disease as a starting point in the exploration, the exchange between Ferdinand and his doctor is in some ways reminiscent of dialogues on the subject of lycanthropy such as John Deacon and John Walker's *Dialogicall Discourses of Spirits and Divels* (1601) where Orthodoxus seeks to return Lycanthropus to physical and spiritual health, while Lycanthropus insists 'I my selfe am *essentially transformed* into a woolfe'.[40] Certainly, the Doctor takes up the official position on transformation being an effect of imagination, and follows the lead into the terrain of the psyche:

> DOCTOR In those that are possessed with't there o'erflows
> Such melancholy humour, they imagine
> Themselves to be transformed into wolves,
> Steal forth to churchyards in the dead of night,
> And dig dead bodies up – as two nights since
> One met the duke, 'bout midnight in a lane
> Behind Saint Mark's church, with the leg of a man
> Upon his shoulder; and he howl'd fearfully,
> Said he was a wolf, only the difference
> Was, a wolf's skin was hairy on the outside,
> His on the inside; bade them take their swords,
> Rip up his flesh, and try. Straight I was sent for,
> And having ministered to him, found his grace
> Very well recovered.   (5.2.8–21)

The recovery is shortlived and within the same scene Ferdinand presents himself in a state of furious hallucination:

> FERDINAND I will throttle it! [*Throws himself upon the ground*]
> MALATESTE O, my lord, you are angry with nothing!
> FERDINAND You are a fool. How is't possible
>   I should catch my shadow unless I fall upon 't?

> When I go to hell I mean to carry a bribe;
> For, look you, good gifts evermore make way
> For the worst persons. (5.2.33–7)

Ferdinand, psychically tormented by his hairy inside, now identifies himself *and* others as wolvish. He is 'like a sheep-biter' but in his eyes his physican is worryingly hairy, needing his 'beard sawed off, and his eyebrows / Filed more civil' (5.2.50–1). Ferdinand and his doctor finally, in different ways, acknowledge his disease: 'possess'd with't. / ... they imagine / Themselves to be transformed into wolves' (5.2.8–9). The doctor does not, quite, define Ferdinand as possessed with devils, though the term possessed is used of the disease. Rather, Ferdinand is 'out of your princely wits' (5.2.48).

Certainly, *Malfi* uses lycanthropy to signify deathly mental decay. Yet, at the same time the scene strongly develops the medical exchange to draw out clear symbolism of morality, rule, tyranny and potentially religious implications. Ferdinand is not just out of his wits, but out of his 'princely wits' and perceives the healer, always of resonant politicised status, as uncivil. The play uses Ferdinand as lycanthrope to suggest both the ambiguous power of wolfishness and its crucial association with rule – with tyranny, and specifically with the threat to social relations. The play's language and Ferdinand's actions suggest that the understanding of Ferdinand's lycanthropy as melancholy or disease is accompanied by a sense of its social and civic implications. He is tormented by internal hairiness, he murders his sister and her children, and he is also the violent – not so much animalistic as specifically wolfish, untameable, degenerate, possibly cannibal – heart of the civil system. Ferdinand's lycanthropic frenzy is specifically a mania generated by the court, and overtly an index of its moral crisis. And although the play's representation of the marriage of Ferdinand's sister to Antonio may offer a progressive moral and political counterweight to Ferdinand's regressive, archaic court, it also offers an opportunity to bring Ferdinand close to the cannibal acts of lycanthropes in his effecting their destruction.

There is no doubt that the play's animal transformations, centrally that of the wolf, constitute its dominant political as well as psychic or emotional vocabulary. Indeed, the emotional dynamic of the play turns on Ferdinand's failure of self-diagnosis in the first part of the play, where he attributes to others, his victims, his wolf-like preying and secrecy, and in the second part of the play where his self-recognition as a wolf simply presses him into fully acting out despotism. Blended in one vocabulary, the psychic and political draw their force from one another.

The political force of Ferdinand's lycanthropy extends and layers more densely the question of the nature of the werewolf explored in *Stubbe Peeter*. It should also remind us that in Gervase of Tilbury's twelfth-century account of lycanthropy his main example was of the political pain of a disenfranchised French nobleman; in Gervase's example, as in Webster's less sympathetic theatrical character, we see the political blended in the personal. However, a significant part of what enriches *Malfi*'s lycanthropy is the cultural presence of Latin antecedents for the story of wolvish rule. The stories of Romulus and Remus, more fully explored in the next chapter, and particularly Ovid's Lycaon had strong associations with the wolf, on the one hand, and with rule on the other and, for contemporaries, clearly added a dimension to the imaginative place occupied by lycanthropy.

The transformed forms in the *Metamorphoses* are significant, too, in offering understandings of the relationships between werewolves and the world that live outside Christian culture. In Ovid's *Metamorphoses*, animal-transformation signifies a highly diverse range of meanings. The story of the punishment of the tyrant Lycaon and Zeus' punitive visit is retold in Golding's translation. Here, Zeus speaks to describe Lycaon's conduct:

> And yet he was not content, but went and cut the throat
> Of one that lay in hostage there which was an *Epirot*:
> And part of him he did to roast, and part he did to stew.
> Which when it came upon the board, forthwith I overthrew,
> The house with just revenging fire upon the owner's head.
> Who, seeing that, slipped out of doors amazed for fear and fled
> Into the wild and desert woods where, being all alone,
> As he endeavoured (but in vain) to speake and make his moan,
> He fell a-howling. Wherewithal for very rage and mood
> He ran me quite out of his wits and waxèd furious wood,
> Still practising his wonted lust of slaughter on the poor
> And silly cattel, thirsting still for blood as heretofore.
> His garments turned to shaggy hair, his arms to rugged paws;
> So is he made a ravening wolf whose shape expressly draws
> To that the which he was before. His skin is hoary grey,
> His look still grim with glaring eyes, and every kind of way,
> His cruel heart in outward shape doth well it self bewray.
> Thus was one house destroyèd quite, but that one house alone
> Deserveth not to be destroyed; in all the earth is none
> But that such vice doth reign therein   (262–82)[41]

This description is part of the narrative of human degeneracy prefacing the body of Ovid's text and, atypically in the *Metamorphoses*, Lycaon's crime does fulfil an exemplary function because of his transgression of the boundary between God and man – not merely by murder, deceit and cannibalism-by-proxy, but by using human flesh to test whether Jove would react with divine knowledge.[42] Golding's interpretation emphasises the reciprocity between wolf and Lycaon: his wolf-form registers, in its very wolvishness, his earlier nature and even appearance. Although he struggles for some time to articulate his grief and rage in language this is definitively taken from him and although he might (reversing Ferdinand's condition) continue to experience himself as human on the inside, as a wolf he is 'thirsting for blood as heretofore', and to others he has always been beastly. Jonathan Bate tells us that Christian allegorisations of Ovid read Lycaon's plot to make Zeus a cannibal as Herod's plan to murder the infant Jesus.[43] However, as this extract indicates, if Golding, famously, reshapes Ovid to fit his Calvinist views, the relationship is not one way. An Ovidian sense of metamorphosis, with its survival of human characteristics in strangely appropriate animal form, comes in a reciprocal exchange to inhabit Golding's translation.[44]

Golding's evocation of political and civic crisis emerges in comparison with Sandys' balder summary of 'Lycaon, King of Arcadia', as a

> cruell and inhumane Prince: who feasted... Jupiter... with the flesh of a stranger. Which discovered, he overthrew the table; and rushing into the streets, so incensed the Citizens, that they betooke them to their weapons, and by his conduct drove him out of the City: who living like an out-law in the woods, committing daily rapines and robberies, was therefore said, together with his sonnes, to have been changed into wolves.[45]

Sandys gives neither the sense of transgression against the god nor the full metamorphic power of the ruler 'made a ravening wolf whose shape expressly draws / To that the which he was before'. We lose the sense that Lycaon becomes a wolf while retaining 'human' characteristics like his ironically 'savage' face: 'His look still grim with glaring eyes, and every kind of way, / His cruell heart in outward shape doth well it selfe bewray.'[46] For an English reader, Golding's Lycaon being translated into an animal expression of his crime at the same time as he remains ambiguously human, and so responsible for his actions, maintains the paradox of the werewolf. In Golding, Ovid's Lycaon articulates the qualities of the Reformation-period werewolf – a border-creature powerful and violent in a problematically inward, recursive, cannibalistic and, ultimately, civic and political sense.

The connection between wolves and rulers is clear beyond Golding. Thus Edward Topsell's sixteen-side entry on the wolf in his *History of Foure-Footed Beasts* includes another Lycaon. Topsell writes:

> There was another *Lycaon*, the son of Pelagius, which built the Citty *Lycosra*, in the Mountaine *Lycaus*, this man clled *Jupiter Lycaeus*. On a time he sacrificed an infant upon his altar, after which sacrifice he was presently turned into a wolf.[47]

So, Topsell locates the name in relation to infanticide (an occupation of Renaissance and Reformation werewolves) but also an infanticidal figuration of tyranny and civil crisis. The connection between wolves and rulers is made in a distinct mode by Topsell when he discusses the wearing of wolf-skin:

> the skins of wolves after they were dressed by Curriers, we do read that there were garments made wherewithal great princes and Noblemen were cloathed, the bare being inward next to their bodies, and the rough being outward, these were used in journies and huntings, and they were the proper garment of the guard of Tyrants.[48]

In early modern culture, where clothes were felt to be so steeped in the significant traces of a person that they were used in magic, such a comment is significant. In using this as his conclusion, Topsell registers strongly the link between wolves and tyranny made by both the classical stories, but also develops an association between dead wolves (not werewolves) and the accrued power of the ruler – a point to which we will return.

To what extent can we see these historical, and, particularly, Ovidian stories as providing a catalyst to the interpretation of other werewolf texts? Herod, who we meet again in the next chapter, like Ferdinand, is hairy on the inside in the sense of holding within himself the Ovidian werewolf. Can we say that Ovid's politicised werewolf is a dominant presence, or do the cannibal desires of Stubbe Peeter and Ferdinand work less systematically? Both *Stubbe Peeter* and *The Duchess of Malfi* blend vocabularies of wolf-lore and werewolf lore with a sense of the werewolf or lycanthrope as an expression of civic crisis. Yet, clearly, *Malfi* extensively develops melancholic and political ideas in a carefully interwoven discourse. *Malfi*'s engagement with lycanthropy is characterised by being primarily textual and intellectual, but also political. While it draws on textual relations that could be described as both popular and elite it contrasts with *Stubbe Peeter*'s use of narrative to primarily explore the animal–human border and the local, witnessed, wolf-transformation. While *Malfi* is evidently knowing in its blending of Ovid and melancholy, the readers of Stubbe Peeter stories, too, might have read Ovid. The folkloric and popular ideas of metamorphosis might be less immediately engaged with Ovid, but as Caroline Walker Bynum reminds us, they also have relationships with Ovid's sources far back in time.[49] The two texts suggest a continuum of associations for readers which might include Ovidian metamorphosis, theological engagement, political sensitivity but also a familiarity with local, print and oral, discussions of transformation.

An illuminating contrast with English print and theatre narratives is to be found in the rich and detailed analysis of the connections between werewolf trials and encounters with wolves in Franche-Comté made by Caroline Oates.[50] Shaped by its direct address to the problem of actual wolves or werewolves, the study uses textual records of encounters with suspect wolves, the sudden appearance of people in the forest just after the disappearance of the wolf, the nature of testimony. This material is local in its application and draws on traditions of belief in ways strikingly distinct from the English context. In comparison to court records and local stories, the English werewolves – Golding's Lycaon, Ferdinand, the English accounts of Stubbe Peeter – are seen more clearly as distinctly emphasising the political and 'popular' aspects of werewolf narrative which, itself, emerges as a productively diverse genre and one which, in both its political and its 'folk' versions, leads us towards the question of the spheres in which these issues of human–animal transformation, and politico-spiritual jeopardy, were circulated and discussed.

IV Men-woolfes: metamorphosis in process

Overall the representation of wolf-transformation in English texts is suggestive with regard to the status and significance of metamorphosis for writers and readers. Werewolf transformation has a huge range of resonance and therefore it is probably helpful to discuss just a few areas in English culture illuminated by these stories – the animal–human border; the place of the wild and the civil; the key question of the life of these texts in the interwoven oral and literary spheres.

Where a European reader might fear, hate (or, as James VI and I seems to, pity and despise) wolves and werewolves, and dread as well as being fascinated by the magic and persecutions associated with them, the English reader would know werewolves through other texts. Yet, significantly, the werewolves of *Stubbe Peeter* and *Malfi* are live, threatening, frightening presences; their largely textual and literary life has not made them arid or merely allegorical. The evidence discussed suggests that several aspects of the werewolf's presence in seventeenth-century culture gave it life for contemporaries.

The figure of the lycanthrope or werewolf featured in a fairly wide range of texts and in each of the cases discussed here it shows metamorphosis in process, with *Stubbe Peeter*, Verstegan's account of the same story and *The Duchess of Malfi* as well as the demonologically focused discussions in James VI and I's *Daemonologie* all either posing or answering the question of the nature of man–beast transformation. Within this debate the church's official view, that transformation was illusory, was supplemented, and at times over-ridden, by witness testimony, tales and classical werewolf texts which had different assumptions and other religious positions which challenged church orthodoxy. The werewolf texts, therefore, habitually present man–beast transformation as an unresolved, or at least multiply explained, phenomenon and one which readers are encouraged to consider.

The sustained focus on the conundrum of man–beast transformation in terms that treat it as though it was an unresolved paradox registers the confusion and multiplicity of positions within the church, notwithstanding the regular restatement of the official position. It is also an aspect of the texts which keeps the werewolf undecided – and so in a state much more exciting than a simple theological impossibility could ever have been. Clearly, the werewolf narratives discussed here articulate a crisis in the issue of where the border of the human is to be placed. Yet, the clarity of the theological debate on the alteration of God's creation coexists with attention to experience and manifestation. Any judgement on what happens in wolf-transformation must take account not simply of the question of body and soul, but of the hard-to-judge nature of witness statements and the complicated categories such as 'shape' and 'likeness' which, as the longer narrative of Stubbe Peeter shows, are the significant terms, *besides* 'body' and 'soul'. Certainly, to look forward for a moment, these stories configure the human very differently from the way in which Descartes was to split mind and body. Such stories offer insights into the cultural circulation of questions about the designation of the border between the human and the animal that religious premises and, later, Descartes' analysis, do not.

At the same time, it is evident that the werewolf and the wolf overlap in terms of lore, yet the wolf is the denizen of the natural world, the werewolf, contrastingly, is understood as springing from the heart of political discontent and civic collapse. As we will see in the next chapter, the werewolf is not the only evidence that the wild in early modern culture was not always the opposite of the civil but might also serve to tell an audience about the crisis or pain of that civilisation. It was not only Christian writing that might be both drawn to and resistant to shape shifting.[51] The wild's ability to signify civility, in or out of crisis, permeates high and 'domestic' early modern representational modes. As Kate Soper notes, the 'natural' devolves easily into colloquial discourse, so that 'the poets' nature [is and is not] the kind of thing we eat for breakfast'. Yet, what is humanly cultivated still in such colloquial discourse lodges itself in the realm of 'nature', as in Milton and Jonson's gardens and the werewolf in the wild, Soper, though not concerned with historical discourses, enables us to recognise that the early modern figuration of the werewolf involves an expansion of the categories of culture and civility – including religious belief – to be understood as *generating* wildness and wolvishness at the heart of culture. At the same time, the imagination of the transformation into wolf expands the category of the natural, more particularly the wild, from the waste around the city to its governmental heart. The simultaneous quality of these expansions, the secret incorporation of the human (civil) in the wolf and the natural (wild) in the citizen is only one of the meanings of these narratives of human transformation.

Giorgio Agamben has argued that the special nature of sovereign power means that 'in the person of the sovereign, the werewolf, the wolf-man of men, dwells permanently in the city' and this, like the figure of Lycaon, most succinctly expresses the intensity of political control as indexed by its opposite dissolution from the very central point of that power.[52] Yet, for all that Agamben identifies both the wolf's tendency to figure its opposite and the power of the figure of the werewolf to figure the violent heart of the state, that important strand is only part of what is happening in these stories. These senses are also tied to other dimensions, including other offences to God or the gods. The multiple significances of the werewolf fuel a tendency for these figures to be, as we have found, ambiguous and particularly to be always in process, unresolved between human and animal. The werewolf inhabits stories fuelled by the storytelling impact of myth and folklore so that the politics of the werewolf is the figuring both of the political crisis and of troubled limits of the human, and so the natural, in metamorphosis. For all that both *Stubbe Peeter* and *The Duchess of Malfi* articulate crisis as at the heart of the polis, as has just been indicated, they also test the limits of the human in modes calculated to fascinate audiences. The discourse of civic crisis, in these stories, is saturated by additional possibilities and alive to contemporary contexts.

It seems clear that these English texts of metamorphosis require consideration of the sphere of theology but also of the complex hubbub of commentary and discussion, both oral and written. This noise seems to be continuously present activating metamorphosis as something that generates meanings and expresses ideas in seventeenth-century culture. We can think of examples from the unease concerning infant baptism to the ideas concerning the manipulation of colour in poultry farming discussed in Chapter 3. In terms of suggesting a world of debate beyond the text, werewolf stories are clearly significant and through them we can begin to understand a little about what the textual evidence of metamorphosis can disclose about vernacular debate, oral and written.

In terms of reading contexts, it seems possible the interest in witchcraft from the 1590s witch trials onwards stimulated interest in reading about werewolves. Although, as James Sharpe notes, many English witches were involved in 'personal and local' disputes, Lawrence Normand and Gareth Roberts, discussing the 1590 trials, illuminatingly argue that, with regard to the North Berwick witch hunt, 'elite and popular culture interacted' with printed explorations of the witchcraft embracing both domestic disputes and 'elite fears' of 'demonic conspiracy' against James I.[53] The printed material Normand and Roberts examine brings together worlds which appear startlingly different but as the texts reveal, share strikingly similar concerns. Whether or not these or other witch trials influenced purchasers and readers of werewolf material, Normand and Roberts' insight about the effect of printed accounts in shifting between or mixing together different discourses on a supernatural subject is very helpful in thinking about werewolf metamorphosis in early modern English culture, for it invites us to recall classical writing on the werewolf – and particularly the fascination with Ovidian metamorphosis which so clearly marks elite culture and, through translation, vernacular readers.

One reason, of course, that the emergence of witch trials in England is a significant context for these texts is the clearest difference between England and Scotland or France: the absence of wolves in England. Observers who saw no wolves also, therefore, saw no werewolves and, for all that rumours persisted and, for example, a house in Wormhill, Derbyshire is said to have a window designed to look out for approaching wolves; none were seen. A vital referent was lacking for English, as opposed to Scottish, domestic wolf-transformation. The specifically non-native status of the stories discussed here invites us, therefore, to consider where such figures were housed in English conversation, storytelling and thought, and it may be that the werewolf occupies a suggestive position in the dynamic of oral and literate storytelling about transformation. As the later namesake of the playwright John Webster noted in 1677, witchcraft beliefs, and potentially supernatural beliefs more generally, tended to be passed on orally. The philosophers have not passed on the poison recipes witches learn 'secretly and by tradition', and 'so these secrets of mischief are for the most part kept in obscurity, amongst old women, superstitious, ignorant and melancholy persons', and so 'commonly one learns it of another according to the Proverb, Popery and Witchcraft go by tradition'.[54] When describing old wives' tales or traditional beliefs contemporaries describe a cast including Robin Goodfellow, fairies, 'Raw-head and bloody-bone', hobgoblins and elves – to name some associated with the nursery.[55] As Andy Wood notes, John Aubrey mourns that since the Civil War ordinary people have learned to read and the 'many good Bookes' have 'putt the old Fables out of dores; and the divine art of Printing and Gunpowder have frighted away Robin-Good-fellowe and the Fayries'.[56] However, Aubrey may have been dramatizing the separateness of print and oral traditions in his youth. Certainly, the findings of Adam Fox suggest that the influence of print is to be found even in 'the anecdotes and remembrances of local folklore', and Fox describes the 'written word' as 'restructuring the nature of spoken tradition and communication'.[57] If the interrelationship between speech and writing reshapes oral knowledge which can, in turn, be remembered differently in writing, then a mixed sphere of oral and written can also, clearly, provide a reading context in which stories can thrive and be elaborated. The werewolf might be only ambiguously present in local tradition, and the printed stories, yet it seems to have had a life in print and beyond. In building up a mosaic of the writing of metamorphosis in seventeenth-century England the place the werewolf seems to have had in the interwoven sphere of written and oral is a key part of what werewolf texts tell us about English understandings of metamorphosis. These stories, like those of protests against baptism and the showing of monsters in commercial contexts, suggests that in many different ways metamorphosis was discussed as well as written.

In the layered contexts of the question of the status of nature, the complex relationship between wolf and tyrant, and the oral and the written, we can return to Sir Philip Sidney's remarks in Nuremberg in 1577, discussed at the start of the chapter. Sidney clearly dissociates himself from a belief that wolves are supernaturally absented from England and when the work of his interlocutor, Philip Camerarius, was translated into English in 1621, Sidney's words found printed form in Europe. In the same volume Camerarius also lends his support to the orthodox understanding of werewolf transformation as the fantasy of 'melancholy and brainsick persons'.[58] Sidney's printed conversation ends with a delineation of the true explanation for the absence of wolves – an explanation that touches upon many of the aspects of wolf-lore we have canvassed. Long ago, Sidney explains, there '*was an ordinance made by the King*' stating that:

> *such persons as not of set purpose but unwittingly had committed an offence deserving any grievous punishment (save the forfeiture of their lives) should be thus punished: namely, That they should stand banished and discredited until they had brought the tongue and head of some wolves by them slaine, in greater or lesser number, according to the sentence of the Judges. This amends was imposed upon them, and this tribute they payed for with their heads.*[59]

In this system of good, as opposed to tyrannical government, the confusion of categories is deftly located in the hard-to-define inadvertent crime. The wolves are not the paradox but a part of the solution because this paradox is righted, Sidney implies, when the tribute (not sacrifice) of wolf heads saves human heads. Sidney, then, preserves the association between tyranny and wolvishness which we have explored while extending the idea to fit the reverse case of the good, lawful, ruler's relationship to the wolf. Just as the tyrant devolves into the wolf, for the Protestant humanist, as we see, good law made by a good king expels it. Sidney's wolves are conversational, yet printed; allegorical, yet natural and historical and from the perspective of Sidney's wolves, the werewolf becomes a way of talking about political and historical pain – a way that, we see, utilises the powerful question of transformation.

CHAPTER FIVE

Transformation rewritten? Extreme nurture, wild children

13 Bear, Edward Topsell, *Historie of Foure-Footed Beasts* (1607).

every real story... contains openly or covertly, something useful.
                                                    Walter Benjamin

something wildly by us performed
Winter's Tale (5.1.128)

'I shall not examine', writes Jean-Jacques Rousseau, whether in the earliest times man 'was hairy as a bear... walking on all fours', his gaze restricted to the earth.[1] Rather, he plans to discuss the dexterous biped who we find 'walking on two feet, using his hands as we do ours, directing his gaze over the whole of Nature, and with his eyes surveying the vast expanse of Heaven'.[2] Just as Rousseau seems about to decisively turn his back on the blended human-animals that this study has investigated, something draws him back to the disavowed hairy quadruped. He recalls that '[t]here are even Savage Nations, such as the Hottentots' which allow children to walk upon four legs for so long that they have trouble getting them to walk upright. And history, like geography, has stories to tell. He remembers:

> the Child found in 1344 near Hesse where he had been raised by Wolves, and who subsequently said at the Court of Prince Henry that if it had been up to him alone, he would have preferred to return among them rather than to live among men. He had become so accustomed to walk like these animals, that wood Splints had to be tied on him which forced him to hold himself upright and keep his balance on his two feet.

Extending the argument, Rousseau recollects another 'Child found in 1694 in the forests of Lithuania', who 'lived among Bears', showed 'no sign of reason, walked on his hands and feet, had no language, and made sounds which in no way resembled those of a human being'.[3]

For Rousseau, these wild children offer condensed, if compromised, dramas of human perfectibility. This characterisation of wild nurture has been powerfully influential, so much so that wild children come to us as infants of the Enlightenment, shaped by Rousseau and others. They arrive in our libraries in the education section linked to Kaspar Hauser, Mademoiselle le Blanc and the Wild Boy of Aveyron brought into being by Enlightenment questions about the subject, learning, language, morality.[4] However, this chapter argues that in England in the seventeenth century, these children and stories had distinct cultural meanings. Particular ideas are explored in stories closely attending to the outcomes of changes wrought in encounters between human infants and the 'wild'.[5] So, we will meet Rousseau's forest children of Hesse and Lithuania again. Indeed, in the very text Rousseau may have reached for to make his wild children, the child of Hesse nourished by wolves is an instance of the wild's ability to foster children of 'marvellous agility'.[6]

As this chapter argues, the stories told about children found in the wild share common elements. What follows explores some of these stories, discussing both 'fictional' and 'true' tales of children changed in order to tease out the shifting understandings of such transformations but also in order to explore the question of what, ultimately, might be being transformed. The chapter takes as its point of departure Walter Benjamin's advice to consider both the official and the covert implications of the story.[7] In focusing on stories, initially on fictions and then on 'true' discoveries that might be called ethnographic, this chapter works in some detail with tales that bought the wild child to seventeenth-century readers. We will begin by thinking about a foundation myth, Romulus and Remus, and the romance of Valentine and Orson. To start the enquiry, though, let us turn not to a story, but to an interpretation of a story, reordered in an image.

I Foundations and romances: twinned lambs

In the 1660s the King's Privy Gallery at Whitehall housed a painting described as 'Brugle. Souldiers fyring of houses and plundering. A Winter piece.'[8] The painting is by Pieter Bruegel the Elder and it tells a story. It represents soldiers violently pillaging and firing a Flemish village. They are grabbing loot – tubs, barrels, domestic animals – from desperate and resisting villagers who rush to hide their possessions. Under this scene is an original which depicts Matthew 2.16, the execution of Herod's tyrannical decree that male children must die, an event usually known as the Massacre of the Innocents. At some point between 1621 and its purchase at Breda in 1660, there had been a thematic re-orientation that leaves us with the scene of plunder we have today.[9] Probably the English viewers in the 1660s were unaware that beneath the looting and shock at the loss of property lies a visual festival of infanticide, clearly visible in the several unrevised versions Bruegel executed.[10]

There are three stories encapsulated in the picture: the Bible story of the massacre; the story in the repainting (plunder), and, crucially, the story of that revision. The nature of the reworking itself indicates a perceived physical similarity between children and bundles, barrels and small farm animals. Babies are roughly the same size as the domestic objects and beasts that replace them, and the scene of plunder offers a coherent replacement narrative. However, just as we have seen in the substitution of cats for babies at the font, discussed in Chapter 2, the change has implications.[11] The effacing and replacing of the children clearly recognises the value of the painting which the redaction seeks to retain and, perhaps, enhance. The viewer is excused the contemplation of infanticide and the secularised image implies the acceptability of the scene substituted. The exchange of animals for infants deals with the problem of adult cruelty and tyrannical rage by removing human status not from the perpetrators but from the victims while the more visually engaging adult faces and poses are left in sole occupation of the field; the viewer is offered adult rage, spared infant sorrow, and the interposition of animals, pots and parcels hygienically separates the two. These decisions tell us something about what viewers and owners could accept in terms of representation. The Biblical story was effaced, we have to assume because of what was changed, on the grounds of its showing the murder of infants. The Massacre of the Innocents tells the story of a tyrant's will causing the murder of a society's weakest members, but also its most valuable – its future. It offers a harsh lesson about the civic order. The removal of massacre from this scene excises its compulsion that the viewer must see and know adult violence. The repainting removes the crucial components of knowledge, viewing and complicity by simply removing the children. The earlier story of the image is so effectively removed as to make the viewer innocent.

It is coincidence, surely, that the concealed massacre was imported to England at the Restoration and lodged at the heart of power. Yet it is tempting, in the light of what is to come, to see the story of the lost knowledge of the painting as resonant with the self-consciously fictional and 'factual' narratives of children 'found' in the wild in English writing. These stories, too, offer overt and undisclosed knowledge. They mix violence, scandal and wonder in ways that both disclose and obscure events. The question of what forms of knowledge stories, rather than as in this instance an image, tell about a social world, is the theme of the rest of the chapter. In the stories of Romulus and Remus and Valentine and Orson, to which we now turn, the infant is not, of course, lost (as in the 'Winter Scene') but apparently found. In order to explore the qualities of change in the fictions of wild children, discussion of the two stories follows the contours of the tales, following the protagonists' path from wild nurture to a renewed role in the human world.

The story of the 'wonderfull foundation' of Rome by the twin brothers suckled by a wolf was familiar to Renaissance readers from Thomas North's translation of Plutarch's *Lives* (1579).[12] The story North gives is also the story we know, recently summarised by Michel Serres: 'Romulus and Remus, the abandoned Alban twins, nurse at the dry breast of a she-wolf; I say "dry breast" because in Latin the she-wolf, *lupa*, refers to a prostitute from a brothel... Romulus, then, kills Remus, and founds Rome.'[13] Plutarch, however, gives not one, but several, versions of Rome's foundation, presenting a complex sequence of increasingly scandalous stories of the uncertain origins of Rome. These are put in etymological terms, that tie the events to words that might have become 'Rome'.

Three main possibilities are given for Rome's name. First, the city might be called after 'Roma' the ringleader of women in the Trojan fleet in flight from Troy; this 'Roma' set fire to the ships and so forced men to stay. Second, Plutarch tells a tale 'of *Romulus* birth, nothing true nor likely'. In the house of Tarchetius, a cruel king of Alba, 'there rose up in the harthe of his chymney the forme & facion of a mans priuie member'. An oracle indicates that the king's daughter is to have congress with the apparition and bear 'a sonne, that should be famous for his valliancie, for strength of bodye, and his happie successe'.[14] When his daughter delegates the childbearing to her waiting woman, the progeny, 'two goodly boyes or twynnes', are exposed on the 'bancke of the river: thither came a shee woulfe and gave them sucke, and certaine byrdes that brought litle crommes and put them in their mouthes'. Ultimately, 'a swyne heard' takes the children.

Rome's supernatural foundation is from the start sent awry by women's sexual straying – with the union of ghost-penis and serving maid bringing forth unsurprisingly unusual offspring. Combining miracles, a priapic ghost, rage and revenge this story mixes scandal with the wonder of nurture by the most vulnerable and most dangerous of the creatures – birds and wolves. Echoing the first story in which women's intervention alters the course of political affairs, the chimney-penis articulates coitus as both scandalous and marvellous, but definitively detached from the social and familial rule of men.

The third story, apparently favoured and best known to the seventeenth-century auditor, again begins with two feuding brothers. Amulius takes the kingdom from his brother, Numitor, and, fearing that his brother's daughter might take his kingdom from him, vows her to Vesta as a nun. When she, nevertheless, gives birth to two sons (claiming the father was Mars, though some assert it was in fact her uncle himself disguised in military dress), her uncle has the children exposed by a river bank. The river carries them away to a place where there is a fig tree. At this place also beasts 'chewe their cudde', ruminate, and so possibly give the place its name though, we read, that equally might derive from 'that the two children dyd sucke the teate of the woulfe' called Ruma by the 'auncient Latines'. Again, 'they write, there came a she woulfe & gaue them sucke: and a hitwaw also which dyd helpe to norishe and keepe them'. Yet, others:

> holde opinion that the name of the nurce which gaue the two children sucke with her breastes, gaue occasion to co[m]mon reporte to erre much in this tale, by reason of the double signification thereof. For the Latines doe call with one selfe name shee woulfes *Lupas*, & women that geue their bodyes to all co[m]mers: as this nurce the wife of *Faustulus* (that brought these children home to her house) dyd use to doe.[15]

Larentia, the woman in question, was the wife of Faustulus, 'chief neate heard to *Amulius*'. They brought up the fratricidal twins.[16]

Here, at last, is the outline of the story which is most familiar to us and which was taken up by English readers and writers – and the complication survived. Readers of Topsell were made aware of the double nature of the story and its grounding in etymology:

> *Lupa* and *lupula* were the names of noble devouringe Harlots, and from thence cometh *Lupanar* for the stewes. It is doubtful whether the nurse of *Romulus* and *Remus* were a harlot or she Wolf, I rather thinke it was a harlot than a Wolfe that nursed those children. For we read of the wife of Fostulus, which was called *Laurentia*, after she had plaied the whore with certaine shepheardes was called *lupa*.[17]

Topsell retains the question of language and, ultimately, thinks the 'harlot' a more likely explanation. However, while that the maternal figure is a 'harlot' might be seen as a more plausible option, it also suggests the danger within society is the one expressed by this fable. Topsell's prioritisation of the whore reminds us that if the wild is dangerous, so is the civil – in complex and potential more damaging ways. If wild suckling involves ingestion from a world beyond the social, the other is nurture from a figure who transgresses the familial basis of society.

Women burning boats, a tyrant's reaction to the shadow of a 'mans priuie member', a nun, raped by her uncle, twins born to a Vestal nun and then suckled by wolf or whore; these features make it inescapable that Plutarch's stories foreground masculine political and sexual violence and feminine sexual scandal. The two boys through whom Rome is founded don't appear from nowhere. Each story of their parentage begins with a mixture of marital and political disruption. Whether they are cast out from Troy, engendered by a spectral penis in the household of a tyrant or incestuously engendered by a brother's usurper with a nun, they bring a perturbing inheritance. The story of rescue confuses the twins' ingestion of wildness through wolf-nurture by adding the possibility that they are nursed by a prostitute. Larentia, as a figure for prostitution, is further confused: she is also a wife and so figures contradictorily in relation to the family. It is embedded within these nested narratives of scandal that North's Plutarch presents the marvellous rescue and nurture of the twins. The stories are marvellous but also monstrous – and in each of the three stories Rome's genesis is a scandalous miracle and, as moderately educated readers would know, the brothers grow up to repeat the fratricidal pattern. Overall, as they circulated, the Romulus and Remus stories raise questions about what happens when an infant is nurtured in a 'wild' environment, but also ask what is inside and what outside culture, implicitly questioning the nature and location of the outside. The story of wolf-nurture, is, then, simultaneously a forward-looking tale of the power of the wild once taken into the subject and a recursive narrative which reiterates sexual and civil wrong-doing.

Clearly, as Topsell's discussion suggests, the problem of Romulus and Remus was transported to English culture. Indeed, the story of Romulus and Remus seems to have been known very widely in the early seventeenth century. North's Plutarch was not merely a resource for writers but a resource for knowing history, modelling manners and shaping narrative; it was recommended by Henry Peacham's *Compleat Gentleman* (1622) and, as Louis B. Wright noted long ago, it was transported across the Atlantic by early emigrants.[18] Peacham recommends Plutarch '[f]or Moralitie and rules of well living', but also as history – a source of 'delight... imprinting a thousand forms upon our imagination'.[19] As the evocation of Romulus and Remus in *The Duchess of Malfi* and in other texts suggest, the story of Rome's political foundations must have been felt by contemporaries.

The powerful scandal of the tale combined with its political centrality as a foundation myth means that the story of the wild and murderous brothers found a place as a well-known narrative resource. As the library of Edmund Berkeley Esquire (who died in 1718) suggests, Shakespeare's plays, what is almost certainly North's Plutarch, and a version of the tale to which we will now turn, that of Valentine and Orson, might live alongside one another.[20] If the story of Romulus and Remus had many retellings and put into English culture a highly problematic version of Rome's foundation, the story of Valentine and Orson, shaped as a romance, dealt with some of the same issues and itself had a powerful and enduring hold on English readers and storytellers.

Valentine and Orson is an ancient tale, enduringly widely known and finding various forms in print that suggest an intertwined oral circulation. Deriving from no identifiable source or extant manuscript, versions of the story of the two brothers reached many cultural corners, carried many different kinds of meaning. The earliest English version discussed by its editor, Arthur Dickson, is a four leaf black letter fragment found, intriguingly, in the library at Hardwick Hall – home to both the Ovidian cushions discussed in the introduction and, in terms of scholars, Thomas Hobbes. Dickson dates this copy between 1503 and 1505.[21] Changed, as Erica Fudge has discussed, to accommodate Reformation, the story circulated from *The Hystory of the two Valyaunt Brethren* (1555) to the Restoration (further 'Abbreviated' for 'young Men and Maids, whose Impatience' was felt to require a mercifully reduced eight-chapter format), and beyond.[22] In 1637 it appeared in a version that was much recycled as a popular staple.

The 1637 text probably inhabited a realm where oral and literate overlapped. At this point it is compendious, providing, as the editor says, 'many faire models & lively Pictures' so 'no man' need 'thinke his time ill spent, or his labour lost where the matter affordeth such copiousness of pleasure'. The text provides 'the cares and troubles of kings, . . . the battles of Martiall Champions . . . Courtly Tournaments and Combats of Princes' but also 'strange births & savage educations'.[23] Moreover:

> Herein is also contained the true difference betwixt art and nature, for in *Valentine* is comprehended the education of art: and in *Orson* the true working of Nature, for being both one Emperors Sons, the one of them brought up in a Princes Pallace, the other amongst savage beasts, now makes the currant passé with the more admiration of the *Reader*, mark but the carriage of wild *Orson*, & you shall find that Nature hath a being above art, but yet Nature bettered by Art, hath a more noble Working.[24]

Thus, the question of 'nature' and 'art' offers the frame within which this text and others place discussions of infant nurture in the wild. Yet, as the quotation above partly begins to suggest, this relationship is complex; to be brought up by the 'nouriture' of a bear is wild, but is nevertheless a process of becoming – the bear's nurture is, perhaps, a kind of art that duplicates even as it challenges, the human process.

The details of the story are both fascinating and too numerous to be adequately detailed, so what follows restricts itself to taking up the 1637 version's exploration of questions of strange births, animal nurture, savage education. For our purposes, the story begins with the marriage of Bellysant, King Pepyn's sister, to the Emperor of Greece. Once in his court she is assailed by a lustful archbishop who, when rejected, tells the Emperor she is unchaste. The Emperor believes the archbishop's tales; his revulsion at her revelation that she is pregnant with his child precipitates her flight into France. Alone in a French wood, with only the assistance of the Virgin, she successfully delivers twin boys. However, 'as she laye under the tree, ther came unto her a beer', it was 'marvellously great and horrible' and, taking her child into his mouth, speedily 'went his way into the thicke of the forest' (see fig. 14: Orson and bear, *Valentine and Orson: The Two Sonnes of the Emperour of Greece* (1637). She searches for this child, but the narrator announces 'she shal never see her child unto the tyme that by a myracle he be yelded unto her agayne'.[25] While she begins a fruitless lifelong search, her other child is found under the tree by none other than her brother, King Pepyn, who sends it on to Orleance to be 'baptyzed' and 'nourysshed'.[26] Rather than eat the other child, the bear in a 'myracle'

Foundations and romances: twinned lambs 169

preserves it. The child, 'all rough because of the neutrifaction of the beer, as a wild beast' grows up in the woods, fearing 'nothing in the worlde'.[27] By the age of fifteen he is a fully fledged cannibal 'wylde man':

> None dusrt passé through the forest for hym, for both men and beastes he put unto death, and eate their flesh al rawe as the other beastes did, and lived a bestual life and not humayne. He was called Orson because of the beere that had nourished him, and he was also as rough as a beere.[28]

Meanwhile, Valentyne, brought up by King Pepyn and longing always to know whether he is a bastard, proves himself against the Saracens.

Thus tested, Valentine the Christian knight takes on Orson, offering him new life as a Christian. '[T]hy soule is in great daunger', he tells Orson but 'I shall make the be baptized, and shall teche the the holy fayth. And shall geve the flesh, and fysshe, bread and wine ynough for to eate.'[29] Although he lacks language, Orson is convinced. He falls to his knees and 'stretcheth forth his handes' in a gesture of obedience. Valentyne binds Orson's hands to his body and leads him 'as a beast tyed, without that ever this same Orson didde hym any harme' – ' a thing myraculous'.[30] As Fudge discusses, Orson is duly baptised and given godparents. He learns, too, to be nourished like a Christian; cooked meats replace cannibal violence and he becomes a kind of Christian berserker – a wild man for God.

Further details are key to our analysis here. Orson, though baptised, remains hairy and lacks language, vowing never to marry the princess he has rescued until by God's will 'he shall speke good language'.[31] On the same night Orson is engaged to Fezonne, Valentine has an angelic vision – emphatically a vision sent from God – telling him where to go to 'knowe' 'of what fader, thou wast engendred, and of what moder was borne and chylded'.[32] Soon after, Valentine calls Orson to him and 'cut and toke away the threde' tying his tongue, and he 'began to speke very ryght'. Released into full and articulate possession of language, Orson tells the story of his life in the forest – a tale that, far from being the recollection of a few grunts, is so rich that they 'were herkenynge hym the moost part of the night'.[33] Ultimately, many, many adventures later, Valentine dies and soon after Orson suffers a bereavement after which he 'ete but brede and rotes, and small froytes that he founde in the wodde where as he did remayne'.[34]

How might the details of this story have spoken to the wide range of readers in and after 1637? Looking back from Orson's final destination as a hermit we can see that the fates of the twin boys were, like those of Romulus and Remus, shaped by the catastrophic and miraculous events attendant on their mother's scandal. That Orson returns to the 'wood' as a hermit at the end of his life is a clue to some of the paradoxes that shape Orson, and something to which readers would have been attuned. While the 'forest' of his birth shaped Orson in his first incarnation, through the strange 'neutrifaction of the beer', so, in redemptive response to his wild past, the forest he returns to is not the same but its answering pair; it is a location similarly set apart from the social yet in this case signifying an exceeding of the human, where the first had been the location of his animal-nurture.

The early wood is the place of the first of Orson's transformations by what the story calls 'art' – a term including learned behaviour and culture. As Michael Whitmore notes, early childhood was a time when 'human animal' might be seen as 'constitutively incomplete' and lacking 'all the cognitive attributes of its natural kind' and in this state animal-nurture powerfully changes young Orson, compromising his soul even as it endows him with huge strength.[35] As Richard Bernheimer writes, the distinguishing features of the medieval wild man were symbolic, characterised by the 'loss or absence' of human faculties, primarily: speech, conceptualisation, a bestial pelt signalling both strength and absence of full humanity, absence of knowledge of God.[36] In Orson's case, hairiness signifies the transformational nature of the animal qualities he has absorbed as nursing and environment shape him and he shares with Bernheimer's wild men the absence of the divine knowledge that makes possible not only salvation but meaningful education, reason, thought – in short, the Renaissance story of the human.[37]

Valentine's education articulates a trajectory towards full humanity through human (cooked) nourishment, baptism and language. Against the foil of this simple process, Orson's time in the wild and later redemption spreads out for careful scrutiny the rites of passage, acquisitions and markers of the human which Orson mainly achieves but signally, in sainthood, exceeds. It is through his encounter with Valentine, the simply inducted human, that Orson is able to know himself as human. The binding and leading of Orson after his silent but complete submission to Valentine suggests the beginning of his education and marks the shock of the decisive change in which his wild powers – strength, lack of inhibition, bestial power and knowledge – are taken back into the civic community. We know, though the protagonists do not, that this wild child originates not in wilderness but is produced by contradictions and crises in sexual, familial, religious and civic life. Using his extraordinary strength in the service of God, Orson's gradual path to canonisation allows, silently, the complete recuperation of the cannibalism committed when he (presumably) knew himself as a bear knows itself. Orson's recuperation is woven into the narrative through his baptism, education and eating. Yet, even in his new-found faith, his difference remains in the heightened, extreme, versions of the human state that make him first an extraordinary warrior for God and later a hermit.

Crucially, while the two brothers are alive, they balance each other as wild and civil humans, their lives ever more interknit as knowledge of their past binds them close. The two brothers both complete each other and mirror each other, evoking Jacques Le Goff's understanding of the marvellous as a quality etymologically and conceptually tied to the mirror.[38] At Valentine's death, this pairing dissolves and Orson, transformed by bestial nurture; redeemed by baptism, is, arguably, at this point a third time transformed in taking up the life of a hermit. Hermits, like the hermit of Cratcliff in his sacred cave that still survives high above the Derbyshire paths, were linked to great houses and the subject of some attempts at rule and regulation by the church. Alone in high and distant places, the pre-Reformation hermit lived a life that rarely touched that of other humans, existing in a sustained liminality. The text is at pains to show that the wildly nurtured Orson, while wholly redeemed, nevertheless exceeds the human.

Jacques le Goff argues that the roots of the marvellous are pre-Christian ideas, accommodated in the medieval period between the Godly miracle and Satanic magic.[39] Orson's transformations perhaps register a tour around this understanding of the marvellous, starting with the bestial nurture of his wild time, he becomes a Christianised marvel, a 'between' figure: hairy, yet baptised; strong beyond manhood yet strong for Christendom. Ultimately, the remaining ambiguities of his status are resolved as miraculous – a register of his deeds as a Christian knight but also of his marvellous, sub-human and so super-human, status.

The story of Valentine and Orson is possibly the longest exploration of an infant transformed by the wild that was widely known – and loved. As we find from the illustrations, the part of the story discussed here was a key attraction for readers. In comparison with the focus on dynasty in the story of Rome's foundation, Valentine and Orson foregrounds the Christian entry into society from the wild with its attendant emphases on baptism, language and food which, as we shall see, also feature in the 'true find' versions of the story of the child found in the wild. Most significantly, though, Valentine and Orson, like North's circulating Romulus and Remus, is a story of how the ingestion of the wild makes a human in excess of the mean in Orson's case, once alone, both a willing exile from mainstream society and (notwithstanding an unwittingly cannibal past as a bear) a saint. Orson's trajectory registers on the one hand the power of the key transformations of Christian life, and concomitantly the almost as great power of 'art', or nurture, acculturation, outside or without these shaping events. In this way speaking perhaps more immediately to the society in which it circulated than Romulus and Remus, it shares with that story an emphasis on the power of the wild to make the child strange. The narratives offer not merely successful re-entry but central places in the societies they inhabit. Before turning to the question of where readers might find wild children in their own worlds, let us compare accounts of such changelings and foundlings that claim the authority of 'truth'.

II   Found in the woods: Kenelm Digby, Bernard Connor

'[E]xperience teacheth us in all beastes, that the smell is given unto living creatures, to know what meats are good for them, and what are not'.[40] So, exploring the sense of smell, Sir Kenelm Digby came to the topic of a child found in the forest. In his *Two Treatises* (1644) Digby offers an atomist discussion of the 'sensible qualities'.[41] In some ways Digby's story of John of Liège is now familiar to us, but in Walter Benjamin's terms may well have some new work to do.

The story is offered as partly from John himself and partly from 'severall (whom I dare confidently believe) that have had it from his own mouth; and have questioned him with great curiosity, particularly about it'.[42] As a 'litle boy' being caught up in that country's regular 'warres' and 'molestations from abroad', 'John' was taken with fleeing villagers into the woods for 'shelter' from troops. The danger past, the villagers returned home, 'excepting this boy; who, it seemeth, being of a very timorous nature, had images of feare so strong in his fansie; that first, he ranne further into the wood then any of the rest'. Staying there, John 'afterwardes apprehended that every body he saw through the thickets, and every voice he heard was the souldiers'; he 'so hidd himselfe from his parents, that were in much distresse seeking him all about, and calling his name as loud as they could'.[43] However, having spent 'a day or two' doing this, they 'returned without him' and 'he lived many yeares in the woods, feeding upon rootes, and wild fruites'. So, Digby narrates the story of his loss in the forest as though he has some access to the feelings not only of the boy but his parents.

Returning to his lead, the sense of smell, Digby seems to take up the boy's testimony, and '[h]e said, that after he had beene some time in this wild habitation, he could by the smell judge the tast of any thing that was to be eaten' and scent humans.[44] He stays in this situation, through fear umastered by his 'litle reason' 'still shunning men' until, in a 'very sharpe winter', so harsh 'that many beastes of the forest perished for want of foode', he was forced close to the village, among the cattle (it is not clear whether he was hunting) to forage and 'sustaine wretchedly his miserable life'.[45] In this way:

> he was upon a time espied: and they who saw a beast of so strange a shape (for such they took him to be; he being naked and all over growne with haire) beleeving him to be a satyre, or some such prodigious creature as the recounters of rare accidents tells us of; layed waite to apprehend him. But he that winded them as farre off, as any beast could do, still avoided them, till att the length, they layed snares for him; and tooke the wind so advantageously of him, that they caught him: and then, some perceived he was a man though he had quite forgotten the use of all language: but by his gestures and cryes, he expressed the greatest affrightednesse that might be. Which afterwardes, he said (when he had learned anew to speak) was because he thought, those were the souldiers he had hidden himselfe to avoid, when he first betooke himselfe to the wood; and were always lively in his fansie, through his feares continually reducing them thither.[46]

John's heightened sense of smell can be overcome by human knowledge of the acuity of animal senses combined with human reason. Smell, Digby later says, is useful in relation to food because the small atoms of smell are less damaging than the large atoms of taste – it is less damaging to inhale the smell of rotting food, meat, than to eat it. John illustrates this example very well – smell is needed for food and safety and he loses the sense as he returns to the world for, after 'good keeping' and 'full feeding', his 'acuteness of smelling' left him.[47]

This analysis of smell suffices to prove Digby's point, but the story gives much more than an analysis of the work of smell. In describing changes brought about by contact with the wild, Digby tells us that the hunters who caught John found him so hairy that they thought him a satyr or 'prodigious creature'. John's fearful imaginings keep him in the wild, lost in 'the forrest of Ardenne'.[48] The imaginations of those who catch him, inhabited by stories of wild men, also shape the situation; they 'snare' him like an animal but, we are told, anticipate that he might be a satyr; they seem initially to have difficulty understanding that he is truly human. Yet, of course, these feelings are ascribed or ordered (we cannot know which) in the potentially multiple processes of transmission – itself a storied process. John, who re-learns language, is by Digby given a subjectivity which knows both his state of mind in the woods and in the present. He has a human memory which enables his potentially animal past to be reshaped as human, or as a human experience of the life and attributes of beasts, though contrasting with his present situation. Thus, the marvellous is present but located in the imagination of those who ensnare John: he is neither a satyr nor prodigious. The categories Le Goff discusses with regard to the 'marvellous', specifically its situation between the miraculous and the Satanic, are present in this story carefully encased in peasant subjectivity, uneducated and so subject to error. The story plays out the disabusing of the peasants in a reworking of the marvellous into a short-lived moment of wonder in an encounter with the unknown. Imagination, which piques the curiosity of the hunters but also deceives them, has more seriously deceived John himself in keeping him in the woods.

Digby's story insists that John is now re-integrated into human society and, crucially, has regained language. It is a story of the experience of smell, but also of the power of fear and fantasy. John was changed by wildness and fear into something between a beast and a man, explicable as a 'satyr' yet by the time the witnesses see him, not only can he speak but recall his motivations as a shivering, desperate forest-dweller whose heightened sense of smell has facilitated survival. John can tell his own story, and it is corroborated by witnesses. However, some details are unresolved. His re-entry into civilisation is, intriguingly, 'among strangers' though 'born in some village of the countrey of Liege'.[49] Presumably he remembers this? Yet more mysterious is that the feelings of his parents seem to be fully known even though, 'among strangers' he is not reunited with them and this is a detail to which we will return later.

John's story radically reworks some aspects of the stories of wild children while retaining others. By the time the *Two Treatises* was published Digby was prominent amongst the early English Cartesians. When Descartes published *Discourse on the Method* in the vernacular in 1637 Digby read it within four months and sent it on to Thomas Hobbes with a recommendation that 'if he were as accurate in his metaphysicall part as he in his experience, he had carried the palme from all men living'.[50] Engaging energetically with Descartes on the ground of experience, Digby was working abreast of William Harvey and became well known and read throughout Europe; the *Two Treatises* was a landmark publication.[51] Digby's approach was constituted by a particular mixture of allegiances and qualities. An experimentalist who found that his experiments supported Aristotle's view of the developing foetus, the inventor of sympathetic powder, a Roman Catholic and an atomist, Digby wrote to Hobbes a month before his recommendation of Descartes about the question of 'foreknowledge', in which he clearly had faith.[52] In a way that is consonant with his practical sense of 'experience', but also with his willingness to take on many different ways of thinking about learning, Digby is happy to use the example of the wild child, as he says, as an example of the role of the small atoms in smell, and in animal and human adaptation. Digby, though, also seems fascinated by other aspects of wild upbringing – the power of imagination and fear, the effects on human status. Digby's John is shaped in part in the interest of atomism and Baconian experience, but he also generates broader questions about the nature of the human, the changes made by the wild and the question of how children find themselves in the forest.

Digby is not alone in setting the wild child within an experimental, partly Cartesian, frame. At the end of the century Bernard Connor, an Irish physician and natural philosopher, made an excursion into vernacular history, and in his *History of Poland* (1698) gives three accounts of wild nurture. Like Digby, Connor writes about the changes effected by an encounter with the wild in terms of changes in being and senses. Connor came to discuss wild children because having cared for the sons of the Chancellor of Poland at the French court, he came to work for a year as physician to the King of Poland where he seems to have gathered materials for the *History*.[53]

The wild children are found in a section on Lithuania, a 'vast Tract of Land' between Poland and 'Moscovy', torn by the Northern wars of the 1660s.[54] Here, there are some 'in the great Woods who still worship Serpents &c as they used to do', Connor tells us, before turning his attention to the woods' other surprises.[55] He writes, 'I was assur'd by the King himself, several Senators and other Great Men of the Kingdom; and moreover, it is the common and undisputed Report, that Children are oftentimes nourish'd and brought up by Bears in these Parts.' Thus, travellers' tales are validated by royal imprimatur:

> It was assur'd me often at Court, and it is certainly believ'd all over the Kingdom that Children have been frequently nurtur'd by Bears, who are very numerous in these Woods. There was one kept a Convent in my time who was taken among them, as I have describ'd in my Latin Treatise, *Of the Suspensions of the Laws of Nature*. He was about ten Years of Age (which might be guess'd only by his Stature and aspect) of a hideous Countenance, and had neither the use of Reason, nor Speech: he went upon all four, and had nothing in him like a Man, except his Human Structure: But seeing he resembled a Rational Creature, he was admitted to the Font, and christen'd; yet still he was restless and uneasy, and often inclin'd to flight. But at length, being taught to stand upright, by clapping up his Body against a Wall, and

holding him after the manner that Dogs are taught to beg; and being by little and little accustom'd to eat at Table, he after some time became indifferently tame, and began to express his Mind with a hoarse and unhuman Tone; but being ask'd concerning his course of Life in the Woods, he could not give much better account of it, than we can do of our Actions in the Cradle.[56]

Baptism makes little difference. Bipedism and speech are imperfect (a contrast with Digby's example) and the child seems more like a 'tame' wild creature than a fellow human. From the framing of the narrative it seems possible, at least, that Connor was aware of Digby's account. However, where Digby presents a relatively smooth transition to humanity for John, Connor's first example remains compromised by animal nursing; his entry into human contact is explicitly violent, his training in bipedism is like a dog, he lacks the humanising memory of Digby's child.

Like Digby, Connor foregrounds the role of the witness in the two further stories he presents. The first is a translated letter sent to him in response to a request for information, and then giving his own account of another boy. His correspondent, 'his Excellency Monsieur *de Cleverskerk*, now Embassador here to his Majesty King *William* from the states of Holland' offers 'an Account of a Boy that I saw in Warsaw in the Year 1661 who had been brought up by Bears' and fairly recently 'taken' at 'a Bear-hunting'.[57] Visiting the boy in the Nunnery where he was held, the correspondent paints a scene of the twelve- or thirteen-year-old boy playing:

> As soon as I came near him he leap'd towards me as if surpriz'd and pleas'd with my Habit. First, he caught one of my Silver Buttons in his hand with a great deal of eagerness, which he held up to his Nose to smell; Afterwards he leap'd all of a sudden into a Corner, where he made a strange sort of Noise not unlike to Howling.[58]

The correspondent goes on to describe the cries of the boy feeding, his leaping and how he 'walk'd about upon all-four' then, 'rais'd himself upright with a great Spring, and took the Bread in his two Hands, put it up to his Nose, and afterwards leap'd off from the Bench upon the Ground, making the same odd sort of Noise as before. I was told that he was not yet brought to speak, but that they hop'd in a short time he would, having his Hearing good.'[59] Emphasising the boy's use of his senses, and particularly smell and agility, the correspondent offers a complex account of the boy. He walks on all fours, is 'not yet brought to speak' and, troublingly, seems to experience his being in the mode of an animal. The witness certifies a physical and experiential condition, and further notes 'there are several parallel Examples in History'. Besides the experimental or experiential data, he accounts for the boy's presence in the woods and, like Digby, Connor cites testimony. Described as the Dutch ambassador J. P. Van den Brande de Cleversclerk explains:

> I have been inform'd in this Country, that whenas the Tartars make frequent Incursions there, which they perform with such extraordinary Swiftness, that they can over-run great part of the Country in a very short time... being arrived at the propos'd Place, they immediately quarter themselves in a great Circle, whereby, as it were in a Net, they take all that come within their Clutches, and carry them into Slavery. So that either the Men or Women, finding themselves thus ensnar'd, and endeavouring to escape, have oftentimes not leisure to take care of their Infants, and therefore probably this Boy might have been left behind in the like manner, and found and born away by the Bears[60]

We will return to the question of the family. At this point, unlike Digby or Digby's informants, this correspondent is uncertain about how a child might arrive in the forest, plumping for a likely explanation in a dramatic scenario of extreme and sudden violence. So, again, the frame could be seen as partially Cartesian, partly an anecdote of a wonder. Certainly, it canvasses the limits of human innateness and explores the question of bestial change experienced by humans.

The social status and reliability of the witness is again emphasised in Connor's final account; the witness, 'M. Christopher Hartknoch of Passenheim in Ducal-Prussia', has written two books on Polish affairs. This story, 'which perhaps might hardly be credited by Posterity', involves the discovery of two boys one of whom is 'taken' by soldiers, brought to Warsaw, and 'christen'd' Joseph. Like the earlier captive he is judged to be between twelve and thirteen, 'his Manners wholly bestial'. Thus, he 'fed upon raw flesh' and 'like Dainties which Bears are us'd to feast with' and moved 'like them, upon all-four'. Indeed, 'after his Baptism' he was only taught with difficulty 'to go upright' and 'there was less hopes of ever making him learn the *Polish* language, for he always continued to express his Mind in a kind of Bear-like Tone'. He is employed as a kitchen carrier, 'but yet could he never be brought to relinquish his native Wildness, which he retain'd to his dying-day; for he would often go into the Woods amongst the Bears, and freely keep company with them without any fear, or harm done him, being, as was suppos'd, constantly acknowledg'd for their Fosterling'.[61] The description mixes some experiential concerns with the figurative language of wild nurture, the child a changeling, almost, a 'fosterling' of the bears, returning to his 'native wildness'.

Connor records the relationship of the children to food, the senses, bipedism, language and to that initiation so crucial to the civil life of Orson – baptism. Yet, in comparison with the fictions the real creatures remain unrecalled to subjecthood. Each story of boys caught on the brink of adulthood shows them in crucial ways failing to achieve human status, with Joseph quite explicitly retaining an affinity with not only the woods but the bears. Indeed, at the same time as focusing on the human in a Cartesian way Connor's whole discussion is framed in ways that would have been recognised by Topsell and that seem to use certain accepted ideas about the natural history of bears – most particularly their association with extreme and transformative nurture:

> littered blind without eies, naked without haire, and the hinder legs not perfect, the forefeet folded up like a fist, and other members deformed by reason of the immoderate humor or moystnes in them, which also is one cause, why the womb of the beare cannot retaine seed to the perfection of her young ones.[62]

Topsell makes clear the association between bears and a naturalised metamorphosis which works on the infant bear, and above all, associates the bear with nurture. Bear cubs, coming forth early because of the problematically moist womb of the bear, require shaping by the female bear which, labouring in a way characterised by Topsell as between nature and culture, makes these strange mis-shapes into proper bears.[63] More importantly, the making of the bear articulated here mixes natural and the social moulding in a significant way. If the bear is able to complete nature's work, is a part of the apparently bodily, natural, process of infant formation transferred into the realm of culture? Topsell implies rather than poses that question, leaving it that the nurture of the bear intervenes in the process of the development of the young of a species in a way which is transformational.

Connor's stories are distinguished by the eyewitness accounts of boys failing to make the return to human sociability. He also recirculates in print aspects of bear lore, imbuing them with characteristics in relation to their encounters with the human:

> They say likewise, that if a hungry He-Bear finds a Child that has been carelessly left any where, he will immediately tear it to pieces; but on the contrary, had it been a She-Bear then giving Suck, she would undoubtedly have carried it safe to her Den, and nourish'd it among her Cubs, which after some time might probably have been rescued from her and been taken by Hunters, as it happen'd in another Case of this nature in the Year 1669, which has been positively asserted to me.[64]

The mythic, metamorphic, power of bear-nurture adds an exotic dimension to stories of wild children. The bear gives physical being, perhaps, to the transformational power of the wild. This power, playing a central and thematic role in the fictions of Romulus and Remus and of Valentine and Orson, is acknowledged also in these post-Cartesian accounts. Connor's account retains bear nurture in part as a wonder, albeit one of which he could give 'several other accounts' which he had 'related' to him in Poland.[65] It is not wasted on Connor that his final example, of the two boys found in the woods, provides a 'real world' story inviting readers to be 'sufficiently convinc'd, that the History of *Romulus* and *Remus* is not so fabulous as it is generally conjectured to be' and:

> As I thought myself it was before I had been in this Country; for considering that Brutes (since philosophers and Divines will allow them no rational Souls) breed up their Young merely out of a Natural Instinct or Sympathy, which I need not describe here, I see no Improbability why they may not likewise bring up those of another Kind, as we have several Instances daily. But I will not insist longer upon these Philosophical Matters, nor examin here whether Examples of this nature refute or establish innate ideas.[66]

Connor has attended to these stories of wild nurture for a reason. Aware of Cartesianism but not its obedient servant, he is using these tales to respond to, rather than embrace, the new criteria Descartes offered for the human. In 1636 Descartes had written that 'As regards reason or sense, since it is the only thing that makes us men and distinguishes us from the beasts, I am inclined to believe that it exists whole and complete in each of us.'[67] Connor seems conscious that he values the beast, and the beast's power to nurture, very differently from Descartes. Using witnesses, emphasising some of the key criteria yet reaching different conclusions, Connor integrates a quasi-Baconian sense of witnessed experiment into the contours of the tale, while at the same time explicitly retaining its mythic dimensions. Significantly, Connor reanimates rather than banishes fable. Indeed, the experiences of the Polish forests serve to revalidate the myth of Romulus and Remus in experiential terms – they 'prove' the possibility of the Roman story. Connor's account is also in a subtly nuanced relationship to Descartes, suggesting that even under the Cartesian dispensation whereby animals lose their 'rational soul', extreme nurture can happen. His expressions suggest that he is unhappy about the Cartesian changes to the status of the animal.

To what extent is it helpful to consider Digby and Connor's discussions as Cartesian reframing, and if so should they be considered as part of a new epoch in telling the story of wild children? The accounts of wild children offered by Digby and Connor are indeed reshaped by an interest in experience and experiment which suggests the emerging influence of Bacon and, potentially, Descartes. We know Digby read and met Descartes. Connor, who had been at the centre of Cartesian debate in Paris and who regarded himself as a physician and experimentalist with 'neither a Genius, nor a Talent for History', was aware of the later seventeenth-century reception of the ideas. It seems possible, even likely, that Connor had himself read Digby's *Two Treatises*. However, although Digby and Connor's texts clearly evidence a rededication of the narrative of wild nurture, and frame more rigorously and precisely questions about the nature and definition of the human and the effect on those qualities of time in the wild, these are not Cartesian texts. Rather, as G. A. J. Roger says of Kenelm Digby, if we can hear Descartes in the writing then we can also hear Bacon – and, probably, Plutarch. Clearly, both Digby and Connor had complex responses to Cartesianism and, as Roger argues, Descartes is here a stimulus to thought rather than a body of ideas to which the writer must turn and attend.[68] Neither writer sees the animal as a machine, nor is the dominant comparison for the human body a machine; rather, their wild children are set in layered scenes of social, fabulous, educational and religious significance. Their ability to be recalled to the human world is tested by baptism, nurture (often literally food) as well as the, potentially but not definitively, more Cartesian concerns with language and reason.[69]

Each writer seeks to recover and elucidate the experience which has rendered these humans so distinct from their own kind, and to specify the nature of the change. The 'true' stories of children lost in the wild are differently inflected from the fictional accounts examined earlier, but remain dramas of transformation. Digby and Connor are concerned to locate the border where human and animal flow into one another. They are clearly working to find routes to restore human status more certainly to those who in religion, reason, speech remain prisoners of the changes wrought by the wild, and they are concerned with how the restoration of the human might be measured or assessed. Both writers register these transformed beings as extraordinary and are at pains to provide stories explaining how these children came to live as animals. The figures they describe might have extra accomplishments, but they recognise clearly that these turn into deficits once they are resettled in human society. Wonder, for these two, is not necessarily limited, as it is for Descartes, to 'a sudden surprise of the soul' but rather a condition more sustained and a pervasive

14 Orson and bear, *Valentine and Orson: The Two Sonnes of the Emperour of Greece* (1637).

response to the whole event.[70] Moreover, Connor is uncertain concerning Descartes' restriction of the sensitive soul and clearly seeks to extend the remit of animal ability so that while they might be automata, yet they are sufficiently sophisticated as machines to nurture humans. So, while Digby and Connor are not working in a fundamentally Cartesian frame, they see themselves as writing with reference to his work. Most notably, writing fifty years apart, neither is primarily Cartesian but each allows wonder at the power of a human to be changed by animal encounters and life, seen not only in the response of witnesses, but, in a more mediated way in their own retelling.

15 Bear suckling humans, Bernard Connor, *History of Poland* (1698), vol. 1.

III Storytelling

There is, in fact, a text that examines the mechanics of the stories of children found in the wild. *The Winter's Tale* analyses the ways in which stories about foundlings, and also about bastards who might be abandoned, produce effects of truth. It is placed late in this chapter not because it offers an answer to the problematic of transformation through the wild evoked in fictional and naturalised form, but because, amongst many other aspects of the play excluded from this analysis, it investigates the 'wild' child in the figure of Perdita and, specifically, interrogates the storytelling surrounding and the motivations for losing children to, or finding them in, the wild. *The Winter's Tale*, then, is distinctively analytical amongst the stories of transformation by the wild in returning the fantasy of the wild child to the social world that produces it. In the light of the texts examined earlier, we can see the way *The Winter's Tale* consistently puts in question myths about the family, the child and the foundling. That the play concerns itself with the lost and found child and the impact on the family of the way the child is treated was noticed by an early auditor, Simon Forman:

> In the Winters Talle at the glob 1611 the 15 of may [Wednesday]

> Observe ther howe Lyontes the King of Cicillia was overcom with Jelosy of his wife with the kinge of bohemia his frind that came to see him . . . / Remember also howe he sent to the orakel of apollo & the Aunswer of apollo, that she was giltes, and the king was Jelouse &c and howe Except the Child was found Again that was loste the kinge should die without yssue, for the Child was carried into bohemia, and there laid in a forrest & brought up by a sheppard. And the king of bohemia his sonn maried that wench & howe they fled into Cicillia to Leontes, and the sheppard having showed the letter of the nobleman by whom Leontes sent a was [it was? away?] that child, and the Jewells found about her, she was knowen to be Leontes daughter and was then 16 yers old.

> Remember also the Rog that cam in all tottered like coll-pixci . . . beware of trustinge feined beggars or fawninge fellous.[71]

So goes Simon Forman's account of a performance of *The Winter's Tale*. Forman notices jealousy, guilt and guiltlessness, the role of the oracle, the child in the forest, the shepherd, the jewels and letter, Perdita's age at marriage and the 'colt-pixie', Autolycus. In the audience at the Globe, Forman was following the family romance in which Leontes loses and regains 'the child', and, as Stephen Orgel and Holgar Schott Syme suggest,

Forman may well be representative in his focus on abandonment and recovery. As Orgel notes, and as the fictional accounts of the wild child we have examined emphasise, the ordering of lineage was the central concern of family in seventeenth-century England. As Orgel also notes, through systems of service and periods in great houses, children of many ranks were deliberately sent away and reclaimed. However, Orgel does not address the question of those other children which the same society 'lost' but did not recover. These children, investigated by Laura Gowing, had a start in life that was determined by a central cultural concern with the uncertainty of paternity.[72]

In such a world Forman might be expected to notice the 'issue' of a child lost and found.[73] What seems, in the light of other evidence, less usual in a text focusing on children in the wild, is the play's emphasis on the analysis of explanatory narratives and their freight of assumptions and expectations. *The Winter's Tale* examines the way accounts, tales, stories, legends and kinds of speech set expectations, and therefore, as established by Stanley Cavell's reading of the play's accounting and recounting vocabulary, it allows audiences to analyse how tales make knowledge.[74] Thus, in the first part of the play Perdita's place in the family is accounted for in roughly three vocabularies – those of the joke, scandalous account, parish dispute or courtroom; in the register of the sacred; in terms of story of exposure in the wild.

The audience meet Perdita through Paulina's assertion that the child, 'prisoner of the womb', is 'by law and process of great nature thence / Freed and enfranchised, not a party to / The anger of the King' (2.3.58–61).[75] However, the child is in fact rapidly immersed in a discourse of scandal as Antigonus is forced to plead the baby's case with her father. Antigonus tells Leontes, 'You are abused, and by some putter-on' and threatens, 'If this prove true' and Hermione is 'honour-flawed', he'll 'geld' his daughters (2.1.141, 143, 147). Such language, addressing the accusation in the everyday sense of sexual scandal, casts the problem in one language familiar to the audience – that of sexual transgression and punishment. Perdita's legitimacy is explored in the language of parish dispute. The use of this language, and its believability and apparent, and convincing, 'veracity' is part of the play's examination of how expulsion from the family can be effected on the flimsy evidence of a story or stories. In relation to this language the actual demonstration of the baby seems questionable evidence and Paulina becomes a 'mankind witch', a 'most intelligencing bawd' (2.3.67–8). It is in such a discursive framework that Leontes, a father, might assert 'No, I'll not rear / Another's issue' (3.1.192–3). The opening moments of Perdita's story, then, canvasses legitimacy in vocabulary most often found in ballads, jokes and court records.[76]

In contrast to the language of scandal, the oracle of Apollo gives access to supervening, heavenly, truth. The oracle's involvement aligns with wonder events usually mired in courts, money and slander. The story it tells is of a future, potentially ruined by the loss of a child. *The Winter's Tale* raises the stakes of paternity by, first, adding kingship to kinship to intensify the importance of lineage and, secondly, using the oracle to decide the truth and set a task for the rest of the play. If the crisis in the state is precipitated by a drama of marital sexual cruelty, the heavens are nevertheless interested in the outcome. The gods are insistent that the audience know Hermione as 'chaste', Perdita legitimate, Leontes, 'a jealous tyrant', and the family 'without an heir' if 'that which is lost be not found' (3.2.130–4). Most significantly, that the audience know the 'truth' guides them to assess not accept the proliferating stories adopted by the characters, from Leontes' vulgar accusation to Autolycus' stories, like that of 'Mistress Tail-Porter'. As Michael Whitmore comments, in the acts to come the audience see 'veracity' as an effect of the tale in the mind of the auditor, not truth.[77]

In Act 3 the audience is given a plethora of stories to evaluate, even as the stage is crammed with events as the child enters the wild. Here the interplay of stories of 'lost' and 'found' gives us a bravura, interrogative reworking of ready-made, pre-known stories about these events.

> ANTIGONUS ... Blossom, speed thee well;
> [*He lays down the baby and a scroll*]
> There lie, and there thy character; there these,
> [*He lays down a bundle*]
> Which may, if fortune please, both breed thee, pretty,
> And still rest thine. [*Thunder*] The storm begins – poor wretch,
> That for thy mother's fault art thus exposed,
> To loss, and what may follow! Weep I cannot,
> But my heart bleeds, and most accurst am I
> To be by oath enjoined to this. Farewell;
> The day frowns more and more – thou'rt like to have
> A lullaby too rough. I never saw
> The heavens so dim by day.
> [*Storm, with a sound of dogs barking and hunting horns*]
>   A savage clamour!
> Well may I get aboard! – This is the chase;
> I am gone for ever!   *Exit pursued by a bear.*
> *Enter an Old Shepherd*   (3.3.45–57)

Antigonus sees the infant as 'for thy mother's fault . . . thus expos'd' (3.3. 50) and so, though 'most accurs'd', he remains 'by oath enjoin'd to this' (3.3. 52–3).[78] Then the storm and bear destroy him. The bear, rushing into the plot, provides the dramatic pretext ensuring that Perdita's identity becomes a mystery to the characters and herself. At the same time, the bear's arrival before the audience links the stories of lost and found children. The same scene which ties together the narratives of exposure and the foundling for the audience separates them for the characters, partially closing the first part of the narrative but also making a bridge between the two parts of the play, between lost and found, past and future.

The Winter's Tale shows us the exposure of the child, the removal of the witness, the threat of the bear and the discovery of the child in a single episode and as a central scene. In this scene the audience is given the information usually missing in the story of a foundling as, splicing together lost and found, the narrative of discovery overlaps with its usually absent backstory: the tale of abandonment (lost, of course, to the characters). At the same time as Antigonus exits, taking with him the knowledge of Perdita's earlier life, the shepherd enters. With the knowledge of that 'truth' and the overarching 'truth' offered by the oracle, the audience is put in a position to analyse the way the shepherd who finds the child responds by putting her in a story.

The shepherd is rustic, pastoral, and registers incursions into his world, having seen young men at 'hunt' (3.3.63):

> SHEPHERD They have scared away two of my best sheep, which I fear the wolf will sooner find than the master; if anywhere I have them, 'tis by the sea side, browsing of ivy. Good luck, and 't be thy will, what have we here? Mercy on's, a bairn! A very pretty bairn – a boy, or a child, I wonder? A pretty one, a very pretty one – sure some scape; though I am not bookish, yet I can read waiting-gentlewoman in the scape. This has been some stair-work, some trunk-work, some behind-door work; they were warmer that got this than the poor thing is here. I'll take it up for pity; yet I'll tarry till my son come; he hallooed even now. Whoa-ho-hoa!
> *Enter Clown*
>
> (3.3.64–76)

The shepherd becomes a storyteller in explaining the foundling using stories he knows and that seem true. Once again, the most obvious explanations are those of rumour – illicit unions, cases in the courts, ballads. As Frances Dolan notes, the shepherd imagines a 'waiting-gentlewoman' as opposed to the servants and widows of the pamphlet and ballad literature.[79] However, he evidently uses stories of infants found out of place, without ties to a

Storytelling 187

wider social fabric. Although the shepherd is 'not bookish' stories he has heard tell him how to interpret such an oft-told situation as a babe found, alone but with certain signs, in a wilderness location. The shepherd uses Perdita's baptismal 'bearing cloth' (3.3.111), her accompanying treasure and tokens to fit a story, in this case an earlier prediction that he would be 'rich by the fairies' – and so by this 'changeling' (3.3.113–14). The prophecy comically mimics the oracle given to Leontes but is, as the plot unfolds, equally true in its way. The shepherd, like Antigonus and Leontes, uses familiar narrative to structure experience. Equipped with knowledge of the actual situation, enhanced by the view of Apollo, the audience is forced to see the hackneyed, potentially hollow, shape of the circulating tale of sexual scandal.

Moreover, once the auditors are alert to the play's dual focus on the plot and the interrogation of those stories which set it in motion, then they are in a position to recognise the familiar narrative elements of a child found as Forman puts it, 'laid in a forrest'. The sheep, wolf and the hunters establish connections to other tales – of babes not found by shepherds but taken 'wild' by bears and wolves or by hunters of those wild animals. The elements of wildness that momentarily enter the text, the storm and the bear, are also extremely familiar if we approach the play with stories of wild nurture in mind. In terms of the play's use of the wild and its dangerously transformative powers, it makes the point that Perdita's humanity is not compromised by a relationship with the bear. Moreover, the nature of the bear's violence is carefully contrasted with the degenerate human violence that has brought Perdita to Bohemia. Even though the bear has 'half dined on the gentleman' (3.3.103), as the clown says, bears 'are never curst but when they are hungry' (3.3.125–6); it is 'curst', in a potentially anthropomorphic expression, for reasons of nature.

The bear is wild, perhaps, but also potentially bound in to the play's attention to the mechanics of plot – in this case not narrative, but theatre. Act 3 begins with the Mariner telling Antigonus, 'this place is famous for the creatures / Of prey that keep upon it' (3.3.12–13), a description as accurate for the London Bankside, with its bear garden, as the Bohemian sea coast. The longstanding critical puzzle of how to imagine the relationships amongst bear- and bull-baitings and the adjacent theatres has been addressed by two recent critics. Setting baitings and theatre alongside one another as 'culturally isomorphic events', Stephen Dickey situates baitings and theatre as adjacent, comparable, allegorising one another.[80] However, as well as seeing theatre and baiting as cognate events, as Michael D. Bristol argues, we need to take a step back from the drama to consider understandings underpinning representations of bears and see such expectations and ceremonies as these as shaped both the drama and the audience's knowledge.[81] Both are compatible with a third strand in which the bear, besides being local and located in the church year, was part of the wildlife that furnish stories like Valentine and Orson – as violent and aggressive or as enigmatic nurture.

The world of the shepherd is not the wild world of shipwreck and bear, rather, as the storm gives way, a pastoral world emerges, once again a storied world, inhabited by creatures and figures of pastoral, romance, classical transformation and the commercial world of cheap print. The classical gods rub shoulders with Autolycus' commercial world of 'wakes, fairs, and bear-baitings' (4.3.99–100), and the satyr of stories and masques finds a form both concrete and intertextual in an offered dance by 'three carters, three shepherds, three neat-herds, three swine-herds that have made themselves all men of hair', and 'call themselves saltiers' (4.4.319–23).[82] As J. H. Pafford comments, the word 'saltier', somewhere between 'sault' (jump) and satyr, oscillates between designating the nature of the hairy costumes and the agility of the dancers.[83] In their turn to the wild, the shepherds take on the extra physical power of those figures – humans, animals, wild humans – that inhabit it; yet, simultaneously, one at least claims to have danced before the king and the whole episode may be yet another intertextual reference – to the satyr dance in Ben Jonson's masque, *Oberon*.[84] In this dance, then, the play recalls both the wild men of the woods and its own status as theatre.

We have seen that *The Winter's Tale* investigates the nature and place of the wild, and evokes the danger of the wild in stories of the wild from Perdita's exposure to its reconsideration in the final act. Yet, of course, the threatened true wildness does not, quite, materialise. Bohemia turns out to be a pastoral environment and even the bear, which lends a momentary wildness, is both familiar from stories and, possibly, from the play *Mucedorus*, as well as being nearby, at the bear garden.[85] The deferral of the wild, and the question of what it might mean, is addressed as the play ends. When Florizel and Perdita are fleeing Polixenes' rage at his son's planned marriage to the pastoral Perdita, Camillo sends them to Sicilia: 'A course more promising / Than a wild dedication of yourselves / To unpathed waters, undreamed shores' (4.4.562–4). In the averted prospect of Florizel and Perdita's further flight, beyond mere pastoral into the wilds of uncharted discovery, the globe's unknown places far beyond the reach of kinship and lineage, the play both reminds the audience of the effect of the loss of children and orchestrates the couple's re-entry into civilisation. The actual appearance of Florizel in Sicilia permits the progressive re-attachment of experience, the senses and feelings to reason that takes place through the fifth act enabling, from Simon Forman's point of view, the 'wench' to be 'known to be Leontes daughter.' In effecting this, *The Winter's Tale* gives us a relocation of the wild at the moment when Leontes recognises not Paulina or Hermione but Florizel:

> Your father's image is so hit in you,
> His very air, that I should call you brother,
> As I did him, and speak of something wildly
> By us performed before. (5.1.126–9)

In recognising another man as a brother, the place of sexual rivalry and deceit amongst men is both acknowledged (Florizel is not, here, a son but given an equal place in a reordered patriarchy), and the wildness of anxiety about generation precisely reallocated to the father, maker and hearer of sexual yarns. In terms of the replacement of the wild where it belongs, Leontes' acknowledgment of Florizel and of the past places the 'wild' at the command centre for both family and state, and in a degenerate not a natural form. This is perhaps the recognition most significant to Perdita's story in that, without it, none of the lost things wrapped up in 'Perdita' can be found again. At the same time, Leontes' acknowledgement is the final move in the play's relentless questioning of the truth of stories – the wildness of Bohemia is pastoral; the wildness of bear, ocean and storm are natural; the wildness of the wild child is a more complex and morally loaded kind of wildness made at the heart of the family and the state. It is this, human wildness that puts babies in the path of bears. This wildness is opposed to the blending of culture and nature in nurture, literally, breastfeeding. Thus, the jealous Leontes says of Mammilus 'I am glad you did not nurse him. / Though he show some signs of me, yet you / Have too much blood in him' (2.1. 56–8).

Finally, approaching the play from the point of view of the wild child invites a reconsideration of one detail which is foregrounded as part of Perdita's story, and which she speaks as part of her interpretation of the world – the 'gillyvors' (4.4.81). Famously, Perdita's garden is 'barren' of gillflowers because she suspects them sexually; 'nature's bastards', whose streaks suggest 'an art which in their piedness shares / With great creating nature' (4.4 84, 87–8). Usually, and appropriately, understood as a commentary on the changing or improving of nature through human 'art', but also, of course, a commentary on the relationship between Florizel and Perdita, the range of stories evidenced by these promiscuous gillyvors can be expanded.[86] It is worth pausing on Polixenes' pedagogic reply that 'we marry / a gentler scion to the wildest stock', to make 'a bud of nobler race' (4.4. 92–3, 95).

Polixenes is at pains to explain the need for the civil to be pied or streaked through contact with the wild – a lesson refused by the foundling Perdita with her trinkets, papers and baptismal robe. *The Winter's Tale* takes the story of the child transformed in an encounter with nature but equips that child with religion (both the oracle and the baptismal certificate), a pastoral, rather than wild, exposure; language, education, family. She even has that arch-pastoral retrieval of the wild, a disguised prince to match her own lost (and found) royalty. Perdita's story, then, is of a child saved from the wild lodged in a play deeply immersed in, and interrogating the social basis of, stories of wild children.

By the time Perdita and Polixenes discuss the sexual politics of gardening, the audience know Perdita as a child saved from the wild and equipped to refuse its dangers. Yet they are reminded of the advantages that men find in a bit of wild transformation. The politics of this exchange is complex and it echoes both the mystery of the wolf in the story of Romulus and Remus, and the rape of the Sabines. Clearly, though, by this point the play's audience are schooled to recognise stories at loggerheads when they see them – as they do in the gillyvors. Theatre, then, sets the terms on which *Winter's Tale* reassesses the truth-telling powers of tales of romance, scandal and the marvellous. The theatrical arc of the play uses multiple voices to voice, reshape and juxtapose the narratives of sexual scandal found in the courts, in ballads, jokes and stories just like those carried and sold by Autolycus into a new structure. The play edits into view and foregrounds throughout the frightening adult storms and emotions that precipitate and surround the crisis of nurture leading up to abandonment. Yet, if it investigates the adult scandals underpinning abandonment it does so, ultimately, under the sign of the marvellous and it is this connection between the low, forensic, suspicious and the extraordinary, marvellous and redemptive that it shares with romance and, arguably underpinning those shapes, creation myths. Presumably simultaneously with the supernatural resolution of scandal and civic disharmony, the story of exposure offers its own re-workings. Working with requirements for the audience to shift modes of apprehension between interwoven, yet conceptually distinct, understandings of drama, the scene invites a response positioned between the forensic and the miraculous but in a strikingly different theatrical mode from the drama at Leontes' court.

Like Autolycus, *The Winter's Tale* speaks as if it has 'eaten ballads' (4.4.186). Amongst the many stories in the play several address the central concern articulated by Forman of 'issue'. Weaving together but also challenging the stories motivating adult conduct, *The Winter's Tale* follows a child into the wild – almost – and redeems it untransformed. In doing so it offers both a reprise of the stories of the child found in the forest and an analysis of what drives those stories. It definitively traces and ties the story of the wild child to the everyday stories of sexual transgression, bastardy, abandonment and foundlings. While the other stories examined here, both the fictional and the 'true', either efface the events leading to abandonment or cast them as extreme, rather than quotidian, in joining up the stories of sexual scandal with those of children marvellously discovered in the wild, *The Winter's Tale* makes unmistakably clear that the 'wildness' in the story is in the casting out from society. For *The Winter's Tale* the transforming encounter with the wild is produced by the violence of sexual storytelling: the stories provide scripts which send the child out to be transformed. For *The Winter's Tale* the children transformed by the wild come from civil society, not from the woods.

IV Autolycus, the wolf and the wild children

What do the diverse stories discussed in this chapter suggest about the implications of stories of wild transformation in seventeenth-century England? Autolycus gives us a clue in untangling some of the specific cultural significances of stories of wild nurture in the seventeenth century. Littered under the sign of Mercury, Autolycus is also a twin, of uncertain parentage and the grandfather of Odysseus, who he named. But he is referred to as 'litter'd' (4.3) because, his name tells us, he is 'the wolf himself'. Autolycus is the wolf himself; thief, trickster, liar. As such, he would seem to be the opposite of the truth-telling Delphic oracle which can divine and truly state the personal, familial and political state of affairs. And, indeed, when we read Edward Topsell's condensed wolf-lore it appears that Apollo and the wolf are indeed enemies; for '*Apollo* himself was called *Lycostonos*, a Wolf-killer, because he taught the people how to put away Wolfs'. However, Topsell continues, directly, '*Homer* calleth *Apollo Lycegenes*, for that it is said immediately after he was born of his mother *Latona*, he was changed into the shape of a Wolf, and so nourished; and for this cause there was the image of a Wolf set up at *Delphos* before him.'[87] Apollo is a wolf-taker, a wolf, and himself one of the children whose lives and destinies were shaped by wolf-nurture. He also accepts sacrificed wolves, Topsell tells us. And so the wolf-hater, we find, is also the wolf himself.

That Autolycus and Apollo, lies and truth, are both, if differently, identified with wolves and that Apollo himself, in Homer, is the subject of wolf-nurture and wolf-transformation is suggestive in terms of the kinds of knowledge produced and obscured in the stories of wild children. In *The Winter's Tale* Apollo and Autolycus are in opposite relations to lies and truth. Perdita encounters Autolycus in a pastoral context, but the stories he brings are from the heart of the social world. Apollo, too, tells us that the play's problem is lodged not in Bohemia or beyond, but in the heart of culture, the king's court. In different ways, Autolycus and Apollo recognise that the threat which leads to the exposure of children is lodged not in the wild, where transformation might take place, but in the society that uses stories to expel them. Autolycus' name is not in itself a confusion but rather directs us to a confounding of forms of wildness belonging to forest and family and which *The Winter's Tale* explores.

If we return to the tales of wild children bearing in mind Walter Benjamin's comment that 'every real story... contains openly or covertly, something useful' we can, I think, follow these tales into one further precinct of knowledge. In the discussion with which this chapter opened Rousseau put to work the wild child of Hesse as an example in his consideration of the perfectibility of the human. Ultimately, this child became an part of the undertow of intransigence and superiority of the uncivil in some of his thinking and so an example in the debates of the Enlightenment. In material in which Rousseau might well have found it, the writings of the early seventeenth-century humanist Philip Camerarius, this story performs rather different exemplary functions. An infant is carried away and subsequently nourished and raised by wolves:

> in times of winter and cold, they made a ditch, which they carpeted with herbs and branches of trees, where the infant could lie environed in a way to endure the times then they trained him to walk on hands and feet and to run with them so often that by usage he walked and ran like a wolf. He was brought little by little to walk on two feet.

Such was his immersion in this life, we are told, that later he often, when it was in his power, chose to 'consort with wolves rather than people'.[88] Camerarius puts the boy under a heading of 'marvellous agility' and he does, it seems, learn to run with wolves. More widely, he explains that such 'stories verify the common saying that custome is second nature'. The story is made useful by its double exemplarity. Overtly, it illustrates the power of custom (a concept evidently close to the transformative 'art' of animal-nursing in Valentine and Orson), but also of extraordinary agility.

While the latter meaning allows in the charge of the 'marvellous' that all these stories contain, yet in the making of an 'overt' meaning for the story, both Rousseau and Camerarius leave that quality unaddressed. Rousseau uses the child exemplarily, as does Camerarius, but in each case the overt meaning offered sets aside the enigmatic core which might fascinate and motivate a reader – such as the wolves' careful making of a nest for the child and their training of him.

If we test this story against the literal meaning of Benjamin's comment on 'usefulness' it is evident that, like those of Digby in the 1640s and Connor in the 1690s, its implications are partially exemplary, yet these stories' evident tendency to exceed their notional illustrational purpose suggests that the tales might, in Benjamin's terms, teach us something covertly. In each 'true' and mythic case there is a surplus in something that exceeds or evades becoming part of the particular tale's proffered exemplary concern. In all cases, the anecdotal, marvellous and mythic elements imbue the reading experience crystallised in the question of infant transformation. Other factors include length, story, number of stories, numerousness of witnessing, troubling intransigence of the transformation and, consistently with the clear exception of *The Winter's Tale*, an uncertainty of origins and ambiguity of the process of loss in contrast to that of being found.

As Benjamin's formulation hints, the form of a story might suggest knowledge of a less overt kind. The clearest example is, perhaps, the repainting of the Massacre of the Innocents as a winter scene. There is definitely a knowledge screened by the rededication of the image. But, as many viewers did not know of that repainting, it is uncertain how such 'covert' knowledge can be brought to bear on the image as it stands. However, the stories of children found in the wild might carry, or for their contemporary reader call up, other knowledge and experience.

The precinct of knowledge within most immediate experience of children lost and found that a reader or auditor was likely to have was of children abandoned and found in their parish. These are the stories that Autolycus, Leontes, Antigonus and the Clown all know. The stories of these children, or rather of their parents, exist in court records, ballads and pamphlets and the financial imperative of the parish to get support from the father is indicated by the fact that, from 1624 onwards, the midwife had to try to discover the name of the father. As Laura Gowing and John Boswell have discussed, alongside the abandoned and the found, there were also those who were stillborn and buried and those who were murdered.[89] The meaning of a child 'lost' was complicated, often obscure, and at stake in many cases at law.

The parish narratives are not present in any of the texts we have examined as a reason why an infant might be exposed or abandoned. Nor are these texts explicitly 'about' such a scenario which is explored to some extent in Plutarch's version of Romulus and Remus and fully in *The Winter's Tale*. It is worth turning, just briefly, to texts discussing how children might find themselves in a forest or, more mundanely, in English woodland. Two contrasting tales of infanticide are the strange catalogue of murders in *The Bloudy Mother* (1610) and the much later gallows confession of the desperate widow, Mary Goodenough, in *Fair Warning to Murderers of Infants* (1691).[90] If, in *Fair Warning*, the murderess is a penitent widow, driven by sorrow, *The bloudy mother, or The most inhumane murthers, committed by Iane Hattersley upon diuers infants, the issue of her owne bodie* tells the story of a man and his servant whose adulterous relationship continued for years and generated, it seems, a number of infants, murdered one after another by their progenitors and, the pamphlet hints, with the knowledge, or at least suspicion, of the wider community who have at various times stumbled upon Jane in the throes of labour. Published just a year before Forman saw *The Winter's Tale*, the maternal cruelty of Jane Hattersley makes her deed an emblem of the unreliability of women taken to extremes of cruelty. Yet, within the text itself there is some sense that the community knew of some of the instances of the violence which might involve, at best, Jane's failing to prompt children to live – and the situation was allowed to continue. Jane, 'more than Tyger like stopt the breath' of a whole sequence of infants, and, described as having 'a heart of steele, and eies of marble'. The author finally reaches for the full classical comparison. She is a 'Chimera, with a Lions upper-part in bouldnesse: a goats middle part in lust: and a serpent's lower part in sting and poyson'.[91] The metaphor the pamphlet uses is, perhaps significantly, metamorphic; every part of Jane contributes to her mythic monstrosity. A contrasting narrative of poverty and desperation shapes Mary Goodenough's status as a penitent in *Fair Warning* but the texts clearly use maternal infanticide to explore the wild violence that *Winter's Tale* allocates to a man. Seventeenth-century people knew infants lost and found in their neighbourhoods as potentially examples of infanticide and a multi-faceted problem spanning the vexed question of parish relief for such mothers and children, the naming (and financial responsibility) of fathers, the stillbirth, neglect, exposure and murder of infants by women desperate to escape the harsh punishments of an illegitimate birth – loss of income, status, reputation.

Crucially, though, for all that these texts were widely known in seventeenth-century England, and playgoers and readers knew them, the stories of children found in the wild, with the exception of *The Winter's Tale* and the Rome texts, do not know their found children as subject to exposure or potential infanticide. However, once we set in one frame 'lost' and 'found' genres, we can see distinct forms of usefulness at work in relation to overlapping material. Perhaps, in Benjamin's terms, we can speculate that in the stories of wild children knowledge of abandonment, exposure and infanticide is present not, usually, at a level of overt narrative but may be registered in the excessive elements that characterise the tales and, perhaps, in the very violence of the transformations undergone by the outcast and ruined children made 'wild' and, again, made human in their fraught reintegration into human society.[92]

In sum, several kinds of cultural transformation are at work in these stories. At the same time that the later seventeenth-century 'true find' stories rework elements of the earlier myth to examine the transformed individual in terms of the debates within natural philosophy intensified by Descartes, the stories continue to do other cultural work. This study considers mainly the literary and cultural presence and work of ideas of transformation. In the case of the wild child we need also to attend to a kind of transformation in general excluded from this study – the alchemy of storytelling and the enigma of how distinct cultural concerns might be part of a web of related concerns. Although it is evidently a fundamental cultural and literary function of metamorphosis to translate between social and cultural spheres and so to make knowledge available, and concealed, that is not a case easily made with regard to specifics. In the case of wild children, the evidence suggests that these children figure the relationships between the human and the wild, often the beast. By the same token, therefore, they express the ties between the human and society; the key areas of loss and acquisition of human status being evoked in discussions of language, baptism, food, reason and to an extent posture. Furthermore, in doing this, they seem to both express and obscure (by casting in the mode of traveller's tale, setting an exotic scene, evoking wonder) more culturally familiar events of exclusion and abandonment. Finally, the stories of children changed by the wild are, it seems, generated by the way that the society that recycled the tales in English print shaped itself and what it acknowledged, what it sought to conceal as 'something wildly by us performed'. To know the work of metamorphosis in these ethnographic and mythic stories in Benjamins' terms is, then, to recall the exotic tales they tell to that other textual and experiential knowledge a reader would have of exposure, abandonment, infanticide.

Coda: Descartes and the disciplines

> HAMLET ... What a piece of work is a man, how noble in reason, how infinite in faculties, in form and moving how express and admirable, in action how like an angel, in apprehension how like a god: the beauty of the world, the paragon of animals.
> (William Shakespeare, *Hamlet* 2.2.303–7)

> Now, in just these two ways we can know the difference between man and beast... [T]here are no men so dull-witted... that they are incapable of arranging words together and forming an utterance... whereas there is no other animal... that can do the like... This shows not merely that beasts have less reason than men, but that they have no reason at all.
>
> ... [I]t is nature which acts in them according to the disposition of their organs. In the same way as a clock[.]
> (René Descartes, *Discourse on the Method*)[1]

These statements express opposed views of the relationship of animal and human. A world where animals are 'automata' has no place for Hamlet's evoked transformation of 'a man' upwards to 'angel', or down to 'animal'. Hamlet's words are part of the analogical thinking that made man indeed a paragon, not only in our sense of an example of excellence but 'a match, a compare, an equall' – a 'comparison'.[2]

Hamlet gives a view familiar to seventeenth-century readers. Lodowick Bryskett's longer exploration of man as a touchstone asserts that 'man is the perfection of all creatures under heaven, and placed as the center betweene things divine and mortall'.[3] Man's central position between gods and beasts made movement between these poles the central drama of life. Pagan and Christian philosophers, Bryskett argues, try to show men:

> how great is the perfection of mans mind, make them know how unworthy & unfit it is for a ma[n] to suffer those parts that he hath common with brute beasts to master and over-rule those by which he is made not much

inferiour to divine creatures: and causing them to lift up their minds to this consideration, instruct them to dispose and rule through virtuous habits those parts which of themselves are rebellious to reason, as they may be forced to obey her no otherwise then their Queene and mistris.[4]

Reason, in the service of virtue, 'through Fortitude, Temperance, Justice, and Prudence, with the rest of the virtues', leads to 'civill felicitie, to wit, that perfect action or operation according to vertue in a perfect life'.[5] In Bryskett's thinking on virtue the soul and reason are not so much mixed together as indivisible. He is happy to reason that the longing for immortality is indeed a sign that 'our soules are immortal':

> For if it were otherwise, we should be of all other creatures that nature produceth the most unhappie: and in vaine should that desire of immortalitie (which all men have) be given unto us.

The human task, 'as a creature intellective,' is to 'apply their minds' to find the 'contemplative simplicitie' for which they were 'borne apt'.[6] Thus, Hamlet and Bryskett both understand the universe as vital. They reach for the Aristotelian idea of the soul to offer an account of angel, human and animal. In doing so each also implies a moral and civic world in which human reason is given by the divine and, used properly, allows the human to find the divine again.

Hamlet and Bryskett imagined the transformative raising and beastly lowering of human status as a given, an assumption underpinning their words. However, it would seem that by 1637 or soon after, things were otherwise. The *Discourse on the Method* was published in French with the specific aim of wide dissemination, and Descartes elaborated his thinking that humans alone had reason in subsequent correspondence. In 1646 he wrote to the Duke of Newcastle that 'I cannot share the opinion of Montaigne and others who attribute understanding or thought to animals' which 'act naturally and mechanically, like a clock'. To another correspondent he notes, 'my opinion is not so much cruel to animals as indulgent to human beings – at least those who are not given to the superstition of Pythagoras – since it absolves them from the suspicion of crime when they kill animals'.[7] This is taken from a letter to Henry More, in Cambridge, in 1649 and although Descartes is evidently satirically attacking the doctrine of the transmigration of souls, he is also attacking the idea of an ensouled universe at one of its most vulnerable points. We see here the way Descartes is engaged in heated contemporary debates, promulgating a tendentious response to Michel de Montaigne's assertion that animals have reason and morality, and, at the same time promoting the idea of the world as a machine – a potentially devastating challenge to the Aristotelian three-soul system. These twin objectives were irreconcilable with the flight and fall Hamlet's vital world offers its human.[8] But was metamorphic thinking and writing so soon to be banished?

The answer usually given to this question is that, in general, yes, by the mid seventeenth century Cartesianism mechanism had taken root and an ensouled, living, universe was residual culture. Descartes' decisive rethinking removed the sensitive soul from the Aristotelian model and put in place a stripped down machine-world operated by human reason and expressed in language. Descartes' understanding of animals as automata, part of his articulation of the world, including the human body, as a machine has long been recognised as participating in a stripping away of the fabric of correspondence and story to reveal a purer investigative process and language. From this vantage point, Bacon's writing and Descartes' beast-machine sit alongside texts like Jonston's *Natural History of Quadrupeds* (1657) which has been seen as 'true' natural history, at last, because it removes the storied casing in which the animal was joined to the human world, or Malphigi's microscopic examination of insects, which, in Chapter 3, we heard praised by Edward Tyson for his close observation of the silkworm.[9] Tyson himself has been claimed as a true exponent of the new science in being the father of comparative anatomy.[10] As Peter Harrison summarises the accepted position, '[o]ver the course of the seventeenth century the behaviors of brutes ceased to be "signs" which bore specific meanings for human observers', but came to be understood as 'effects of particular internal operations'.[11] However, it is not clear that the material we have been examining entirely supports this conclusion.

Certainly, within a few months of publication the *Discourse on the Method* was under discussion in England.[12] Kenelm Digby wrote to Hobbes about Descartes within months of the publication of the *Discourse* and the letter was copied by the churchman, William Sancroft. As we have seen, Sir Kenelm Digby's *Two Treatises* (1644) responded to Descartes. Discussing animal language Digby notes the 'vanity' of earlier philosophers who 'would have it believed that beasts have compleat languages, as men have, to discourse with one another in'.[13] He notes that for humans 'speaking or talking is an operation of reason . . . by another instrument; and is nowhere to be found without reason' – a perfectly Cartesian sentence. He continues by deriding 'those irrational Philosophers, that pretended to understand the language of beasts, allowed them, as well as the ability of talking to one another'.[14] Digby dramatically counter-poses old and new. However, by taking as an example a relatively tendentious claim to understand animal language he is able to leave ambiguously open less counter-intuitive ideas about animal communication. Whether or not they accepted Cartesian views, thinkers and writers who engaged with Descartes had to find ways to work with Cartesian ideas while maintaining their own views and values.

In this regard it is worth looking at a thinker we have not previously examined but who initially loved Descartes and then fell into revolt, or perhaps revulsion: the Platonist, Henry More. As Marjorie Hope Nicolson noted, before he came to loathe Descartes, More had enthused a generation of Cambridge students with his version of Cartesianism.[15] Let us briefly consider some of the reasons for his change of view. He writes to Descartes of his 'abhorrence' for the 'deadly and murderous sentiment' whereby he withholds 'life and sense from all animals'. The 'gleaming rapier-edge' of Descartes' 'genius' he finds misapplied in transforming animals – 'metamorphosing them into marble statues and machines'.[16] He notes, 'I perceive clearly what drives you to hold that beasts are machines. It is simply a way of demonstrating the immortality of our souls.' More, contrastingly, is prepared to grant animals 'bodies activated by immortal souls', taking his cue from 'Pythagoras, Plato, and others'.[17] More, strongly influenced by Marsilio Ficino, saw the world as animate rather than mechanical and, accordingly, he here polemically restates a version of the Platonic position on the soul in articulating his repugnance at Descartes' beasts.

Descartes' views on speech and the human and on the resemblance between animals and clockwork were clearly and repeatedly stated, and his English readers debated them. Evidently, Descartes' radical and precise re-ordering of nature forced respondents on to his ground but, simultaneously, elicited equally clear articulations of opposing positions. In 1691 the English naturalist, John Ray, wrote on the question of language, the animal-machine and the related question of whether animals could feel pain. Writing in support of his position that the investigation of nature follows God's ordained path for humans, Ray argues that the heart pulses by 'no Mechanical but a Vital motion' and he goes on to discuss the 'sensitive soul'.[18] Clearly, he is unsympathetic to what he takes to be Descartes' formulation of the animal as machine. 'You will ask me', he writes, 'who or what is the Operator in the Formation of the bodies of Man and other Animals? I answer, The sensitive Soul itself, if it be a spiritual and immaterial Substance, as I am inclined to believe.' He can 'hardly admit' that it could be 'material, and consequently the whole *Animal* but a mere Machine or *Automaton*'.[19] The scandalous nature of the opinion that 'the Soul of Brutes is material, and the whole Animal, Soul and Body, but a mere Machine' is actually, and for Ray shockingly 'the Opinion publickly owned and declared of *Des Cartes, Gassendus, Dr Willis* and others'. Ray counters:

> I should rather think Animals to be endued with a lower Degree of Reason, than that they are mere Machines. I could instance many Actions of *Brutes* that are hardly to be accounted for without Reason and Argumentation[.][20]

Finally, moving from speech to pain, Ray writes:

> Should this be true, that Beasts were *Automata* or Machines, they could have no sense or perception of Pleasure or Pain, and consequently no Cruelty could be exercised towards them; which is contrary to the doleful significations they make when beaten or tormented, and contrary to the common sense of Mankind[.][21]

For Ray, animals must be understood as having 'feeling of Pain and Misery' like humans – not merely as 'sensation'.[22] His arguments for animal reason and the sensitive soul are explicit in response to Descartes' attack, rather than, as in Bryskett, implicit. The transformative path between human and animal remained open.

The claim that 'Beasts were *Automata*' shocked Descartes' readers because they interpreted it, as we see, as so radically denying animals being in the world. It is possible to make the case, as has John Cottingham, that it was consciousness or self-consciousness that Descartes denied to the animal, not feeling. Cottingham further notes that humans as much as animals were, for Descartes, machines. A human, though, had the advantage of being a 'thing that thinks' – and so 'doubts, understands, affirms, denies, is willing, is unwilling, and also imagines and has sensory perceptions'.[23] Thus, Cottingham argues that Descartes' idea of an 'automaton' did not imply a lack of life. However, contemporary readers of Descartes were immersed in a vital universe peopled with animals imbued with significance to humans; every part of the universe was alive. Predictably, in such a context both More and Ray took Descartes view of animals as 'automata' to imply inanimacy. Indeed, Descartes' English readers are consistent in understanding his animal- 'automata' as starkly lifeless and that they did so, and with textual justification, was also a factor in setting the terms of the seventeenth- and, indeed, eighteenth-century debate.

We have to ask how typical Digby, Ray and More might be. Erica Fudge is clearly right to note that although the 'beast-machine hypothesis' was not accepted, Descartes 'mechanical philosophy' was influential.[24] However, it is worth reconsidering some of the evidence about when it was

Coda: Descartes and the disciplines

accepted; what acceptance might constitute, and who accepted it rather than working in relation to it. A substantial part of the English writing on Descartes engages the topic of the beast-machine and the associated questions of language. The Cartesian doctrines mediating the relations of animals and humans were widely and justifiably understood (as by our writers) as definitional to Cartesianism. Indeed, when an English edition of Descartes' works was published in 1694, ensuring the availability of his writings to well-off vernacular readers, the beast-machine seems to have taken up a great deal of the attention of those responding. This doctrine was first made available by the French publication of the *Discourse on the Method*, further disseminated in English and a collected edition of Descartes' works was published by subscription in 1694.

The lavish *An Entire Body of Philosophy According to the Principles of the Famous Renate Des Cartes*, aimed at an affluent vernacular general reader, has trouble dealing with that philosopher's most famous, infamous, text 'A Dissertation of the Want of Sense and Knowledge in Brute Animals'.[25] Cordoned off in its own separate 'book' and, in a volume featuring illustration, accorded only two (one of which shows a dog and a clock), it was clearly seen as trouble. The dedication tells us that the 'Author's opinion' on animals 'being not commonly received; requires the Protection and Patronage of some Person, *Eminent for his learning*'. The best that can be hoped is that the patron, by 'favouring that Opinion, if not totally recommend it as an uncontroversial Position', will be able to 'stamp it so as to make it currant with the Ingenious'.[26] Overall, in the material we have examined, the beast machine hypothesis was considered by non-philosophical writers as the central tenet of Cartesianism and these writers responded to, rather than accepted, the thesis.

The specialised reception of Descartes' 'entire body' of thought by the 'ingenious' gave his work a place in the debates on optics, physics and atomism. Stephen Clucas' detailed analysis of natural philosophical writing in English has implications also for the material considered here. Discussing specifically the Aristotelian concept of 'form' in relation to mechanist ways of thinking Clucas writes that although 'dynamic or energic models of atomic interaction increasingly *replaced* form as an explanatory device in the latter half of the seventeenth century', yet 'earlier "transitional"' thinkers, including Digby, have:

> a vision of natural process [which] had still to be negotiated through theoretically eclectic conceptual vocabularies. It is the delicate conceptual negotiations of these tenuous sub-visible boundaries – between ... soul-like

substantial form and mechanical force – which are in need of careful examination, for it is here, if anywhere, that a scientific revolution in natural philosophy took place.[27]

Clucas' findings in the realm of natural philosophy where, undoubtedly, mechanistic philosophy was important, nevertheless seem to support the evidence of the broadly literary vernacular writing discussed in this study. In terms of those vernacular writings, as we have found when reading even in the most steepedly philosophical of those texts, Sir Kenelm Digby's *Two Treatises*, the presence of Descartes' ideas seems to co-exist with other attitudes – if Digby is equivocally Cartesian on animal language, he is an Aristotelian when it comes to generation. That Cartesian ideas coexist with others, whether easily or uneasily, is clearly true for other texts we have examined by John Ray, Bernard Connor and even Edward Tyson.

At the same time, populist texts, late in the seventeenth century and beyond, strive to be a near-impossible thing, a little bit Cartesian. Cartesian ideas are made to mesh with associative ideas, as, for example, in William Ayloffe's discussion of reason as 'an Emanation from the Divinity' in a world whose 'wonderful Springs' are hidden as though behind the 'Dial Plate of the Clock'. But this is no call to investigate – our job is not to take apart the mechanism but to 'admire what whilst we are here below we can never understand'.[28] In such texts terminological integration makes a stew of Cartesianism. A year earlier, commenting on animal nurture of children, Bernard Connor deals differently with the need to acknowledge Descartes without forcing it on his reader. He speculates momentarily on how mechanical a creature can be, before tactfully passing over the question, writing 'I will not insist longer upon these Philosophical Matters, nor examin here whether Examples of this nature refute or establish innate ideas.'[29] Connor, writing history for as wide an audience as possible, is careful to remain agnostic on the question of the animal's sensitive soul. If this is the reception of Descartes then it is Descartes lite.

To return to Peter Harrison's discussion of animal virtues, there is no doubt that Descartes' views were unavoidably important for natural philosophers by the end of the seventeenth century. Yet, Clucas' research qualifies what is often seen as simply an absorption of Cartesianism. As Clucas suggests, the English natural philosophers struggled to find ways to make the new philosophy work for them. Harrison, too, is careful to point out that although in his view, Descartes' understanding of animal–human difference took effect because it answered certain philosophical problems, it was very 'counter-intuitive'.[30] It has been found so in modern times. How much more unlikely must it have seemed in a world where animation, but also symbolic and other 'character' that humans used to present animals to themselves, and even exactly the stories Descartes mocks, like the Pythagorean changed states, were held true. The assumptions seventeenth-century readers brought only added to the feeling that Descartes' unanthropomorphic views were harsh and outlandish – though also fascinating.

Without entering the terrain of natural philosophy it is possible to say that in the evidence discussed here Descartes' publication of the *Discourse on the Method* did not put paid to the transformative world of Hamlet and Bryskett. Indeed, a substantial quantity of the material that Peter Harrison cites as belonging to the 'old' world of Aristotelianism, correspondence and the storied web of association is itself published in the very late seventeenth century.[31] In terms of vernacular writing, while there is no doubt that ultimately Cartesian ideas were accepted and absorbed, the writing discussed in *Writing Metamorphosis* raises questions about what that might mean for writing beyond the philosophical or 'ingenious'. It also raises the question of *when* 'acceptance' might have happened. How we respond to this question, even if we can't definitely answer it, has some impact on our understanding of the terms on which we research sixteenth- and seventeenth-century culture – and particularly the question of metamorphosis.

It seems that the period we have been examining was paradoxical in that, as discussed in the Introduction, while Michel Foucault can legitimately claim Johann Jonston's *Natural History of Quadrupeds* (1650) as symbolising the 'sudden separation . . . of two orders of knowledge', at the same time Jonston's contemporaries seem to have continued uninhibited in their analogical thinking and we find a mixed mode in James Duplessis' eighteenth-century compilation of extraordinary phenomena.[32] When can we say that the 'gleaming rapier-edge' of Descartes' 'genius' had isolated the human in an island of reason, remote from fellow animals?

Although there can be clear divisions amongst some seventeenth-century specialist texts and others which might engage a general reader, as we have seen, there is not, in late seventeenth-century England, a sense of discipline. Thus, while there might be specialist treatises on atomism in the seventeenth century, a reader would not approach a vernacular text using the disciplinary protocols which, for us, give forms of knowledge 'their privileged vantage point, provided that they remain separate'.[33] We can at least speculate that it was the Enlightenment emergence of the discipline which instituted the beast-machine in a new way because, by isolating it as an object of study, it was split from its non-rigorous contexts – in part from those interpretations which had consistently infringed its claims to be systematic, even hermetically so. Cartesian thinking truly isolates the human in reason and renders the animal obsolete with the assistance of a disciplinarity which both isolated philosophy, history and mathematics in separate spheres and instituted Descartes' thought at the foundation of several of the disciplines, but split into sections. For all that Descartes' ideas were important and debated at learned societies, it seems that the Cartesian split came to have force through the creation, and above all institution, of the disciplines – a movement often characterised as the inauguration of the modern world.

Philosophers, social scientists and others have long recognised the complex effects of disciplinary thinking in modernity. The material analysed here is not disciplinary, and only in the case of the repeated rededication of the narratives of wild children have we traced it into a disciplinary afterlife in its appropriation by Rousseau and other Enlightenment thinkers. As is suggested by the Enlightenment use of the material on wild children, the same disciplinary movement which institutes Descartes' philosophy, and particularly the beast-machine, as a founding text of modern philosophy, renders obsolete, or re-designates as exotic 'lore', texts which are intractable to disciplinary approaches. In the case of the wild child, seventeenth-century texts become available as either exotic or 'raw' data, available to support disciplinary arguments. Thus, much of the material we have explored, not only by Ovid and Edward Fenton on transformation, but also, probably, Jacob Rueff and John Ray, on 'nature', cease to have analytical or truth-telling power to express knowledge in a world where investigation of nature is driven by disciplines (which change 'nature' itself as an object of investigation). The writing examined here which *is* taken up as antecedent to disciplinarity, such as that of Sir Thomas Browne, is also non-disciplinary. It is so in the double sense of not, necessarily, seeing itself as a part of a 'new science' (Bacon would be an exception to this) and of seeing itself as in communication with other kinds of contemporary writing. Disciplinarity remakes the material of the Aristotelian universe as 'fugitive identities and occulted genealogies', as Luisa Calè and Adriana Craciun argue, but that is not because before the disciplines, in the period we are examining, there was an undifferentiated morass of material. Rather, at the same time, readers were educated in disciplinary habits which confirmed boundaries between kinds of knowledge by educating readers in disciplinary techniques.[34]

As Calè and Craciun note, it was this process that saw the museum of the eighteenth-century collector, Sir Hans Soane, first become the foundations of the British Museum and then, later, be split amongst distinct departments and institutions, dividing 'Ethnography' from 'Zoology', 'Mineralogy' from 'Palaentology'.[35] Thus, as Jan Golinski implies in his analysis of the disciplines, the seventeenth-century text might offer us a history of the uses of things; it might offer us a map of the world, but it did not know the world through the disciplinary map of knowledge.[36] And as he further argues, the 'breach' separating early modern investigation and modern 'science' can be temporally located in the long Enlightenment, over a long period spanning roughly 1780–1850. Modernity, then, is part of what can be understood as emerging from the prolonged Enlightenment institution of disciplines. We can ask what might form modern writers' understandings of temporality or epoch, and there are some distinctions between disciplines in protocol and therefore the temporal placing of modernity.

The parts of philosophy and the history of philosophy that concern themselves with Descartes, however, use his writings within a specific disciplinary framework and disciplinary temporality. For all that Jacques Derrida laces his use of the term 'epoch' with doubt, he writes of 'a certain mutation between Montaigne and Descartes' and 'a certain "epoch", let's say, from Descartes to the present' including 'Kant, Heidigger, Lacan and Levinas'.[37] In asking about the speech and gaze of animals what is at stake, he argues, is that they 'involve thinking about what is meant by living, speaking, dying, being, and world as in being-in-the-world'.[38] The linguistic terms used here, drawn from philosophy and specifically from the philosophers with whom he engages, make it crystalline that he sees animals as a philosophical problem. They have always been troubling in humans' ability to manipulate them but a fall, with the force of a Biblical catastrophe, befell animals, humans and philosophy simultaneously with Descartes' redefinition of the human–animal border. Since this time, Derrida indicates, it has been impossible, in the terms of Emmanuel Levinas, to be 'face-to-face' with an animal.[39] For Derrida, this scandal troubles the foundation of modern philosophy which rests upon the Cartesian cogito. He writes:

> Thinking concerning the animal, if there is such a thing, derives from poetry. There you have a thesis: it is what philosophy has, essentially, had to deprive itself of. It is the difference between philosophical knowledge and poetic thinking.[40]

For all that there is much poetry in Derrida's rich discussion of the animal, his study's central concern is the legacy of Descartes' violent casting of the non-human animals into silent oblivion. Derrida's focus is the violent effects of our having deprived ourselves of philosophical doubt concerning animal–human relations with regard to the subsequent history of European philosophy. Derrida clearly loves 'poetic thinking' but it is not his subject and the temporality, or epochs, of such thinking are emphatically not his concern. That he does value such 'poetic' thinking, though, is seen in his use of Montaigne. The canon and temporality of philosophy, in the sense of the responses of, for example, Levinas to Kant and to Descartes, are under discussion in *The Animal That Therefore I Am*. Without contradicting any of the arguments in Derrida's text, the 'poetic thinking' explicitly excluded from philosophical debate can legitimately, indeed, within the logic of Derrida's argument, *must* have a distinct, if related, epochal temporality from post-Cartesian philosophy.

In Bruno Latour's acute analysis of the networks of science, the impetus to change the division of the world into humans and things needs to be recognised as constituting modernity. As Latour characterises modernity, it 'is often defined in terms of humanism, either as a way of saluting the birth of "man" or as a way of announcing his death', but this 'overlooks the simultaneous birth of "nonhumanity" – things, objects, or beasts'.[41] As he makes clear, 'science', politics, philosophy and literature have been, and are, the stuff of the world – the desired separation of material by discipline comes at the cost of potentially marginalising the very knowledge it privileges. For Latour, explicitly and implicitly for Derrida, the Cartesian split between the animal and the human ruptures an earlier fabric, but if in some ways Derrida leaves that world aside, or designates it the zone impacted by the effects of the new philosophy, Latour pays helpful attention to that world. If we accept the thesis of modernity as a rupture with what went before, then we can ask when that rupture might have happened. In terms of the small part of thinking and writing that this study engages with, it seems that the time when it ceased to be possible in 'poetic thinking' to allow for metamorphic possibilities must be a little later than Descartes' lifetime or the end of the seventeenth century. For such thinking, perhaps, as Derrida hints, there is no sudden break (just possibly no complete break) but rather the gradual effect of the modern, not merely the enduring discussion and sedimentary accepting as central, if not desirable, of the Cartesian remodelling of human–animal relations, but also the gradual institution of disciplines which split wolf from werewolf, dispatched Sir Hans Soane's eighteenth-century collection to different libraries and museums, and made animated stones, werewolves, wild children seem to us – fantastic.

Writing Metamorphosis has looked at a thread in the fabric of writing and thinking – metamorphosis. In tracing metamorphosis through different kinds of writing from the first English *Book of Common Prayer* (1549) to Bernard Connor's discussion of the nurture of Romulus and Remus in his *History of Poland* (1699) Descartes has not been the dominating or pervasive presence that might have been anticipated. As we see, writers seem to consider the responses of readers when having recourse to Descartes. The anticipation of conversation beyond the text and the sense of animism versus mechanism as something debated, not necessarily with knowledge, in many spheres of culture is strongly present in texts canvassing metamorphosis and it is, I think, only with the gradual disciplinary separation of the mechanical world from this sphere of debate that the metamorphic world becomes strange and unreal. *Writing Metamorphosis* hopes to show more clearly some of the connections and possibilities that shaped a pre-disciplinary, shiftingly metamorphic time.

Notes

Introduction: writing metamorphosis

1. See Erica Fudge, *Brutal Reasoning: Animals, Rationality, and Humanity in Early Modern England* (Ithaca and London: Cornell University Press, 2006) 84–122 and *passim*.
2. 'metamorphosis, n.'. OED Online. September 2012. www.oed.com.ezproxy.lib.bbk.ac.uk/view/Entry/117313?redirectedFrom=metamorphosis. See also John Florio, 'Metamorphosi[], *a transformation, or changing of one likenesse or shape into another*', *Queen Anna's World of Words* (London, 1611) 311.
3. Caroline Walker Bynum, *Metamorphosis and Identity* (New York: Zone, 2001) 19.
4. Louise Gilbert Freeman, 'Vision, Metamorphosis, and the Poetics of Allegory in the *Mutabilitie Cantos*', *SEL* 45.1 (2005) 65–93.
5. See for example Paul Barolsky, 'As in Ovid, So in Renaissance Art', *Renaissance Quarterly* 51.2 (1998) 451–74; 473; see discussion in Richard F. Hardin, 'Ovid in Seventeenth-Century England', *Comparative Literature* 24 (1972) 44–62.
6. Raphael Lyne, *Ovid's Changing Worlds* (Oxford University Press, 2001).
7. See summary discussion in Craig W. Kallendorf, 'Renaissance' in Kallendorf ed., *A Companion to the Classical Tradition* (Oxford: Blackwell, 2007) 30–43; Charles Martindale, *Roman Literature and Its Contexts: Redeeming the Text* (Cambridge University Press, 1993) 4; Philip Hardie, *The Epic Successors of Virgil* (Cambridge University Press, 1993) 3, 2; Jean Seznec, *The Survival of the Pagan Gods* (Princeton University Press, 1953 rpt London: Harper 1961) 219–323; Malcolm Bull, *The Mirror of the Gods* (London: Allen Lane / Penguin, 2005).
8. Martindale, 'Reception' in *Classical Tradition*, ed. Kallendorf, 303–9.
9. Justin Smith ed., *The Problem of Animal Generation in Early Modern Philosophy* (Cambridge University Press, 2006).
10. See Erica Fudge's important essay, 'Writing the History of Animals: a Left-Handed Blow' in *Animals and Society: Critical Concepts in the Social Sciences*, ed. Rhoda Wilkie and David Inglis, vol. 1 (London: Routledge, 2006) 13–18; Joyce Salisbury, *The Beast Within: Animals in the Middle Ages* (London: Routledge, 1994).

11. Caroline Walker Bynum, *Metamorphosis and Identity*, 163–86; Marina Warner, *Fantastic Metamorphoses, Other Worlds: Ways of Telling the Self* (Oxford University Press, 2002).
12. Walker Bynum, *Metamorphosis and Identity*, 20, 188.
13. Marina Warner, *Fantastic Metamorphoses*.
14. *Ibid.*, 5.
15. Santina M. Levey, *An Elizabethan Inheritance* (London National Trust, 1998) 18–19, 493.
16. See Anthony Wells-Cole, *The Art of Decoration in Elizabethan and Jacobean England* (New Haven and London: Yale University Press, 1997); Folger MS x.d.48 (n.p.) quoted Santina M. Levey, *Elizabethan Inheritance*, 11.
17. See Malcolm Bull, *The Mirror of the Gods*, 85.
18. Lucy Hutchinson, '[Final Meditation]' in *Memoirs of the Life of Colonel Hutchinson*, ed. N. H. Keeble (London: Dent, 1995) 337; Ovid, *Metamorphoses*, trans. Arthur Golding, ed. Madeleine Forey (London: Penguin, 2002) Book 10, ll. 58–60 (Bk x. 58–60). Forey's tactfully modernised edition is at present by far the best printed text that readers are likely to access and is therefore used throughout.
19. Natalie Zemon Davis, 'Towards Mixtures and Margins', *AHR* 97.5 (1992) 1409–16; 1411.
20. See Brian Cummings, *The Book of Common Prayer: the Texts of 1549, 1559, and 1662* (Oxford University Press, 2011); Madeleine Forey, 'List of Golding's Works' in *Metamorphoses*, trans. Golding, xxix.
21. Joyce Salisbury, *The Beast Within*, 162.
22. Brian Cummings, 'Introduction' to *The Book of Common Prayer*, xxxiv.
23. Gervase of Tilbury, *Otia Imperialia Recreations for an Emperor*, trans. and ed. S. E. Banks and J. W. Binns (Oxford University Press, 2002) 812–15; James VI, *Minor Prose Works of King James VI and I*, ed. James Craigie (Edinburgh: Scottish Text Society, 1982) 42–3.
24. I Corinthians 15.21–54, Douay translation quoted in Caroline Walker Bynum, *The Resurrection of the Body* (New York and Chichester: Columbia University Press, 1995) 3–4.
25. Henry Charles Lea trans. and ed., *Materials Toward a History of Witchcraft*, ed. Arthur C. Howland, vol. 1 (New York and London: Thomas Yoseloff, 1957) 178–80; 179–80. An alternative translation is 'Whoever believes that it is possible for any creature to be transformed for better or worse or changed into another species or likeness except by the creator who made all things and through whom everything was made, is without doubt an unbeliever.' Regino of Prum, *Libri duo de synodalibus causis et disciplines ecclesiastics* 2.371, ed. Wilfred Hartmann (Darmstadt, 2004) 420–2 quoted and translated by Robert Bartlett, *The Natural and the Supernatural* (Cambridge University Press, 2008) 81.
26. Stuart Clark, *Thinking With Demons: the Idea of Witchcraft in Early Modern Europe* (Oxford University Press, 1997) 191.

27. Bartlett, *The Natural and the Supernatural*, 83–4; Hans Peter Broedel, *The Malleus Maleficarum and the Construction of Witchcraft* (Manchester University Press, 2003) 113.
28. See Henry Charles Lea on the fifteenth-century Inquisitor Nicholas Jaquerius pointing out that there was evidence of the bodily presence of witches at the sabbat. Henry Charles Lea, *A History of the Inquisition in the Middle Ages*, vol. III (London: Sampson Low, 1888) 496, 497. See Hans Peter Broedel, *The Malleus Maleficarum*, 73–90; see also 'Note on Texts' regarding Jakob Sprenger, *Malleus Maleficarum* (Speyer, 1487).
29. Henry Charles Lea, *Materials*, vol. I, 417–24; 418–19. On Calvin see vol. I, 428–31. See summary in Lynn Thorndike, *A History of Magic and Experimental Science*, vol. VI (New York: Columbia University Press, 1941) 525–6, 531.
30. Cora Fox, 'Authorising the Metamorphic Witch: Ovid in Reginald Scot's *Discoverie of Witchcraft*' in *Metamorphosis: the Changing Face of Ovid in Medieval and Early Modern Europe*, ed. Alison Keith and Stephen Rupp (Toronto: Centre for Reformation and Renaissance, 2007) 165–78.
31. Leonard Barkan, *The Gods Made Flesh* (New Haven and London: Yale University Press, 1986) 1.
32. Marina Warner, *Fantastic Metamorphoses*, 2.
33. Arthur Golding, 'To the Reader' in *Metamorphoses*, trans. Golding, l.1, 'Epistle', ll. 7, 65–6.
34. Arthur Golding, 'To the Reader' in *Metamorphosis*, trans. Golding, ll. 3, 28, 1.
35. Arthur Golding, 'To the right honourable and his singular good Lord, Robert Earl of Leicester' in *Metamorphoses*, trans. Golding, 6.
36. Arthur Golding, 'To the Reader' in *Metamorphoses*, trans. Golding, 23.
37. Arthur Golding, 'To the right honourable' in *Metamorphoses*, trans. Golding, 10, 27–8.
38. See Francis Bacon, *Essayes* (London, 1597), *Advancement of Learning* (London, 1605), *The Wisdom of the Ancients*, trans. Arthur Gorges (London, 1619); Francis Bacon, *Works*, ed. James Spedding, R. L. Ellis and D. D. Heath, 7 vols. (London, 1857–74 rpt London: Routledge/Thoemmes, 1996).
39. Francis Bacon, *Descriptio globi intellectualis* (1612) trans. Graham Rees in *Francis Bacon, Philosophical Studies c.1611–1619*, ed. Graham Rees, vol. VI (Oxford: Clarendon Press, 1996) 101. See also 112–13.
40. Walter Lemmi, *The Classic Deities in Bacon: A Study in Mythological Symbolism* (1933; rpt Folcroft, Pa.: The Folcroft Press, 1969) 93.
41. See Sophie Weeks, 'Francis Bacon and the Art–Nature Distinction' *Ambix* 54 (2007) 117–45; 121–2; Peter Pesic, 'Wrestling with Proteus: Francis Bacon and the "Torture" of Nature', *Isis* 90.1 (1999) 81–94; and *The Wisdom of the Ancients* (1609) 6.759 qtd Peter Pesic, 'Wrestling with Proteus', 84.
42. Francis Bacon, 'And a Discourse of the Wisdom of the Ancients' in *The Essays, or Councils Civil and Moral* (London: H. Herringman, 1696) 47.
43. Adam Fox, *Oral and Literate Culture in England 1500–1700* (Oxford University Press, 2000) 1–17; 5. See also Michael Clancy, *From Memory to Written Text* (London: Edward Arnold, 1979).

44. Bruno Latour, *We have Never Been Modern*, trans. Catherine Porter (Brighton: Harvester Wheatsheaf, 1993) 25.
45. Michel Foucault, *The Order of Things*, English edn (London: Tavistock Publications, 1970) 128–9. Johannes Jonston in fact published *Historai Naturalis* in 1650. See William B. Ashworth, Jr, 'Natural History and the Emblematic World View' in *Reappraisals of the Scientific Revolution*, ed. David C. Lindberg and Robert S. Westman (Cambridge University Press, 1990) 303–32; 330, n. 41.
46. Michel Foucault, *The Order of Things*, 129.
47. William B. Ashworth, 'Natural History', 305–6.

1 Classical transformation: turning *Metamorphoses*

1. *Metamorphoses*, trans. Arthur Golding, ed. Madeleine Forey (London: Penguin, 2002). Subsequent references in text.
2. Raphael Lyne, *Ovid's Changing Worlds* (Oxford University Press, 2001), p. 1.
3. William Shakespeare, *A Midsummer Night's Dream*, ed. Harold F. Brooks (London: Methuen, 1979; rpt 1984), 1.2.11–12. Subsequent references in text. This text is used because of the frequency of references to Brooks' 'sources'.
4. Helen Hackett, 'Introduction' to *A Midsummer Night's Dream* (London: Penguin, 1967; 2005) xxxi.
5. Peter Holland, 'Theseus' Shadows in *A Midsummer Night's Dream*' in Stanley Wells ed., *Shakespeare Survey* 47, rpt in *The Shakespeare Library*, ed. Catherine Alexander, vol. II (Cambridge University Press, 2003) 91–102; 93.
6. See Kathryn Schwarz, *Tough Love: Amazon Encounters in the English Renaissance* (Durham, N.C. and London: Duke University Press, 2000). As indicated by Kathryn Schwarz, if Theseus was known to some from his life in Plutarch, he might also be known as an associate of Hercules in Seneca's tragic dramas – as the husband of Seneca's *Medea*, but also as one rescued from the underworld by Theseus. Hippolyta has a bit part in Theseus' story. Theseus and Hippolyta, both, by the late sixteenth century at least, of unstable family and contradictory allegiances in the stories they inhabit, frame the narrative but perhaps for the contemporary audience and reader they don't presage the triumph of heterosexual, even patriarchal, union quite as self-evidently as they do for many critics. See *Tough Love*, 16–20, 39–40, 204–35.
7. For a summary of critical discussion see Peter Holland, 'Introduction' to *A Midsummer Night's Dream* (Oxford: Clarendon Press, 1994) 23–5.
8. Harold F. Brooks ed., *A Midsummer Night's Dream*, lviii–lxxxix and appendices, especially 129–53.
9. For example, at 2.1.43–4 Brooks finds a reference to Phaedra's words from Seneca's *Hippolytus*. See 141 n.118.
10. Larry Langford, 'The Story Shall Be Changed: The Senecan Sources of *Midsummer Night's Dream*' *Cahiers Elisabethains* 25 (1984) 37–52.
11. Harold F. Brooks, 'Introduction' and 'Appendix I' in *A Midsummer Night's Dream*, lviii–cxx, 129–53, lxiii.

12. See William Baldwin, *Beware the Cat*, ed. William A. Ringler, Jr and Michael Flachmann (San Marino: Huntington Library, 1988) 166. Robin Goodfellow's ability to take on shapes occurs in the context of re-animation of the dead, witchcraft and anti-Catholic propaganda.
13. Holland, 'Introduction' to *A Midsummer Night's Dream*, 32–5. As Holland notes the name occurs in Ovid, not Golding.
14. David A. Sprunger, 'Wild Folk and Lunatics in Medieval Romance' in *The Medieval World of Nature*, ed. Joyce Salisbury (New York and London: Garland, 1992).
15. *Ibid.*, 153; *The Greek Alexander Romance* (London: Penguin, 1991) 116.
16. See Jonathan Bate, *Shakespeare and Ovid* (Oxford: Clarendon Press, 1993) 139–40.
17. Brooks, 'Appendix I' in *A Midsummer Night's Dream* 141–5.
18. Holland, 'Introduction' to *A Midsummer Night's Dream* 78.
19. Leonard Barkan, 'Diana and Actaeon: the Myth as Synthesis', *ELR* 10.3 (1980) 317–59; 351–9.
20. Brooks, 'Appendix I' in *A Midsummer Night's Dream* 145–6.
21. Walker Bynum, 129–131 *Metamorphosis and Identity* (New York: Zone, 2001) 129–31.
22. Brooks, 'Introduction', xcix; Peter Holland, 'Introduction', 106. Holland cites Ann Barton in G. Blakemore Evans ed., *The Riverside Shakespeare* (Boston: Houghton Mifflin, 1974) 219. See Patricia Parker, *Shakespeare From the Margins* (University of Chicago Press, 1996) 101.
23. This draws on Jonathan Bate's helpful discussion, *Shakespeare and Ovid*, 135–7.
24. Golding, *Metamorphoses*, Bk IV. 67–201 and cited by Brooks as 'main source' of Quince's interlude 5.1.127 ff; Brooks, 149.
25. See Bate, *Shakespeare and Ovid*, 133.
26. Brooks, 5.1 n. 273.
27. Parker, *Shakespeare From*, 275, n. 10.
28. *Ibid.*, 95–6.
29. *Bulfinch's Mythology* (London: Spring Books, 1964) 9–10.
30. 'A New Sonet of Piramus and Thisbe [.] To The, Downe-right Squier' in *Handefull of Pleasant Delites* (1584), ciir–ciiiv; ciiir; cii4 (STC 1669:02).
31. Nicholas Bownd, *The Doctrine of the Sabbath Plainely Layde Forth* (London, 1595) 242. See Adam Fox, *Oral and Literate Culture in England 1500–1700* (Oxford University Press, 2000) 5, 9.
32. Siobhán McElduff, 'Fractured Understandings: Towards a History of Classical Reception in Non-Elite Groups' in *Classics and the Uses of Reception*, ed. Charles Martindale and Richard F. Thomas (Oxford: Blackwell, 2006) 186, 187; Peter Holland, 'Theseus' Shadows', 91–102.
33. Jonathan Bate, *Shakespeare and Ovid*, 131.
34. Peter Holland, 'Theseus' Shadows' in *MND*' in Catherine Alexander ed. *Cambridge Shakespeare Library*, 91–102.
35. Luke Hutton (attrib.), *The Blacke Dogge of Newgate* (London, 1596).

36. *Luke Huttons Lamentation* (London, 1598). This one-sheet poem, possibly not penned by Hutton, passed through several editions during the seventeenth century: *Luke Hutton's Lamentation*; *Luke Huttons Lamentation which he wrote the day before his death* [c. 1656]; *Luke Huttons Lamentation* (1681–4?).
37. Ian W. Archer, *The Pursuit of Stability: Social Relations in Elizabethan London* (Cambridge University Press, 1991) 9–11.
38. *Ibid.*, 218.
39. Antony Babington, *The English Bastille: A History of Newgate Gaol and Prison Conditions in Britain 1188–1902* (London: Macdonald, 1971) 15.
40. *Ibid.*, 21, 23.
41. *Ibid.*, 45.
42. *Ibid.*, 4, 43.
43. *Ibid.*, 43.
44. 'Articles by the Court of Aldermen, 11 May 1574', E. D. Pendry, *Elizabethan Prisons and Prison Scenes* vol. 1 (University of Salzburg, 1974) 329–36; 330, 335.
45. Archer, *Pursuit of Stability*, 245, 255.
46. *Ibid.*, 229.
47. 'To the Reader' sig Ar, 1596.
48. Barkan, 'Diana and Actaeon', 320, 325–8.
49. *Ibid.*, 317–59; 322.
50. See Philip Schwyzer, *Archaeologies of English Renaissance Literature* (Oxford University Press, 2007) 108–50.
51. See E. D. Pendry, *Elizabethan Prisons*, vol. 1, 107–8.
52. For fascinating discussions of Dante's challenge to Ovidian metamorphosis see Caroline Walker Bynum, *Metamorphosis and Identity*, 182–9; Marina Warner, *Fantastic Metamorphoses, Other Worlds* (Oxford: Clarendon Press, 2002) 35–8.
53. See the evocation in Ciaran Carson's translation, *The Inferno* (London and New York: Granta, 2002) 112–18.
54. Marina Warner, *Fantastic Metamorphoses*, 35.
55. E. D. Pendry, *Elizabethan Prisons*, 107.
56. Paul Griffiths, Simon Devereaux and Paul Griffiths, *Penal Practice and Culture 1500–1900* (Houndmills: Palgrave, 2004) 1.
57. Samuel Kiechel, trans. William Brenchley Rye, *England as Seen by Foreigners* (London: John Russell Smith, 1865) 87, 89. Kiechel (1563–1619) was from Ulm and came from Flushing to Dover in 1585.
58. On the consistent use of the *Metamorphoses* as 'reference points for representing and evaluating emotion in Elizabethan England' see Cora Fox, *Ovid and the Politics of Emotion in Elizabethan England* (New York: Palgrave, 2009) 141.
59. *The Blacke Dogge*, D25.
60. *Ibid.*, D31r; D25.
61. *A Relation . . . of the Island of England* trans. Charlotte Augusta Sneyd (London: Camden Society, 1847) 33–4. Dated by editor 'about 1500'.
62. Tim Wales, 'Thief-takers and their Clients in Later Stuart London' in *Londinopolis: Essays in the Cultural and Social History of Early Modern London*, ed. Paul Griffiths and Mark S. R. Jenner (Manchester University Press, 2001).

63. Patricia Fumerton, 'Making Vagrancy (In)Visible: The Economics of Disguise in Early Modern Rogue Pamphlets', *ELR* 33.2 (2003), 211–27, 216. See also Patricia Fumerton, *Unsettled: The Culture of the Working Poor and Mobility in Early Modern England* (Chicago University Press, 2006).
64. Luke Hutton (attrib.) revised Samuel Rowlands (attrib.), *The Discovery of a London Monster* (London, 1638).
65. *Ibid.*, A4r.
66. *Ibid.*, A4r–5.
67. Arthur Golding, *Metamorphoses*, Book 1 239–94.
68. Hutton / Rowlands, *The Discovery of a London Monster*, A4v.
69. See e.g. Jim Sharpe, 'Social Strain and Social Dislocation' in *The Reign of Elizabeth: Court and Culture in the Last Decade*, ed. John Guy (Cambridge University Press, 1995) 192–211; 203–8.
70. Hutton / Rowlands, *The Discovery of a London Monster*, A4v–A5r.
71. In 1566, twice in 1568, in 1573 as well as being excerpted in 1577 and 1587. See Lee Beier, 'On the Boundaries of New and Old Historicisms: Thomas Harman and the Literature of Roguery', *ELR* 33.2 (2003) 181–200; 181.
72. Archer, *Pursuit of Stability*, e.g. 229, 244, 245 and *passim*; Georgia Brown, *Redefining Elizabethan Literature* (Cambridge University Press, 2004) 224–5.
73. Brown, *Redefining*, 35–6; 39; 43–4.
74. *Ibid.*, 33.
75. Charles Martindale, *Redeeming the Text: Latin Poetry and the Hermeneutics of Reception* (Cambridge University Press, 1993) 4, 10 and *passim*.
76. Liz Oakley-Brown, *Ovid and the Cultural Politics of Translation in Early Modern England* (Aldershot: Ashgate, 2006); Siobhán McElduff, 'Fractured Understandings'.
77. In popular contemporary versions A. D. Melville gives the succinct 'Of bodies changed to other forms I tell'; David Raeburn, 'Changes of shape, new forms, are the themes which my spirit impels me / now to recite'. See Ovid, *Metamorphoses* trans. Raeburn (Oxford University Press, 1986) 1; Ovid, *Metamorphoses: A New Verse Translation* (London: Penguin, 2004) 5.
78. Bate, *Shakespeare and Ovid*; Raphael Lyne, *Ovid's Changing Worlds* (Oxford University Press, 2001) 27–9, 75.
79. Amongst many examples see Edward Topsell, *The History of Serpents* (London, 1608) 6–7.
80. See Lyne, *Ovid's Changing Worlds*, 78–9.
81. Arthur Golding, 'To the right honourable... Lord Robert, Earl of Leicester' in *Metamorphoses*, 3.
82. Lyne, *Ovid's Changing Worlds*, 32.
83. Again, Lyne summarises discussion, see *ibid.*, 30–5.
84. See *ibid.*, 52.
85. Eugene R. Kintgen, *Reading in Tudor England* (University of Pittsburgh, 1996) 98–104, 122–4, 138–140, 199. See also Robert Scribner, *For the Sake of Simple Folk* (Oxford: Clarendon Press, 1981; rev. rpt 1994).

86. John Leon Lievsay, 'Newgate Penitents: Further Aspects of Elizabethan Sensationalism' *HLQ* 7.1 (1943) 47–69.
87. See Martindale, *Redeeming*, 9.
88. *Ibid.*, 4.
89. *Ibid.*, 4.
90. Philip Hardie, *The Epic Successors of Virgil* (Cambridge University Press, 1993) 3, 2.
91. For summary see Craig W. Kallendorf, 'Renaissance' in *A Companion to the Classical Tradition*, ed. Craig W. Kallendorf (Oxford: Blackwell, 2007) 30–43.
92. Jean Seznec, *The Survival of the Pagan Gods* (Princeton University Press, 1953 rpt Harper, 1961) 219–323.
93. Although Bull's discussion is focused on much, much earlier visual rather than verbal materials he makes some telling points concerning the different attitude towards the body implied in mythological art and in Christian thinking. Malcolm Bull, *The Mirror of the Gods* (London: Allen Lane / Penguin, 2005) e.g. 381–2.
94. Martindale, *Redeeming*, 7.
95. Liz Oakley-Brown, *Ovid and the Cultural Politics of Translation*; Siobhán McElduff, 'Fractured Understandings'.
96. Natalie Zemon Davis, 'Towards Mixtures and Margins', *AHR* 97.5 (1992) 1409–16; 1411.
97. Antonio Gramsci, *Selections from the Cultural Writings*, ed. David Forgacs (London: Lawrence and Wishart, 1985) 195.
98. See for example Carlo Ginzburg's study of the miller Menocchio which makes it clear that non-elite readers can encounter texts with an undisciplined intensity which bring to life unexpected meanings. Carlo Ginzburg, *The Cheese and the Worms*, trans. John and Anne Tedeschi (Baltimore: Johns Hopkins University Press, 1980) 28–47; 37.
99. Natalie Zemon Davis, 'Towards Mixtures and Margins', 1411.

2 Sacred transformations: animal events

1. 'Of the Administracion of publyke Baptisme to be used in the Churche' in *The Book of Common Prayer: The Texts of 1549, 1559, and 1662*, ed. Brian Cummings (Oxford University Press, 2011) 47; 142; F. Bulley, *A Tabular View of the Variations in the Communion and Baptismal Offices of the Church of England 1549–1662* (Oxford: J. H. Parker, 1842) 94.
2. 'Notes From the Act Books of the Archdeaconry Court of Lewes', ed. Walter C. Renshaw, *Sussex Archaeological Collections* vol. 49 (Sussex Archaeological Society, Lewes, 1906); 47–65; 53–4; Thomas Edwards, *Gangræna*, vol. III (London, 1646) 17–18 discussed in Ann Hughes, *Gangræna and the Struggle for the English Revolution* (Oxford University Press, 2004) 120. See also 'Certeyne articles conteyning some parte of the evill behauiour of Mr. Buckley, parson of Beccles', *The Letter Book of John Parkhurst Bishop of Norwich*, ed. R. A. Houlbrooke (Norfolk Record Society, 1974 and 1975) 253–4; 254.

3. 'Of the Administracion of publyke Baptisme', *The Book of Common Prayer*, ed. Brian Cummings, 48; to compare texts see F. Bulley, *A Tabular View*, 97–8.
4. See F. Bulley, *Tabular View*, Appendix 7.
5. Exorcism for a female, 'The Rite of Baptism in the Sarum Manual', trans. and ed. J. D. C. Fisher, *Christian Initiation: Baptism in the Medieval West* (London: S.P.C.K., 1965) 158–79.
6. If for a Lutheran a sacrament was, perhaps ambiguously, 'a divine promise marked by a divine sign', for Calvin sacraments were 'instruments instituted by God for conferring grace'. See Diarmaid MacCulloch, *Reformation: Europe's House Divided* (London: Penguin, 2003) 129–30, 251.
7. Diarmaid MacCulloch, *Reformation*, 256–9.
8. *Ibid.*, 256–8, 251, 10, 281.
9. Will Coster, *Baptism and Spiritual Kinship in Early Modern Britain* (Aldershot: Ashgate, 2002) 51. See also David Cressy, *Birth, Marriage and Death* (Oxford University Press, 1997) 97–8; 106–17.
10. Keith Thomas, *Religion and the Decline of Magic: Studies in Popular Beliefs in Sixteenth- and Seventeenth-Century England* (1971; rpt London: Penguin, 1991) 41.
11. Edward Muir, *Ritual in Early Modern Europe* (Cambridge University Press, 2005) 164.
12. Keith Thomas, *Religion and the Decline*, 85.
13. Robert Parker, *A Scholasticall Discourse Against Symbolizing with Antichrist in Ceremonies: Especially in the Signe of The Crosse* (London, 1607) 101, 109.
14. Thomas Bentley, *The Monument of Matrons* (1582) 106; see Mary Fissell, *Vernacular Bodies: the Politics of Reproduction in Early Modern England* (Oxford University Press, 2004) 14–52.
15. Erica Fudge, *Perceiving Animals* (Macmillan: Basingstoke, 2000) 41–3; 43.
16. *Ibid.*, 44; Dorothy Leigh, *The Mother's Blessing* (London, 1616) in *Women's Writing in Stuart England*, ed. Sylvia Brown (Stroud, Gloucestershire: Sutton, 1999) 26.
17. *The Private Life of an Elizabethan Lady: the Diary of Lady Margaret Hoby 1599–1605*, ed. Joanna Moody (Stroud: Sutton Publishing, 1998) 80–1.
18. Nehemiah Wallington, Notebook for 1635, BL Sloane MS 1457fo. 19v.
19. Thanks to Erica Fudge for personal communication concerning forthcoming work. On modernity and these relations see e.g. Anat Pick, *Creaturely Poetics: Animality and Vulnerability in Literature and Film* (New York: Columbia University Press, 2011).
20. Cf. John Bossy's argument against bringing to bear on religious issues contemporary frameworks and attitudes, 'Some Elementary Forms of Durkheim', *Past and Present* 95 (1982), 3–18; 18.
21. HMC *Salisbury* 18 (1940) 26.
22. HMC *Hatfield* 10, 1904, 450–1. I am grateful to students on my BA English module 'Death By Language' 2007–8 for discussion of this and similar material. Particular thanks to Mr Martin Baillie, Ms Clare Day, Mr Ed Lyon.

23. See e.g. Jim Sharpe, 'Social Strain and Social Dislocation' in *The Reign of Elizabeth: Court and Culture in the Last Decade*, ed. John Guy (Cambridge University Press, 1995) 192–211.
24. John Guy, 'Introduction. The 1590s: The second reign of Elizabeth?' in *The Reign of Elizabeth*, ed. John Guy 1–19; 1.
25. A JP in Somerset, Edward Hext, on 25 Sept. 1596 wrote to Lord Burghley a 'litany of complaints about threats to law and order' cited in R. H. Tawney and Eileen Power, *Tudor Economic Documents* vol. II (3 vols. London, 1924) 339–46, quoted Guy, *The Reign of Elizabeth*, 192.
26. HMC (18) 1940, 297–8; on the tobacco, interesting in its own right, see HMC (18) 1940, 'Exeter', 448–9.
27. HMC (18) 1940, 298.
28. William Cotton to Sir Robert Cecil, 15 Jan. 1599/1600 HMC (10), 1904, 9; Henry, Lord Cobham to Sir Robert Cecil HMC *Salisbury*, vol. IX (1902) 383; HMC *Report on the Records of the City of Exeter* (1916) 93–6.
29. Henry Charles Lea, *A History of the Inquisition in the Middle Ages*, vol. III (London: Sampson Low, 1888) 495–6, 502, 504.
30. William Baldwin, *A Marvelous Hystory intitulede, Beware the Cat* (London, 1570). See William A. Ringler, Jr ed., *Beware the Cat* (San Marino, Ca.: Huntington Library, 1988) ix–x.
31. 'Exhortation' in William Baldwin, *Beware the Cat*, 54.
32. 28 October 1568 John son of Thomas Chrismas was baptised at St Nicholas in Sydling; 20 Jan. 1571/2 Robert also son of Thomas Chrismas, daughter Ann on 22 July 1573, son Briant 28 December 1574, Timothy 18 February 1575/6, another Timothy to Thomas 18 Feb. 1577/8. On 10 October 1586 Richard son of Richard Chrismas was baptised at St Nicholas. Savage and Devenish families both had baptisms in the same church in the period. The incumbent rector 1579–1636 was William Crode.
33. *The Casebook of Sir Francis Ashley J.P. Recorder of Dorchester 1614–35*, ed. J. H. Bettey (Dorset Record Society, 1981) 29. Bound over to the next Assizes, on 9 March 1617/18 Chrismas appears there but the cause is not noted.
34. *Ibid.*, 30.
35. *Ibid.*, 34.
36. *CSPD* 20 March 1618.
37. *CSPD* 14 April 1618; 29 April 1618.
38. *CSPD*, 10 May 1618.
39. *CSPD* 10 May 1618 Petition of Leonard Trevellyan, SP14/97/67.
40. *CSPD* 8 May 1618; *CSPD* 14 May 1618, 540.
41. See Malcolm Gaskill, *Witchfinders: A Seventeenth-Century English Tragedy* (London: John Murray, 2005), *passim*.
42. *CSPD* 9 February 1629.
43. *The High Commission Notices of the Court*, ed. John Southernden Burn (London: J. Russell, 1865) 60.
44. SP 16, 201 f59.

45. *CSPD* 20 January 1632 Commissioners for Causes Ecclesiastical to the Council Answer to report of Earl Rivers *et al.*
46. *Reports of Cases in the Courts of Star Chamber and High Commission* (London: Camden Society, 1886/7). This quotes Rawlinson MS A128– Bodleian. See also *CSPD* 1632 20 Jan., 256. The final text seems compromised: e.g. Hardwick should be Harwich. See also *CSPD* summary 'Co.Reg.Car I, vol. vii, p. 357'.
47. On Cotton's Catholic relative see letter from Henry Lord Cobham to Robert Cecil October 1599 in HMC *Salisbury* 9, 383. See also HMC 10 (1904) 9, 17, 378, 450–1; HMC *Exeter*, 18 (1940) 297–8, 448–9.
48. Christopher Haigh, *The Plain Man's Pathways to Heaven* (Oxford University Press, 2007) 172–4; and on mocked ceremonies *passim*.
49. Keith Thomas, *Religion and the Decline of Magic* (London: Allen Lane, 1971 rpt, Penguin, 1991) 37–41; 40; 41.
50. Cressy, *Travesties in Tudor and Stuart England* (Oxford University Press, 2000), 184.
51. *Ibid.*, 183.
52. See *A History of Oxfordshire*, 42–3 where what seems to be the drinking incident is cited as MS.Top. Oxon c.56, 59. See also Haigh, *Plain Man's*, 172.
53. Cressy, *Travesties*, 182.
54. I am very grateful to Donna Landry for discussion of this point.
55. *Mercurius Aulicus*, Mon 21 Oct., 1219.
56. See Keith Lindley, *Popular Politics and Religion in Civil War London* (Aldershot: Scolar Press, 1997) 87–90; John Morrill, 'The Church in England, 1642–9' in *Reactions to the English Civil War 1642–1649* ed. John Morrill (Macmillan: Basingstoke) 89–114; 94.
57. E. M. Symons ed., 'The Diary of John Greene (1635–57) II', *EHR* 43 (1928) 598–604; 602; 603.
58. John Morrill, 'The Church in England', 95.
59. *Ibid.*, 104 and *passim*.
60. London Metropolitan Archives, 952 /56; 952 /57.
61. *Ibid.*, 956/33.
62. *Ibid.*, 956/35.
63. *Ibid.*, 956/36; 956/37; 965/35; 958/94.
64. MJ/GBR5 (Gaol Delivery Registers) 1644–1656 fos. 13v, 16v–17r.
65. Lindley, *Popular Politics*, 291; 301.
66. Hughes, *Gangræna*, 180.
67. John Morrill, 'The Church in England'; Keith Lindley, *Popular Politics*, 1–2 and *passim*.
68. Thomas Edwards, *Gangræna* vol. I (London, 1646) 17.
69. Thomas Edwards, *Gangræna* vol. II, 17–18.
70. *Ibid.*, 18.
71. Hughes, *Gangræna*, 131–83; 131; 183.
72. *Gangræna*, vol. I, 17, 18.
73. I. M. Green, 'The Persecution of "Scandalous" and "Malignant" Parish Clergy during the English Civil War', *EHR* (1979) 507–31.

74. John Walter, '"Affronts & Insolencies": The Voices of Radwinter and Popular Opposition to Laudianism', *HER* 122.495 (2007) 35–60; 38, 39.
75. *Mercurius Britanicus* 11 Nov.–18 Nov. 1644, 457.
76. See Hughes, *Gangræna*, 176–82.
77. 'This profusion of Holy Water is done out of a belief, that Devils are Cats, as Cats are supposed to be Devils, and that neither can endure to wet their feet. I will not trouble myself whether Cats be Devils or Devils Cats; but sure it can never be, that the Devil should be so terrified afraid of Holy Water, when he stands in so much need of a Cooler. Men that are not half so hot as he, nor come out of half so hot a place, drink Snow in their Wine, and shall the Devil be afraid of a little cold water?' *A Whip for the Devil; or, the Roman Conjuror* (London, 1683) 96.
78. John Milton, *A Maske Presented at Ludlow Castle* in *The Works of John Milton*, ed. Frank Allen Patterson (New York: Columbia University Press, 1931) 85–122, 525–6.
79. Izaak Walton, *The Compleat Angler 1653–1676*, ed. Jonquil Bevan (Oxford: Clarendon Press, 1983) 340.
80. Peter Harrison, 'The Virtues of Animals in Seventeenth-Century Thought', *Journal of the History of Ideas* 39.3 (1998) 463–84; 463–70; on fish, 465.
81. Tom Tyler, 'If Horses Had Hands', in *Animal Encounters*, ed. Tom Tyler and Manuela Rossini (Brill, 2007) 13–26; 23.
82. Martin Wainwright, 'Pendle witches progrom haunts water workers after find', *The Guardian* 8 Dec. 2011; www.guardian.co.uk/uk/2011/dec/08/pendle-witches-water-mummified-cat accessed 18.10.2012. I am grateful to Anthony Bale for this cat.

3 Transforming nature: strange fish and monsters

1. William Shakespeare, *The Tempest*, ed. Virginia Mason Vaughan and Alden T. Vaughan (London: Thomas Nelson, 1999). This edition is used throughout so subsequent references are in the text. When other editions are used they are referenced.
2. In his use of myth to challenge assumptions about subject, object and possibility of being see e.g. Michel Serres, trans. Lawrence E Schehr, *The Parasite* (Grasset & Pasquelle, 1980 repub. Minneapolis and London: University of Minnesota Press, 2007), especially 71–3, 231–3.
3. Lorraine Daston and Katherine Park, *Wonders and the Order of Nature* (New York: Zone Books, 2001).
4. Deborah E. Harkness, *The Jewel House: Elizabethan London and the Scientific Revolution* (New Haven and London: Yale University Press, 2007) xv–xviii, 257–8, 258.
5. Stephen Bateman, *The Doome warning All Men to the Judgement* (London, 1581); Alixe Bovey, *Monsters and Grotesques in Medieval Manuscripts* (London: British Library, 2002).

6. Bateman, *The Doome Warning*; Edward Fenton, *Certaine secrete wonders of nature* translating Pierre Boaistuau, *Histoires prodigieuses* (1560) (London, 1569).
7. On Edward Fenton see *ODNB*; Lorraine Daston and Katherine Park, *Wonders and the Order of Nature* (New York: Zone Books, 2001) 192.
8. Fenton, *Certaine*, 3.
9. *Ibid.*, 15.
10. Antoine Goudin, *Philosophy, Following the Principles of St Thomas* (Paris, 1864) 301; qtd Justin E. H. Smith, 'Imagination and the Problem of Heredity in Mechanist Embryology' in *The Problem of Animal Generation in Early Modern Philosophy*, ed. Justin Smith (Cambridge University Press, 2006) 84.
11. Justin E. H. Smith, 'Imagination', 85.
12. *Ibid.*, 80, 82.
13. Aristotle, *De Partibus Animalum 1 and De Generatione Animalum 1 (with passages from II. 3)* trans. David Balme (Oxford: Clarendon Press, 1992). See *De Generatione* II. 1, 734b, 61.
14. Justin E. H. Smith, 'Imagination', 83.
15. Edward Fenton, *Certaine*, 119–20.
16. Ambroise Paré, *The Workes of that famous chirurgion Ambrose Parey* translated out of Latine and compared with the French, by Th: Johnson (London, 1634).
17. *Ibid.*, 962.
18. *Ibid.*, 1000.
19. Edward Fenton, *Certaine*, 38.
20. *Ibid.*, 39.
21. Paré, *Workes*, 998.
22. *Ibid.*, 998.
23. Francis Packard, *The Life and Times of Ambroise Paré* (London: Humphrey Milford, 1922) 63–4.
24. Stephen Jay Gould, 'Father Athanasius on the Isthmus of a Middle State' in *Athanasius Kircher: the Last Man Who Knew Everything*, ed. Paula Findlen (London: Routledge, 2004) 207–38.
25. *Ibid.*, 226; on reception 227.
26. *Ibid.*, 227–30.
27. Helen King, *Midwifery, Obstetrics and the Rise of Gynaecology: the Uses of a Sixteenth-Century Compendium* (Aldershot: Ashgate, 2007) 118.
28. On the afterlife of the baby see Jan Bondeson, *The Two-Headed Boy and Other Medical Marvels* (Ithaca and London: Cornell University Press) 39–50.
29. See Ambroise Paré, *On Monsters and Marvels* (Chicago and London: University of Chicago Press, 1982). Chapter 11 in this version becomes Chapter 9 and the petrified child disappears in the English Paré, *Workes* (1634) 980; James Duplessis, 'A Short History of Human Prodigies & Monstrous Births' MS Sloane 5246, fo. 55v. On the eighteenth-century transmission see also Helen King, *Midwifery, Obstetrics and the Rise of Gynaecology*, 117–18.
30. See Jan Bondeson, *The Two-Headed Boy*, 39–50.

31. Jacob Rueff, *The Expert Midwife* trans. (London, 1637) 1–2.
32. *The husbandlye ordering and governmente of poultrie* (1581), chapters 82 and 83.
33. Philip Skippon, *An Account of a Journey* in *A Collection of Voyages and Travels* vol. VI (London, 1732) 564.
34. Thomas Browne, 'Observation on Eggs' in *The Works of Sir Thomas Browne* ed Geoffrey Keynes, vol. V (London: Faber & Faber, 1931) 321–2.
35. Paré, *Workes*, 966.
36. Edward Topsell, *The Historie of Serpents* (London, 1608) 120.
37. Paula Findlen, *Possessing Nature: Museums, Collecting, and Scientific Culture in Early Modern Italy* (Berkeley and London: University of California Press, 1994) 19.
38. See Topsell, *Historie of Serpents*.
39. *Ibid.*, 1–5; 1.
40. *Ibid.*, 6–9.
41. Some think the putrid back-bone; *ibid.*, 6–7.
42. *Ibid.*, 6; see *Metamorphoses*, trans. Arthur Golding ed. Madeleine Forey (London: Penguin, 2002) Book 4, 759–63.
43. Topsell, *History of Serpents*, 8.
44. *Ibid.*, 20.
45. *Ibid.*, 1–32.
46. *Ibid.*, 119, 125.
47. *Ibid.*, 119.
48. *Ibid.*, 119.
49. KJV cf. ASV and ASV where 'adder' is substituted for cockatrice in margin.
50. Thomas Browne, *The Works of Sir Thomas Browne*, ed. Geoffrey Keynes (London: Faber and Faber, 1928).
51. Leonardo Da Vinci, *Notebooks*, ed. Irma A. Richter (Oxford University Press, 1952) 167. Qtd Paula Findlen, 'Commerce, Art, and Science in the Early Modern Cabinet of Curiosities' in Pamela H. Smith and Paula Findlen, ed., *Merchants and Marvels: Commerce, Science, and Art in Early Modern Europe* (New York and London: Routledge, 2002) 297–323; 307.
52. See discussions in Horst Bredekamp, *The Lure of Antiquity and the Cult of the Machine*, trans. Allison Brown (1993 Germany; Princeton: Marcus Wiener Publishers, 1995) 77 and *passim*; Daston and Park, *Wonders and the Order of Nature*, 222–3.
53. Francis Bacon, *Descriptio globi intellectualis* (1612) in *The Oxford Francis Bacon, Philosophical Studies c.1611–1619*, trans. and ed. Graham Rees, vol. VI (Oxford: Clarendon Press, 1996) 101. On Proteus see 112–13. See also Peter Pesic, 'Wrestling with Proteus: Francis Bacon and the "Torture" of Nature', *Isis* 90.1 (1999) 81–94.
54. Francis Bacon, *Abecedarium nouum naturae* in *The Oxford Francis Bacon*, vol. XIII, 218 trans. Sophie Weeks, qtd Sophie Weeks, 'Francis Bacon and the Art–Nature Distinction', *Ambit* 54.2 (2007) 101–29; 118.
55. Weeks, 'Francis Bacon and the Art–Nature Distinction', 108.

56. See Sophie Weeks, 'Francis Bacon and the Art–Nature Distinction', 121–2; Charles Lemmi, *The Classic Deities in Bacon* (Baltimore: Johns Hopkins, 1983). See also Pesic, 'Wrestling'.
57. Bacon, 'The New Atlantis: a Work Unfinished' *Works* (vol. III pt 1) (1876; rpt, London: Routledge / Thoemmes, 1996) 164.
58. *Ibid.*, 167.
59. Pierre Belon, *L'histoire naturelle des estranges poisons marins* (Paris, 1551), 18r.
60. Ambroise Paré, *Workes*, 1004, 1003.
61. Findlen, 'Commerce, Art, and Science', 311, 310.
62. Horst Bredekamp, *Lure*; Anthony Grafton, 'Renaissance Histories of Art and Nature' in Bernadette Bensaude-Vincent and William R. Newman eds., *The Artificial and the Natural: an Evolving Polarity* (Cambridge Mass.: MIT Press, 2007) 185–210.
63. Bredekamp, *Lure*, 77; Grafton, 'Renaissance Histories', 188, 194.
64. Julius Caesar Scaliger, *Exoticarum exercitationum liber quintus decimus* (Paris: Vascosan, 1557) fos. 395v–6 quoted in Anthony Grafton, 'Renaissance Histories', 194, 206.
65. Findlen, 'Commerce, Art, and Science', 303–5.
66. Mark A. Meadow, 'Quiccheberg and the Copious Object: Wenzel Jamnitzer's Silver Writing Box' in Stephen Melville ed., *The Lure of the Object* (Massachusetts: Clark Institute, 2005) 39–53; 41.
67. *Ibid.*, 48.
68. Topsell, *Serpents*, 201. I am grateful to Takashi Nishi for discussions of his work on Hercules, Hydra and Shakespeare's *Coriolanus*.
69. *Ibid.*, 201–2.
70. See Findlen, 'Commerce, Art, and Science', 308.
71. Sir Thomas Browne, *Pseudodoxia Epidemica* (London, 1672) Bk 3.7, 130–4.
72. John Evelyn, *The Diary of John Evelyn*, ed. William Bray vol. 1 (London and Washington: Walter Dunne, 1901) 176.
73. Philip Skippon, 'An Account of a Journey' in *A Collection of Voyages and Travels* vol. VI (John Walthoe: London, 1732) 517.
74. John Ray, *Ornithology* (London, 1678), preface.
75. John Ray, *Observations* (London, 1673) 236–7.
76. *Ibid.*, 27, 28.
77. *Ibid.*, 27, 28.
78. Migeul de Asúa and Roger French, *A New World of Animals* (Aldershot: Ashgate, 2005) 210–11.
79. Asúa and French, *A New World*, 213–14.
80. 'Mr Ray to Dr. Hans Sloane' n.d., *The Correspondence of John Ray* (London: Ray Society, 1848) 472.
81. Arthur MacGregor, 'The Tradescants as Collectors of Rarities' in *Tradescant's Rarities*, ed. Arthur McGregor (Oxford University Press, 1983) 17–23.
82. *Coryat's Crudities*, vol. 1 (Glasgow: James Maclehose, 1905) 114.

83. Thomas Platter, *Thomas Platter's Travels in England 1599*, trans. and ed. Clare Williams (London: Jonathan Cape, 1937) 165; Henry Peacham, *Coryat's Crudities*, 114.
84. Platter, *Platter's Travels*, 171.
85. *Ibid.*, 172–3.
86. Virginia Mason Vaughan and Alden T. Vaughan, 'Introduction' to William Shakespeare, *The Tempest*, ed. Vaughan and Vaughan (Surrey: Thomas Nelson, 1999) 3.
87. Charlton Hinman ed., *The Norton Facsimile of the First Folio of Shakespeare* (New York: W. W. Norton, 1968), 408–11 qtd in Alden T. Vaughan and Virginia Mason Vaughan, *Shakespeare's Caliban: A Cultural History* (Cambridge University Press, 1991) 10.
88. *Chronicles of England, France, Spain, Portugal*, 'tr. John Bourchier, Lord Berners reprinted from Pynson's edition of 1523 and 1525 (London, 1812), II, 589 f.' quoted in Robert Hillis Goldsmith, 'The Wild Man on the English Stage', *MLR* 53.4 (1958) 481–91; 481.
89. *The Discription of a Maske, Presented before the Kinges Maiestie at White-Hall, on Twelfth Night last, in honour of the Lord Hayes, and his Bride* (London, 1607); Ben Jonson, *Masque of Blackness*, ed. Stephen Orgel in *The Complete Masques* (New Haven: Yale University Press, 1969) 61–74.
90. The most succinct discussion remains Frank Kermode, 'Introduction' to *The Tempest*, xxii–xxiv; see also Vaughan and Vaughan, 69–73.
91. Alan C. Dessen, *Recovering Shakespeare's Theatrical Vocabulary* (Cambridge University Press, 1995) 212.
92. John Dee, 'Compendious Rehersal' in *Autobiographical Tracts of John Dee*, ed. James Crossley (London: Chetham Society old series, 1851) 5–6.
93. For an overview see Virginia Mason Vaughan and Alden T. Vaughan 'Introduction' to *The Tempest*, 62–6. Examples of the debate concerning the moral valence of Prospero's art include: Walter Clyde Curry, *Shakespeare's Philosophical Patterns* (Lafayette: Baton Rouge, 1937 rpt Gloucester, Mass.: Peter Smith 1968), especially 160–99. Curry's account of Prospero's 'theurgy' is challenged by D'Orsay W. Pearson's argument that Shakespeare was not specifically knowledgeable concerning theurgy and that, rather than seeing Prospero as heir to Iamblichus, Porphyry and others, in representing Prospero Shakespeare follows 'the attitude of both church and state that theurgy is a damnable, unlawful art'. D'Orsay W. Pearson, '"Unless I Be Reliev'd by Prayer": *The Tempest* in Perspective', *Shakespeare Studies*, ed. J. Leeds Barroll, vol. VII (Columbia, S.C.: University of South Carolina Press, 1974) 253–82; 255, 256. John S. Mebane, *Renaissance Magic and the Return of the Golden Age: the Occult Tradition and Marlowe, Jonson, and Shakespeare* (Lincoln, Neb. and London: University of Nebraska Press, 1989), seeking to use philosophy, literature and history as mutually illuminating contexts explores the magus as 'the most fully developed expression of Renaissance hopes for the development of humankind's moral, intellectual, and spiritual potential' (176); an aspiration which, as Thomas Greene explores in his important essay, 'The Flexibility of

the Self', was repeatedly challenged. Thomas Greene, 'The Flexibility of the Self', in Peter Demetz, Thomas Greene and Lowry Nelson ed., *The Disciplines of Criticism* (New Haven: Tale University Press, 1968) 241–64.
94. Barbara A. Mowat, 'Prospero, Agrippa, and Hocus Pocus', *ELR* 11.3 (1981) 281–303; 302, 303. See also Mebane, *Renaissance Magic*, 177.
95. See e.g. Mebane, *Renaissance*, 177–9.
96. J. Peter Zetterburg, 'The Mistaking of "the Mathematicks" for Magic in Tudor and Stuart England', *Sixteenth Century Journal* 11.1 (1980) 83–97.
97. Dessen, *Recovering Shakespeare's*, 215.
98. Abraham Cowley 'To the Royal Society' in Thomas Sprat, *The History of the Royal Society* (London, 1667), B2r.
99. Asúa and French, *A New World*, 209.
100. Edward Tyson, *Phocaena, or the Anatomy of a Porpess, Dissected at Gresham Colledge: with a Preliminary Discourse concerning Anatomy, and a Natural History of Animals* (London, 1686?) 1–2.
101. *Ibid.*, 2–3.
102. *Religio Medici* in *The Works of the Learned Sr Thomas Brown* (London, 1686) I. 13.
103. Tyson, 'Preliminary Discourse', *Phocaena*, 4.
104. *Ibid.*, 5
105. *Ibid.*, 6–9.
106. Thomas Sprat, *The History of the Royal Society* (London: T. R. for J. Martyn, 1667) 83.
107. 'A Relation of Two Monstrous Pigs With the Resemblance of Humane Faces, and two young Turkeys joined by the Breast, by Sir John Floyer, Communicated by Dr. Edward Tyson, Fellow of the College of Physicians, and R.S.' in *Philosophical Transactions* 21 (1699) read at Royal Society 8 Nov. 1699, 431–4.
108. Floyer, 'A Relation' in *Transactions*, 432.
109. *Ibid.*, 433.
110. *Ibid.*, 433.
111. Paré, *Workes*, 982, 983.
112. *Ibid.*, 963. See Montaigne *Essays* Bk 1 ch. 20; Marie-Germaine; Mountebank *Essays* Bk 1 ch. 22; Francis R. Packard, *The Life and Times of Ambroise Paré* (London: Humphrey Milford, 1922) 32–7.
113. James Duplessis, 'A Short History of Human Prodigies & Monstrous Births', MS Sloane 5246 fos. 11, 34, 42, 46.
114. *Ibid.*, fo. 55v.
115. *Ibid.*, fo. 13.
116. See Mary E. Fissell, 'Hairy Women and Naked Truths: Gender and the Politics of Knowledge in *Aristotle's Masterpiece*', *The William and Mary Quarterly* Series 3, 60.1 (2003) 43–74; 46.
117. See e.g. the survey of ovism in Clara Pinto Correira, *The Ovary of Eve* (University of Chicago Press, 1997) esp. 136–82.

118. Vincent Aucante, 'Descartes's Experimental Method and the Generation of Animals' in *The Problem of Animal Generation*, ed. Justin E. H. Smith (Cambridge University Press, 2006) 65–79.
119. *The Embryological Treatises of Hieronymus Fabricius of Aquapendente* (Ithaca: Cornell University Press, 1942; rpt 1967). See 'Proem' for discussion of method, vol. 1.4. 4.
120. Aucante, 'Descartes's Experimental Method', 72–5.
121. *Ibid.*, 67.
122. John Farley, *The Spontaneous Generation Controversy From Descartes to Oparin* (Baltimore and London: Johns Hopkins University Press, 1977) 12.
123. *Ibid.*, 1–7.
124. Sir Kenelm Digby, *Two Treatises* (Paris, 1644); R. T. Peterson, *Sir Kenelm Digby: The Ornament of England 1603–1665* (London: Jonathan Cape, 1956) 195–6.
125. William Harvey, *Anatomical Exercitations Concerning the Generation of Living Creatures* (New York: Gryphon, 1991) 151.
126. Paula Findlen, *Possessing Nature: Museums, Collecting, and Scientific Culture in Early Modern Italy* (Berkeley and London: University of California Press, 1994) 15. This account follows Findlen.
127. Richard Pulteney, *Historical and Biographical Sketches of the Progress of Botany in England from its Origin to the Introduction of the Linnean System*, vol. 1 (London, 1790) 312–13.
128. See Zachary Grey, *Notes on Hudibras*; Samuel Butler, *Hudibras*, 2 vols. (London, 1819); Richard Pulteney, *Historical and Biographical*, 312–13.
129. Georges Canguilhem, 'Monstrosity and the Monstrous', *Diogenes* 40 (1962) 27–42.
130. Daston and Park, *Wonders and the Order of Nature*, 176; Stephen Shapin, *A Social History of Truth* (Chicago and London: University of Chicago Press, 1995) is an important analysis of seventeenth-century to modern conditions of truth as disavowing testimony. On the circular reasoning of some critiques of 'science', see Pierre Bourdieu, 'The Peculiar History of Scientific Reason', *Sociological Forum* 6.1 (1991) 3–26.
131. 'What an Egge is' in Harvey, *Anatomical Exercitations*, 137.

4 Metamorphosis and civility: werewolves in politics, print and parish

1. Henry Boguet, *Discours de Sorciers* (1590) in *A Lycanthropy Reader: Werewolves in Western Culture*, trans. and ed. Charlotte Otten (New York: Syracuse University Press, 1986) 78–9.
2. James VI, *Minor Prose Works of King James VI and I*, ed. and trans. James Craigie (Edinburgh: Scottish Text Society, 1982) 42–3.
3. Gervase of Tilbury, *Otia Imperialia Recreations for an Emperor*, ed. S. E. Banks and J. W. Binns (Oxford University Press, 2002) 812–15. See also Caroline Walker Bynum, *Metamorphosis and Identity* (New York: Zone, 2001) 15–18.

4. John Cotta, *The Triall of Witch-craft* (London, 1616) 34. See also Hayden White, 'The Forms of Wildness: Archaeology of an Idea' in Edward Dudley and Maximillian E. Novak ed., *The Wild Man Within: An Image in Western Thought From the Renaissance to Romanticism* (London: University of Pittsburgh Press, 1972) 3–38; 5, 18.
5. Gervase of Tilbury, *Otia*, 15–18.
6. Caroline Walker Bynum, in her fascinating discussion of twelfth-century werewolf texts, notes what seems an intriguingly similar way in which a large range of discourses, not simply theological, canvass and are sceptical about the status of werewolf transformation. See *Metamorphosis and Identity* (New York: Zone Books, 2001) 82–111; 86. She concludes that medieval explorations of 'body-hopping' 'reflect less a desire to shed the body than an effort to understand how it perdures, less an escape into alterity than a search for the rules that govern change'. Bynum, *Metamorphosis*, 109.
7. P[hilip] Camerarius, *The Living Librarie, or, Meditations and Observations Historical, Natural, Moral, Political and Poetical*, trans. John Molle (London, 1621) 98.
8. Edward Topsell, *The Historie of Foure-Footed Beasts* (London, 1607) 748.
9. William B. Ashworth Jr, 'Natural History and the Emblematic World View' in *Reappraisals of the Scientific Revolution*, ed. David C. Lindberg and Robert S. Westman (Cambridge University Press, 1990) 303–32, especially 306, 316. In a discussion of the relationship between discourses enunciating the symbolic significance of the animal and an 'emerging' emphasis on factually true and empirically testable statements *about* animals William B. Ashworth Jr carefully places Topsell's collection of animal lore in terms of its significant departures from Gesner in importing variously symbolic information. I am grateful to Kevin Killeen for bringing this article to my attention. Readers interested in a fuller discussion of Topsell will find it in Erica Fudge, *Perceiving Animals: Humans and Beasts in Early Modern English Culture* (Basingstoke: Macmillan, 2000) 11–13, 93–6.
10. Robin Briggs, 'Dangerous Spirits Shapeshifting, Apparitions and Fantasy in Lorraine Witchcraft Trials' in *Werewolves, Witches, and Wandering Spirits: Traditional Belief and Folklore in Early Modern Europe*, ed. Kathryn Edwards (Kirksville, Mo.: Truman State University Press, 2002) 1–24; 4.
11. Topsell compares the wolf and the hyena and discusses the progeny of wolves mated with hyenas and panthers – 'wolves do engender not only amongst themselves', *Foure-Footed Beasts*, 737, 745.
12. *Ibid.*, 748–9.
13. *Ibid.*, 737–48; 744. On leagues see e.g. 741, 748. On lions see e.g. 746.
14. Hayden White, 'Forms of Wildness' in *The Wild Man Within: An Image in Western Thought from the Renaissance to Romanticism*, ed. Edward Dudley and Maximilian E. Novak (London: University of Pittsburgh Press, 1972) 3–38; 3.
15. Topsell, *Foure-Footed Beasts*, 735. As Caroline Oates notes in her fascinating discussion of werewolf trials in Franche-Comté, trials offer a contrasting context: for trials to happen there needed to be wolves in the area: 'where there were

no wolves, there were no werewolves'. Caroline Oates, 'Trials of Werewolves in the Franche-Comté in the Early Modern Period' (London: University of London, unpublished Ph.D. thesis 1993) 11. Topsell also recounts the forced species mixture between a wolf and a mastiff at the Tower.
16. *A True Discourse Declaring the Damnable Life and Death of One Stubbe Peeter, A Most Wicked Sorcerer* (London, 1590) 4. Subsequent references are all to this edition. There is also a modernised edition in *A Lycanthropy Reader: Werewolves in Western Culture*, ed. Charlotte F. Otten (New York: Syracuse Unversity Press, 1986) 69–76; 69.
17. *Stubbe Peeter*, 4–5.
18. *Ibid.*, 5.
19. *Ibid.*, 10.
20. *Ibid.*, 19.
21. *Ibid.*, 5–6.
22. *Ibid.*, 7.
23. *Ibid.*, 7–9, 9.
24. *Ibid.*, 5.
25. Caroline Oates presents a different woodcut of the arrest (Augsburg, 1589) showing the arrester slicing off the wolf's paw in a scene reminiscent of many other stories of lycanthropic transformation and witchcraft transformation more generally where the human agent is found to have a wound in the same place as the animal wounded after an attack; 'Metamorphosis and Lycanthropy', 315–16, fig. 3.
26. *Stubbe Peeter*, 15–16.
27. Erica Fudge, *Perceiving Animals*, 51–5.
28. *A True Discourse*, 19.
29. Richard Verstegan, *A Restitution of Decayed Intelligence in Antiquities* (1605) 237.
30. *Stubbe Peeter*, 16.
31. Robin Briggs 'Dangerous Spirits', 1–24; 2.
32. See Nicole Jacques-Lefévre, 'Such an Impure, Cruel and Savage Beast: Images of the Werewolf in Demonological Works' in *Werewolves, Witches*, ed. Edwards, 181–97, 184, 188–9; Briggs, 'Dangerous', 4.
33. Reginal Scot, *The Discoverie of Witchcraft* (London, 1584) Book v, chap. 1, p. 89.
34. John Cotta, *The Triall of Witch-Craft* (London, 1616) 34. Also qtd in Stuart Clark, 'The Scientific Status of Demonology', *Lycanthropy Reader*, 168–94; 181. See Reginal Scot, *Discoverie*, 101 qtd and discussed by Philip C. Almond, *England's First Demonologist* (London and New York: I. B. Tauris, 2011) 103.
35. Clark, 'The Scientific Status of Demonology', in *Lycanthropy Reader*, 179. Clark is discussing Jean de Nynauld. On possession, see Stuart Clark, *Thinking With Demons, the Idea of Witchcraft in Early Modern Europe* (Oxford University Press, 1997) 190–4, 396 and *passim*.
36. Clark, 'The Scientific Status of Demonology', in *Lycanthropy Reader*, 177–81.
37. Clark, *Thinking With Demons*, 166–7, 172–3 and *passim*.

38. Clark, 'The Scientific Status of Demonology', in *Lycanthropy Reader*, 168–94, 176–9.
39. John Webster, *Duchess of Malfi* ed. Leah S. Marcus (London: Methuen, 2009). Subsequent references are to this edition. On the hyena see Joyce Salisbury, *The Beast Within: Animals in the Middle Ages* (London: Routledge, 1994) 141.
40. John Deacon and John Walker, *Dialogicall Discourses of Spirits and Divels* (London, 1601) 131–64; 158.
41. See *The XV Bookes of P.Ovidius Naso, Entituled, Metamorphosis*, trans. Arthur Golding (London, 1593) 4. All quotations from Ovid, *Metamorphoses*, trans. Arthur Golding, ed. Madeleine Forey (London: Penguin Books, 2002) 38–9.
42. See Wendy Olmsted, 'On the Margins of Otherness: Metamorphosis and Identity in Homer, Ovid, Sidney, and Milton' *New Literary History* 27.2 (1996), 167–84.
43. Jonathan Bate, *Shakespeare and Ovid* (Oxford: Clarendon Press, 1993) 26. See also Jean Seznec, *The Survival of the Pagan* Gods (Princeton University Press, 1953) 84–95. For a selection of the identifications of Lycaon and for the different ways in which *Metamorphoses* was interpreted in relation to the Bible, see Ann Moss, *Ovid in Renaissance France* (London: Warburg Institute, 1982) 30–5.
44. See Louis Thorn Golding, *An Elizabethan Puritan* (New York: Richard R. Smith, 1937).
45. *Ovids Metamorphosis*, trans. G. S. (London, 1640) 17.
46. Golding, *Elizabethan Puritan*, 4.
47. Topsell, *Foure-Footed Beasts*, 735.
48. *Ibid.*, 749.
49. Caroline Walker Bynum, *Metamorphosis*, 178.
50. Caroline Oates, 'Metamorphosis and Lycanthropy in Franche-Comté, 1521–1643' in *Fragments for a History of the Human Body* ed. Michael Feher with Ramona Naddaff and Nadia Tazi, Part I (New York: Zone Books, 1989) 305–61.
51. Caroline Walker Bynum, *Metamorphosis*, 96.
52. Giorgio Agamben, *Homo Sacer: Sovereign, Power and Bare Life*, trans. Daniel Heller-Roazen (California: Stanford University Press, 1998) 107. See also Jacques Derrida, *The Beast and the Sovereign*, trans. Geoffrey Benington (Chicago and London: Chicago University Press, 2009).
53. James Sharpe, *Instruments of Darkness: Witchcraft in England 1550–1750* (London, Hamish Hamilton, 1996) 65; Lawrence Normand and Gareth Roberts ed., *Witchcraft in Early Modern Scotland: James VI's Demonology and the North Berwick Witches* (University of Exeter Press, 2000) 1–2. We should briefly mark here the importance of the late Gareth Roberts' contribution to the study of the English Renaissance and particularly to the supernatural despite such a sadly short career.
54. John Webster, *The Displaying of Witchcraft* (London, 1677) 242–3.
55. Adam Fox, *Oral and Literate Culture in England 1500–1700* (Oxford University Press, 2002) 196.

56. John Aubrey, BL, Lansdowne MS 231, F140 quoted in Andy Wood, 'Custom and the Social Organization of Writing in Early Modern England', *Transactions of the Royal Historical Society* 6. 9 (1999) 257–69; 258.
57. Fox, *Oral*, 411; building on Fox see also Wood, 'Custom', 268.
58. P[hilip] Camerarius, *Living Librarie*, 275–8; 276.
59. *Ibid.*, 99.

5 Transformation rewritten?

1. Jean-Jacques Rousseau, 'Discourse on Inequality' in *The First and Second Discourse*, trans. Victor Gourevitch (New York: Harper, 1986) 141. Rousseau's words seem to echo those of St Basil. 'Homilia IX' in *Hexaemeron* II, *Patrologica Graecae* 29.192, quoted in David A. Sprunger, 'Wild Folk and Lunatics in Medieval Romance' in *The Medieval World of Nature*, ed. Joyce Salisbury (New York and London: Garland, 1993) 145–63; 150.
2. See also C. A. Patrides, 'Renaissance Ideas on Man's Upright Form', *JHI* 19 (1958) 256–8; Philip C. Almond, *England's First Demonologist* (London and New York: I. B. Tauris, 2011) 103.
3. Rousseau, *First and Second Discourse*, 201.
4. See e.g. *The History of a Savage Girl, Caught Wild in the Woods of Champagne* (London, 1760); Lucien Malson and Jean Itard, *Wolf Children and the Wild Boy of Aveyron*, trans. Edmund Fawcett, Peter Ayrton and Joan White (London: New Left Books, 1972); Michael Newton, *Savage Girls and Wild Boys: A History of Feral Children* (London: Faber and Faber, 2002).
5. Geoffrey Symcox, 'The Wild Man's Return: the Enclosed Vision of Rousseau's *Discourses*' in *The Wild Man Within: An Image in Western Thought from the Renaissance to Romanticism*, ed. Edward Dudley and Maximilian E. Novak (London: University of Pittsburgh Press, 1972) 223–46.
6. *Les Meditations Historique de M. P. Camerarius* (Lyon, 1610) chap. 15, 36.
7. Walter Benjamin, 'The Storyteller: Reflections on the Work of Nikolai Leskov' in *Illuminations*, trans. Harry Zohan, ed. Hannah Arendt (1955; trans. rpt London: Jonathan Cape, 1979) 83–109; 86.
8. Lorne Campbell, *The Early Flemish Pictures in the Collection of Her Majesty the Queen* (Cambridge University Press, 1985) 14.
9. *Ibid.*, 13.
10. *Ibid.*, 14, 18. Bruegel seems to have done several versions of the story, claimed by some critics to articulate contemporary politics. See Stanley Ferber, 'Peter Bruegel and the Duke of Alba' *Renaissance News*, 19.3 (1966) 205–19. Challenges to Ferber's discussion are summarised by Perez Zagorian, 'Looking for Pieter Bruegel', *Journal of the History of Ideas* 64.1 (2003) 73–96; 80–1.
11. Caroline Walker Bynum, *Metamorphosis and Identity* (New York: Zone Books, 2000) 19.
12. Plutarch, *The Lives of the Noble Grecians and Romanes compared together by that graue learned philosopher and historiographer, Plutarke of Chaeronea* trans.

(from Greek into French) James Amyot, trans. Thomas North (London, 1579). STC / 1712:12.
13. Michel Serres, *Rome: the Book of Foundations* (Stanford University Press, 1991) 9.
14. Plutarch, *Lives*, 21.
15. *Ibid.*, 22.
16. *Ibid.*, 23.
17. Edward Topsell, *The Historie of Foure-Footed Beastes* (London, 1607) 734.
18. Louis B. Wright, 'The Purposeful Reading of Our Colonial Ancestors', *ELH* 4.2 (1937): 85–111, especially 92–5. See also Gustaaf Van Crumphout 'Cotton Mather as Plutarchan Biographer', *American Literature* 46.4 (1951) 465–81. On non-Shakespearean literary use see e.g. Peter Ure, 'Chapman's Use of North's Plutarch in *Caesar and Pompey*', *RES* ns 9.35 (1958) 281–4.
19. Henry Peacham, *The Compleat Gentleman* (London, 1622) 52, 51.
20. 'The Library of Edmund Berkeley, Esq.' *The William and Mary Quarterly* 2.4 (1894) 250–1.
21. Anon., *Valentine and Orson*, trans. Henry Watson ed. Arthur Dickson (London: Early English Text Society, 1937) xi.
22. Arthur Dickson, 'Introduction' to *Valentine and Orson*, ix–xvi; Erica Fudge, *Perceiving Animals: Humans and Beasts in Early Modern English Culture* (Basingstoke: Macmillan, 2000), 58–63; Dickson, 'Introduction', xi–xx; *The Famous and Renowned Histor[y] of Valentine and Orso[n]* (London, n.d. ?1680).
23. *Valentine and Orson: The Two Sonnes of the Emperour of Greece* (London, 1637) A2v; A3r–v.
24. 'The Printer, To the Reader', *Valentine and Orson* (1637).
25. Henry Watson trans., *The Hystory of the Two Valyaunte brethren Valentyne and Orson* (1555) STC (2nd edn) 24571.7. Citations to Dickson ed., *Valentine and Orson*, 33–4.
26. Dickson ed., *Valentine and Orson*, 34.
27. *Ibid.*, 38.
28. *Ibid.*, 38.
29. *Ibid.*, 69.
30. *Ibid.*, 70.
31. *Ibid.*, 119.
32. *Ibid.*, 120.
33. *Ibid.*, 144.
34. Chapter misnumbered: 'Of the merveylous vision of Orson' *ibid.*, 326–7.
35. Michael Whitmore, *Children and Fiction in the English Renaissance* (Ithaca and London: Cornell University Press, 2007) 3.
36. Richard Bernheimer, *The Wild Man in The Middle Ages* (Harvard University Press, 1952), 8–12.
37. *Ibid.*, 12.
38. Jacques Le Goff, 'The Marvellous in the Medieval West', *The Medieval Imagination*, trans. Arthur Goldhammer (1985 rpt; Chicago and London: Chicago University Press, 1988) 27–44; 27.

39. Le Goff, 'The Marvellous', 36.
40. Sir Kenelm Digby, *Two Treatises* (Paris, 1644) 309.
41. *Ibid.*, 303.
42. *Ibid.*, 310.
43. *Ibid.*, 311.
44. *Ibid.*, 311.
45. *Ibid.*, 311.
46. *Ibid.*, 311.
47. *Ibid.*, 311.
48. *Ibid.*, 310.
49. *Ibid.*, 247–8.
50. 'Sir Kenelm Digby to Hobbes, from London' in *The Correpondence of Thomas Hobbes*, ed. Noel Malcolm, vol. 1 (Oxford University Press, 1994) 51. G. A. J. Roger, 'Descartes and the English' in *The Light of Nature* ed. J. D. North and J. J. Roche (Dordrecht and Boston Lancaster: Nijhoff, 1985) 281–302.
51. Lisa Shapiro ed., *Princess Elizabeth of Bohemia and René Descartes* (University of Chicago Press, 2007) 39, 89–90, 126; Peter Anstey, 'Descartes' Cardiology in England' in *Descartes' Natural Philosophy*, ed. Stephen Graukroger, John Schuster and John Sutton (London and New York: Routledge, 2000) 420–44; 428.
52. See also R. T. Peterson, *Sir Kenelm Digby the Ornament of England 1603–1665* (London: Jonathan Cape, 1956) 191–222; 'Sir Kenelm Digby to Hobbes, from London', *Correspondence*, vol. 1, 50.
53. William Hayley, *A Sermon Preached in the Parish Church of St Giles in the Fields at the Funeral of Bernard Connor, M.D. who departed this life Oct 30 1698* (London, 1699) 27–8.
54. Bernard Connor, *The History of Poland*, vol. 1 (London, 1698) 302.
55. *Ibid.*, 341–5, 342.
56. *Ibid.*, 342–3.
57. *Ibid.*, 342, 346.
58. *Ibid.*, 346–7.
59. *Ibid.*, 347.
60. *Ibid.*, 347–8.
61. *Ibid.*, 348–9.
62. Topsell, *Foure-Footed Beasts*, 37.
63. On early modern descriptions of material expelled from the womb see Laura Gowing, *Common Bodies: Women, Touch and Power in Seventeenth-Century England* (New Haven and London: Yale University Press, 2003).
64. Connor, *Poland*, 343.
65. *Ibid.*, 349.
66. *Ibid.*, 350.
67. René Descartes, *Discourse on the Method: The Philosophical Writings of Descartes*, trans. and ed. John Cottingham, Robert Stoothoff and Dugald Murdoch vol. 1 (Cambridge University Press, 1984) 112.
68. G. A. J. Roger, 'Descartes and the English' in *The Light of Nature*, 284–5.

69. As John Cottingham emphasises, comparison between human body and machine 'remained absolutely central to his physiology' occurring in his early *Treatise on Man* and it 'recurs unaltered in the *Description of the Human Body*, written two years before his death'. John Cottingham, *Descartes* (Oxford: Basil Blackwell, 1986) 108.
70. Descartes, 'The Passions of the Soul', *The Philosophical Works* vol. 1 (Cambridge University Press, 1985) 353. 'Wonder is a sudden surprise of the soul which brings it to consider with attention the objects which seem to it unusual and extraordinary. It has two causes: first, an impression in the brain, which represents the object as something unusual, and consequently worthy of special consideration; and secondly, a movement of the spirits, which the impression disposes both to flow with great force towards the place of the brain where it is locatd so as to strengthen and preserve it there . . . ' 353.
71. Simon Forman, Ashm. 208 fo. 210v–211r quoted in J. H. Pafford, 'Introduction' to William Shakespeare, *The Winter's Tale* ed. J. H. Pafford (1962; London: Thomson, 2002) xxi–ii. The manuscript, Ashm. 208, fos. 200–13 contains Forman's accounts of the plays. The manuscript was a 'discovery' of the notorious forger John Payne Collier. As Lauren Kassell summarises it, these accounts are the sole 'discoveries' of Collier not proved fakes, but, on the other hand, she notes 'the content and format are typical of Forman's writings'. Lauren Kassell, *Medicine and Magic in Elizabethan London* (Oxford: Clarendon Press, 2005) 2–3.
72. Gowing, *Common Bodies*, 177–203.
73. Holgar Schott Syme, *Theatre and Testimony in Shakespeare's England* (Cambridge University Press, 2012) 205–6; Stephen Orgel, 'Introduction' to *The Winter's Tale* (Oxford University Press, 1996) 78.
74. See Stanley Cavell, *Disowning Knowledge in Six Plays of Shakespeare* (Cambridge University Press, 1987). See also Gillian Woods, *Shakespeare's Unreformed Fictions* (Oxford University Press, 2013), 175, 195.
75. Quotations are taken from William Shakespeare, *The Winter's Tale* ed. Stephen Orgel (Oxford University Press, 1996) and the chapter also draws on J. H. Pafford's edition of the play.
76. Gowing, *Common Bodies*, 177–203; especially 177–8.
77. Michael Whitmore, *Pretty Creatures: Children and Fiction in the English Renaissance* (Ithaca: Cornell University Press, 2007) 163.
78. The names 'Antigonus' is used in the Alexander romance in connection with the return of a wife. Richard Stoneman ed., *The Greek Alexander Romance* (London: Penguin, 1991) 137–9.
79. Frances Dolan, *Dangerous Familiars: Representations of Domestic Crime in England 1550–1700* (Ithaca: Cornell University Press, 1994) 164.
80. Stephen Dickey, 'Shakespeare's Mastiff Comedy', *SQ* 42.3 (1991) 255–75; 255.
81. Michael D. Bristol, 'In Search of the Bear: Spatiotemporal Form and the Heterogeneity of Economies in *The Winter's Tale*', *SQ* 42.2 (1991) 145–67. See also Julie Sanders' fascinating discussion of Thomas Wentworth's bear pit,

Julie Sanders, *The Cultural Geography of Early Modern Drama* (Cambridge University Press, 2011) 1–8.
82. See Robert Hillis Goldsmith, 'The Wild Man on the English Stage', *MLR* 53.4 (1958) 481–91; 487.
83. J. H. Pafford ed., *The Winter's Tale*, 4.4.327–8 note.
84. Goldsmith, 'Wild Man', 487.
85. On the bear and *Mucedorus* see *ibid.*, 489 n.3.
86. Jonathan Sawday, *Engines of the Imagination: Renaissance Culture and the Rise of the Machine* (London: Routledge, 2007) 182–3.
87. Edward Topsell, *Foure-Footed Beasts*, 741; Homer, *The Odyssey*, trans. Robert Fagles (1996; London: Penguin, 1997) Bk 11. 96; 525.
88. Translated from *Les Meditations Historique de M. P. Camerarius*, 369. N.B. Camerarius' English translator misses out this chapter.
89. John Boswell, *The Kindness of Strangers: The Abandonment of Children in Western Europe From Late Antiquity to the Renaissance* (University of Chicago Press, 1988) 26, 45–9, 432–4 and *passim*.
90. *Fair Warning to Murderers of Infants* (London, 1691).
91. *The Bloudy Mother, or The Most Inhumane Murthers, Committed by Jane Hattersley vpon Diuers Infants, the Issue of her Owne Bodie* (London, 1610), B1r, B3r. STC (2nd edn) / 3717.3.
92. Dolan, *Dangerous Familiars*, 167–70.

Coda: Descartes and the disciplines

1. William Shakespeare, *Hamlet*, ed. Harold Jenkins (London: Methuen, 1982); René Descartes, *Discourse on the Method* in *The Philosophical Writings of Descartes*, trans. and ed. John Cottingham, Robert Stoothoff and Dugal Murdoch, vol. 1 (Cambridge University Press, 1984) 140.
2. John Florio, *Queen Anna's World of Words* (London, 1611) 356.
    See *OED*: 'paragon, n. and adj.'. OED Online. December 2012. Oxford University Press. 12 December 2012 www.oed.com.ezproxy.lib.bbk.ac.uk/view/Entry/13745?rskey=7xLuCu8result=18isAdvanced.
    As a verb: 'paragon, v.'. OED Online. December 2012. Oxford University Press. 12 December 2012 www.oed.com.ezproxy.lib.bbk.ac.uk/view/Entry/137416?rskey=7xLuCu8result=2.
3. Lodowick Bryskett, *A Discourse of Civill Life* (London, 1606) 3.
4. *Ibid.*, 257.
5. *Ibid.*, 258
6. *Ibid.*, 263.
7. 'To the Marquess of Newcastle, 23 November 1643', 'To [Henry] More 5 February 1649', *Philosophical Works* (1991) vol. III (1991) 302–4; 366.
8. See Peter Harrison, 'The Virtues of Animals in Seventeenth-Century Thought', *JHI* 39.3 (1998) 463–84; Katherine Morris, 'Bêtes-Machines' in *Descartes' Natural Philosophy*, ed. Stephen Gaukroger, John Schuster and John Sutton (London and New York: Routledge, 2000) 401–19; 401–4; and John

Cottingham, *Descartes* (Oxford: Basil Blackwell, 1986) 51–2. The nature of Descartes' claims and their impact on the nature of the animal receive an excellent discussion in Erica Fudge, *Brutal Reasoning: Animals, Rationality and Humanity in Early Modern England* (Ithaca and London: Cornell University Press, 2006) especially 147–93.
9. Michel Foucault, *The Order of Things*, trans. (London: Tavistock Publications, 1970) 128–9. Johannes Jonston in fact published *Historai Naturalis* in 1650. See William B. Ashworth, Jr, 'Natural History and the Emblematic World View' in *Reappraisals of the Scientific Revolution*, ed. David C. Lindberg and Robert S. Westman (Cambridge University Press, 1990) 303–32; 330, n. 41. Edward Tyson, 'Preliminary', *Phocaena, or the Anatomy of a Porpess, Dissected at Gresham Colledge: with a Preliminary Discourse concerning Anatomy, and a Natural History of Animals* (London, 1686?) 6–9.
10. See e.g. M. F. Ashley Montagu, *Edward Tyson, M.D., F.R.S. 1650–1708 and the Rise of Human and Comparative Anatomy in England* (Philadelphia: American Philosophical Society, 1943).
11. Peter Harrison, 'Virtues', 483–4.
12. Marjorie Hope Nicolson, 'The Early Stages of Cartesianism in England', *SP* 26.3 (1929) 356–74; 357, 360. See also G. A. J. Roger, 'Descartes and the English' in *The Light of Nature* ed. J. D. North and J. J. Roche (Dordrecht, Boston, Lancaster: Nijhoff, 1985) 281–302.
13. Kenelm Digby, *Two Treatises: In the One of Which, The Nature of Bodies* (London: John Williams, 1645), 389.
14. *Ibid.*, 389
15. Hope Nicolson, 'Early', 361–9.
16. Henry More to Descartes, 11 Dec., 1648, trans. and ed. Leonora D. Cohen, 'Descartes and Henry More on the Beast-Machine – a Translation of their Correspondence Pertaining to Animal Automatism', *Annals of Science* 1 (1936), 48–61; 50.
17. More to Descartes, 11 Dec., 1648, trans. and ed. Leonora D. Cohen, 'Descartes and Henry More', *Annals of Science* 1 (1936), 48–61; 51.
18. John Ray, *The Wisdom of God Manifested in the Works of the Creation* (London, 1691) 30, 31.
19. *Ibid.*, 37.
20. *Ibid.*, 38.
21. *Ibid.*, 38–9.
22. *Ibid.*, 39.
23. Descartes, 'Second Meditation' in *Meditations on First Philosophy*, trans. John Cottingham (Cambridge University Press, 1984) 19.
24. Fudge, *Brutal Reasoning*, 175.
25. René Descartes, *An Entire Body of Philosophy*, trans. Richard Blome (London, 1694); see also Wallace Shugg, 'The Cartesian Beast-Machine in English Literature (1663–1750)', *JHI* 29.2 (1968) 279–92; 283.
26. Richard Blome, 'To the Honoured Sir Henry Hobart' in Descartes, *An Entire Body*, 225.

27. Stephen Clucas, '"The Infinite Variety of Forms and Magnitudes": Sixteenth- and Seventeenth-Century English Corpuscular Philosophy and Aristotelian Theories of Matter and Form', *Early Science and Medicine* 2.3 (1997) 251–71; 270–1.
28. William Ayloffe, *The Government of the Passions* (London, 1700) 1–4, 122–3.
29. Bernard Connor, *History of Poland* (1699), 350.
30. Peter Harrison, 'Virtues', 483–4.
31. Thus, for example, Thomas Robinson develops a 'natural history' based on Moses' 'Philosophical Description of the Creation'. Thomas Robinson, *New Observations on the Natural History of this World of Matter and this World of Life* (London, 1698).
32. James Duplessis, 'A Short History of Human Prodigies & Monstrous Births' MS Sloane 5246. Descartes himself was not above a momentary appeal to correspondence – as on the endlessly canvassed question of birthmarks where he tells a correspondent that a mother, 'by scratching the corresponding area while the desire to eat was upon her, transformed the effects of her imagination to the corresponding parts of the baby', though he goes on to say that mother–baby correspondence can be proven by mechanics. René Descartes, 'To Mersenne, 30 July 1640' in *The Philosophical Writings of Descartes*, ed. John Cottingham, Robert Stoothoff, Dugald Murdoch, Anthony Kenny vol. III (Cambridge University Press, 1991) 148–9.
33. Bruno Latour, *We Have Never Been Modern*, trans. Catherine Porter (Cambridge, Mass.: Harvard University Press, 1993).
34. See Luisa Calè and Adrian Craciun, 'The Disorder of Things', *Eighteenth-Century Studies* 45.1 (2011) 1–13.
35. Peter Murray Jones, 'A Preliminary Check-list of Sir Hans Soane's Catalogues', *British Library Journal* 2.1 (1988) 38–51.
36. Jan Golinski, *Making Natural Knowledge: Constructivism and the History of Science* (University of Chicago Press, 2005) 67–8.
37. Jacques Derrida, *The Animal That Therefore I Am*, trans. David Wills, ed. Marie-Louise Mallet (2006; New York: Fordham University Press, 2008) 6, 13, 14.
38. *Ibid.*, 11.
39. *Ibid.*, 9. For Derrida this seems to be an acute problem in philosophy which has effects in the world so, while philosophy cannot come face to face with an animal, other discourses, though problematic, may be less fully ruined.
40. Derrida, *Animal*, 7.
41. Bruno Latour, *We Have Never*, 13.

Index

Abraham and Isaac 6, 7
Actaeon (*see also* Diana) 7, 21, 32
adder 104
addition 21
adultery 184, 194
Aesop 82
Agamben, Giorgio 157
agility 162, 176, 192
Aldrovandi, Ulisse 98, 101, 107, 110, 112, 113, 132, 134
Amazon 1, 16
anatomy 125, 126, 127, 130, 134, 140, 198
anecdotes (also gossip) 65, 77, 159, 177, 193
animal–god border / relationship 192
animal–human, human–animal transformation 20, 38, 47, 50, 65, 84, 85, 87, 131, 137, 138, 146, 147, 150, 156, 157
  and law 38
  bestiality 129, 130, 141
  fantasy or illusion of 138, 139, 144, 145, 146, 147, 148, 149, 151, 156
animal–human border/relationships 7, 14, 20, 64, 81, 83, 102, 127, 128, 131, 133, 140, 144, 145, 149, 154, 161, 163, 175, 196, 205
animal nurture of humans 166, 167, 168, 169, 170, 171, 175, 176, 178, 179, 180
Animal Studies, history of animals 4, 27
animals (*see also specific creatures*) 24, 48, 56, 59, 81, 82, 83, 84, 90, 91, 111, 124, 126, 127, 128, 130, 133, 137, 139, 168, 172, 173, 175, 196, 206
  abilities 181, 199, 200
  abolished 204, 206
  attributes, personality 141, 174
  bodies 126, 199
  culture / mode of life 126, 164
  pain 199, 201
  reason, wisdom 126, 146: lack of reason 196, 201
  souls 179
  voice / cry 68, 83, 162, 176, 177, 206

animal events (including symbolism, ceremonies; *see also* baptism) 13, 59, 63, 64, 65, 67, 68, 69, 70, 72, 74, 77, 80, 81, 84, 131, 141, 143
anthropocentrism 83, 84
anthropomorphism 64, 68, 82, 84, 127
Apollo 30, 191, 192
Aquapendente, Fabricius d' 132
Archer, Ian 29
Aristophanes 120
Aristotle, Aristotelian 10, 48, 84, 87, 88, 89, 90, 91, 92, 94, 99, 106, 124, 132, 133, 174, 181, 197, 198, 201, 203
Aristotle's Masterpiece 131
art (and nature, relationship) 10, 87, 90, 95, 99, 105, 107, 110, 122, 124, 127, 135, 136, 168, 170, 172, 189
Ashley, Francis 67, 68, 70, 72, 80, 81
Ashworth, William B. 12, 140
atheism 65
atomism 175
Aucante, Vincent 132
audience (*see also* reading; reception) 84, 115, 121, 124, 150, 185, 194
  dramatic irony 186
  judgement/evaluation by audiences 185, 187, 190
authority 129
automata 125, 126, 127, 196, 198, 199, 200
  clockwork 199, 202
Ayloffe, William 202

Bacchus 24
Bacon, Francis 8, 10, 11, 87, 89, 105, 106, 120, 122, 124, 125, 132, 135, 179, 180, 204
baiting (bulls, bears) 187, 188
Baldwin, William *A Marvelous History intitulede Beware the Cat* 67
ballad 26, 29, 185, 186, 190, 193
Banks, Joseph 112
banishment 160

Index

baptism, baptismal liturgy 8, 13, 58, 59, 61, 62, 65, 66, 67, 69, 74, 75, 76, 78, 80, 81, 82, 137, 158, 159, 168, 169, 170, 176, 177, 178, 180, 190, 195
  animals 59, 61, 81
Barkan, Leonard 32
Barthes, Roland 55
Bartlett, Robert 8
basilisk (and cockatrices) 99, 101, 102, 103, 104, 109, 110, 111, 115, 123
bastardy, legitimacy 184, 185, 189
Bate, Jonathan 27, 47, 153
Bateman, Stephen 89
bear 25, 107, 162, 168, 171, 175, 176, 179, 185, 186, 187, 188
  bear garden 170
  Hunks 113
beast machine 180, 198, 199, 200, 201, 203
beastliness, bestial 2, 7, 21, 63, 83, 84
bee 50, 101
beetle 120, 121, 124
Belon, Pierre 107
Benjamin, Walter 161, 162, 172, 192, 193, 195
Berkeley, Edmund 167
Bernheimer, Richard 170
Bess of Hardwick, *see* Elizabeth, Countess of Shrewsbury
bestiaries 88, 89
biology 87, 116
birds (*see also specific creatures*) 165
Black Dog of Newgate (*see also* Hutton) 35, 39, 40, 41, 42
Blanc, Mademoiselle le 162
blending 2, 4, 7, 83, 84
The Bloudy Mother 194
Boaistuau, Pierre *Histoires prodigeuses* 89, 91, 92, 93
boar 56
Bobart, Jacob 133, 134
body-hopping 226
Boguet, Henri 137, 138, 139
Boke of Duke Huon of Bordeaux 21
Book of Common Prayer 2, 7, 11, 60, 61, 64, 73, 74, 75, 76, 79, 81, 82, 83, 207
  Scottish 61
Bosch, Hieronymous 5
Boswell, John 193
botany 134
Bredekamp, Horst 109
Briggs, Robin 147
Bristol, Michael D. 187
British Museum 205
  disciplinary division 205

institution of departments 205: Ethnography 205; Mineralogy 205; Palaentology 205; Zoology 205
Brooks, Harold F. (*see also* Shakespeare, *A Midsummer Night's Dream*) 4, 17, 211
brotherhood 140, 165, 167, 189
Brown, Georgia 4–6, 44
Browne, Thomas 98, 99, 103, 104, 110, 111, 126, 204
Brueghel, Pieter, the Elder 163
  'Winter Scene' 163, 164
Bryskett, Lionel 196, 197, 203, 204
Buckley, Mr 215
building 85
bull 187
Bull, Malcolm 3, 11, 55
Butler, Samuel 134

Calè, Luisa 204
Calvinism 60, 61, 153
Camerarius, Philip 139, 159, 192, 193
Campbell, Mary Baine 87
Canghuilhem, Georges 134, 135
cannibalism 41, 151, 152, 153, 170
Canon Episcopi 8, 138
Cardano, Gerolamo 107, 128
carp 83
cat 4–6, 59, 67, 68, 72, 76, 77, 80, 81, 82, 83, 85, 99, 140, 163
caterpillar 103
Catholicism 4, 60, 61, 65, 66, 69, 72, 74, 80, 81, 83, 114, 145, 174, 212
  Sarum Manual 61
Cavell, Stanley 184
Cavendish, William Duke of Newcastle 197
Cecil, Robert 65, 66
Cerberus 1, 32, 34, 35, 37, 38
chameleon 112
changeling, fosterling 172, 177, 187
Charles I 61, 72
Charles II 61, 163
  Restoration 164
Chaucer, Geoffrey 1, 16
chicken 59
children (and infants; *see also* wild children) 13, 63, 75, 76, 84, 90, 95, 101, 114, 131, 136, 138, 139, 143, 145, 146, 151, 162, 164, 168, 170, 172, 177, 191, 193, 194, 195
  abandonment / exposure (*see also* infanticide) 165, 184, 188, 193, 194, 195
  foundling 183, 186, 190
  lost and found (*see also* wild children) 164, 172, 177, 183, 185, 188, 191, 193, 194, 195
  murdered, *see* infanticide

children (*cont.*)
    investigation of category by contemporary texts 183
    motivations related to 183
    stillborn 193, 194
chimera 194
Chrismas, Richard 2, 68
    family 217
Christmas 75
churching of women 64
Circe 18, 83
civil, civility 143, 144, 151, 154, 156, 157, 167, 190, 197
Civil War 59, 74, 124, 159
classical material 13, 18, 25, 26, 27, 30, 46, 54, 55, 80, 81, 92, 93, 99, 119
    and Christian 4, 55, 84, 139, 215
    and medieval 55
    mediation of (*see also* reading; reception) 46
    texts of metamorphoses (*see also Odyssey*; Ovid) 56, 156, 158, 188
Clucas, Stephen 201, 202
    brilliant 202
cockatrice, *see* basilisk
collections, collecting (museums, cabinets of curiosity, etc.) 86, 87, 94, 96, 99, 101, 106, 107, 111, 112, 113, 114, 115, 127, 134, 206
compendia, catalogues 87, 93, 114, 116, 123, 131
competition 125
concepts, cultural mobility of (including metamorphosis) 6–7, 162
coney-catching 39, 40, 42
Connor, Bernard 175, 176, 177, 178, 179, 180, 181, 207
    History of Poland 175, 207
    relationship to Descartes 202
Cope, Sir Walter 113, 114
Corinthians 7, 8
Coryat's Crudities 113
Cotta, John 138, 147
Cottingham, John 200
Cotton, William Bishop of Exeter 65, 67, 68, 70, 72
Court of Aldermen 30
courts 65, 67, 155, 185
    church 59
    High Commission 69
    Star Chamber 69
Cowley, Abraham 124, 125, 131, 134, 136
cows 64, 173
Craciun, Adriana 204
Cranmer, Thomas 61
creation 52
Cressy, David 72, 73, 74
crime 31, 152, 153, 160, 167

culture 124, 134, 157, 162, 172, 189, 195
Cupid 19
curiosity 86, 87, 114, 115, 139, 172
    curiosities, *see* monsters; wonders
Curry, Walter Clyde 120
custom 192
customs 62

da Vinci, Leonardo 5, 105, 107
Dante 5, 29, 36
    Inferno 36, 38
Daston, Lorraine 87
Davis, Natalie Zemon 6
Deacon, John 150
debate, opinion 80
Dee, John 119, 120, 121
deformity 53
demonology 5, 148, 150, 156
demons, *see* devil
Derrida, Jacques 205, 206
    animal gaze 205
    animal speech 205
    being 205
    being-in-the-world 205
Descartes, René 5, 132, 133, 134, 150, 156, 174, 179, 180, 195, 196, 197, 198, 199, 200, 201, 203, 232
    acceptance / non-acceptance 202, 203, 207
    and disciplines, disciplinarity 204
    animal–human border redefined 205
    Cartesian 125, 175, 177, 178, 179, 180, 181, 198, 199, 204: English Cartesians 174, 201
    Discourse on the Method 174, 196, 197, 198, 201, 203
    An Entire Body of Philosophy 201
    epoch 205, 206
    innovation (conceptual, methodological, linguistic) 198, 199
    legacy 205, 206
    Levinas and/after 206
    living 205
    makes animal philosophical problem 205
    mutation 205
    on reason in animals and humans 197, 204, 205
    'poetic thinking' 205, 206: not philosophy 206; temporality of 206
    poetry 205
    splits philosophy and poetry 205, 206
    thinking things 200
    readers, reception 201, 202
    wonder 232
    writers engaging Descartes 199, 200, 201, 202, 203, 204

Index

desire 143
despair 35
Dessen, Alan 119, 121
devil, devils (*also* non-malign spirits) 31, 35, 36, 40, 41, 60, 79, 83, 101, 102, 103, 119, 122, 129, 130, 143, 144, 145, 147, 148, 219
Diana (*see also* Actaeon) 6, 7, 18, 21, 30, 32, 121
Dickey, Stephen 187
Dickson, Arthur 167
Digby, Sir Kenelm 133, 172, 173, 174, 175, 176, 177, 179, 180, 181, 193, 200, 201, 202
　Two Treatises 172, 174, 180, 198, 202: animal language 198, 199, 202; co-existence of Cartesianism 202; human language 198
Directory of Worship 7, 60, 61, 62, 74, 76
disciplines, disciplinarity 3, 12, 13, 87, 122, 125, 134, 201, 203, 204
　analysis of 205
　institution/temporality of 204, 205
　interdisciplinarity 13
　non-disciplinary 204
　pre-disciplinary, pre-disciplinarity 12, 13, 87, 88, 123, 159, 207
　separate spheres of knowledge 204, 205, 207
　specialist versus disciplinary 203
dog (*see also* Black Dog; Hutton) 14, 31, 34, 59, 65, 66, 71, 72, 76, 128, 138, 140, 176, 201
donkey 21, 91, 128
doubleness, double-dealing 39
doves 62
dragon 98, 99, 101, 102, 104, 107, 115, 123, 124, 125, 133, 134
　do-it-yourself 105, 134
duck 98, 111
Duplessis, James 96, 125, 130, 203

editorial practice 17, 27
Edward VI 4–6, 61
Edwards, Thomas *Gangraena* 59, 79
eggs 88, 94, 95, 96, 99, 103, 111, 112, 115, 124, 125, 128, 130, 131, 132, 133, 134, 136
elephant 114
elite, powerful 84, 158
Elizabeth, Countess of Shrewsbury 6
Elizabeth I 30, 53
emblems, emblematic 6
Enlightenment 87, 162, 203, 204
　long 205
epic 55
Epicurus 52
epoch 6, 124, 125, 180, 205, 207
　of metamorphic writing 198, 203, 204, 207

ethnography, enthnographic 13, 69, 115, 162
etymology 140, 164, 165, 166
eucharist 61
Evelyn, John 110, 111
evidence, literary / other evidence 54, 78, 85, 129, 134, 140, 155, 158, 172, 184, 195
exorcism 60
experiments 112, 113, 124, 127, 148, 175, 177, 179, 180
explanations 148, 151, 156, 166, 177, 184, 186, 187
Eyam 63

fable 10, 11, 13, 59, 111, 159
facts, fact–fiction relationship 40, 164
Fair Warning to Murderers of Infants 194
fall, the 49, 109
family 183, 192
　lineage, issue 184, 188, 191
　paternity 184, 185
　questioned 183
Farley, John 132
fates 23
Fennor, William *Compter's Commonwealth* 44
Fenton, Edward 89, 91, 92, 93, 126, 204
Ficino, Marsilio 91, 199
fiction 129, 164
figure, figural 44, 45
Findlen, Paula 107, 133
fish (*see also individual fishes*) 83, 86, 95, 103, 110, 111, 116, 121
Fissell, Mary 131
flies 90, 111, 114
Floyer, Sir John 127, 128, 129, 130
folklore, folkloric (*see also* popular) 13, 20, 25, 27, 44, 46, 99, 147, 154, 157
font 59
forensic evidence, examination 47, 80, 96, 99, 107
form, forms 11, 201, 202
Forman, Simon 183, 184, 187, 189, 191, 194
fossils 89, 94, 95, 112
Foucault, Michel 12, 203
Fox, Adam 12, 26
Fox, Cora 213
frogs, toads 90, 93, 101
Fudge, Erica 4, 17, 62, 167, 169, 234
Fumerton, Patricia 40
furies 23, 31, 32, 37, 38, 41

Galen 91
generation 4, 47, 87, 88, 89, 91, 92, 93, 94, 95, 96, 98, 99, 102, 103, 116, 118, 123, 124, 125, 126, 127, 128, 129, 130, 131, 135, 140
　spontaneous generation 90, 92, 96, 101, 102, 132, 133, 135, 136

Genesis 6
genre 36, 45, 87
Gervase of Tilbury 7, 9–10, 138, 139, 152
Gesner, Conrad 101, 107, 110, 112, 140
giant 112, 119
Ginzburg, Carlo 215
Globe Theatre 183
Golding, Arthur, *see* Ovid
Golinski, Jan 205
Goodenough, Mary 194 (see also *Fair Warning*)
goose 65, 98, 112
Goudin, Antoine 90
Gould, Stephen Jay 94
Gowing, Laura 184, 193
grace 58
Gramsci, Antonio 56
Greek 93, 103
Greene, Jon 75
greyhound 105
Grimston, Sir Harbottle 71

Haddon Hall 56
Haigh, Christopher 72
Handefull of Pleasant Delites 4, 25
Hardie, Philip 3, 12, 15
Hardwick Hall 167
hare 112
Harkness, Deborah 88
Harman, Thomas *A Caveat or Warening for Common Cursetors* 42
Harrison, Peter 83, 198, 203
Harvey, William 89, 125, 133, 135, 137, 174
hell 12, 29, 31, 34, 35, 36, 37, 38, 41
hen 98, 133, 136
 chick 132
 cock 103, 104, 105, 136
 poultry breeding 98, 158
Henry, Prince, son of James I 113
Henry II 30
Henry III 41
Henry VIII 30
heresy, heretics 8, 9, 30
hermit 169, 170, 171
 of Cratcliff 171
Herod 153, 154, 163
hierarchy 28
Hippolyta, *see* Amazon; Shakespeare, *A Midsummer Night's Dream*
hippopotamus 112
history of art 3, 18
history of science 4, 13, 66, 88, 105, 125, 135
Hobbes, Thomas 167, 174, 198
Hoby, Lady Margaret 62
Holland, Peter 27
horse 65, 69, 70, 72, 77, 78, 82, 84, 91, 128

Hughes, Ann 78, 80, 81
human 7–8, 9–10, 24, 32, 59, 64, 84, 90, 91, 112, 117, 118, 121, 123, 124, 128, 133, 141, 144, 145, 148, 157, 173, 180, 199, 200
 Aristotelian/Cartesian 198, 203
 attitudes to animals (*see also* anthropomorphism) 82, 84, 126
 bipedism / all fours 161, 175, 176, 177, 178, 195
 body 138
 border with monstrosity 117, 118, 129, 149
 black 131
 exceeded 170, 171, 180
 falling below, falling away from, failure to reach human status (*see also* Aristotle; beastliness) 22, 50, 90, 91, 149, 151, 170, 178, 196
 gaze 161
 head 18
 hermaphrodite 131
 innate ideas, qualities 177, 181, 202
 language, speech 162, 169, 170, 174, 175, 176, 177, 178, 180, 195, 196, 201, 205
 men 138
 perfectibility 162
 perfection 196
 position between beast and divine 196, 197
 preference to live amongst animals 162, 177, 178
 relationship with divine and animal 153, 157, 196, 197, 200
 showing animals 139, 140
 transformation 2, 41, 48, 60, 82
 wildness 189
humanism, humanists 56, 206
hunt 173, 176, 178, 185, 186
Hutchinson, Lucy 6
Hutton, Luke
 The Blacke Dogge of Newgate (see also Black Dog of Newgate) 28, 29, 30, 32, 36, 38, 40, 42, 45, 46, 51, 54, 57
 Luke Huttons Lamentation 29
hybridity, mixture 18, 21, 27, 45, 46, 135, 161, 190, 192
hydra 99, 101, 104, 107, 109, 110, 111

identification 150, 151
identity 21, 25, 31, 39, 50, 60, 101, 104, 130, 138, 139, 147, 151, 186
illustrations 87, 96, 98, 110, 131, 145
imprisonment, *see* prison
infanticide 154, 193, 194, 195
Innes, William 70, 71
insects 125, 127, 198
intertextuality 2, 16, 17, 19, 20, 25, 32, 34, 36
Irish myths 26

Index

James VI and I 7, 12, 62, 74, 84, 138, 155, 156
John of Liège 172, 173, 174, 175, 176
jokes 66, 72, 74, 134, 185
Jonson, Ben 157, 188
   Oberon 188
Jonston, Johann 203
   Natural History of Quadrupeds 12, 198, 203
Juno 37
Justices of Peace 66, 67, 76

Kallendorf, Craig 55
Kaspar Hauser 162
Kermode, Frank 120
Kintgen, Eugene 49, 57
Kircher, Athanasius 94, 95

Latin (*see also* classical material) 15, 26, 46, 47, 49, 147, 152
Latona 18
Latour, Bruno 206
   effects of disciplinarity 206
Laud, Archbishop (Laudianism) 59, 72, 74, 75, 78, 84
law, agents of law, punishment 38, 39, 40, 52, 69, 74, 77, 193
   sessions 41, 77
Le Goff, Jacques 171, 174
legend 40, 44
Leigh, Dorothy 62
Levinas, Emmanuel 205
lice 149
Lindley, Keith 77
lion 194
literacy 13, 27
literary criticism 2, 25, 65, 88
literary texts 81, 155, 195
lithopodion 95, 96, 131, 220
lobster 124, 131
Locke, John 125
lunar cycle 138
Luther, Martin 8
Lutheranism 61, 216
lycanthropy 137, 138, 139, 147, 148, 149, 150, 152, 156
Lycaon 41, 137, 152, 153, 154, 155, 157
Lyne, Raphael 3, 4, 12, 15, 47

MacGregor, Arthur 113
machine, mechanical 99, 119, 120, 121, 124, 126, 134, 135, 199
   mechanical life 126, 200
mechanism 198, 199, 200, 202, 207
magic (Hermeticism) 20, 21, 41, 61, 64, 80, 81, 121, 122, 123, 124, 132, 140, 143, 158, 171
Magliabecchi, Antonio 133

Malleus Maleficarum 9, 147
Malphigi 127, 198
man (concept) 126
manufacture 110, 111, 115, 117, 125, 127, 136, 178
Martindale, Charles (*see also* reception) 3–4, 9, 15, 45, 53, 54, 55
marvellous, the 89, 90, 102, 103, 107, 123, 165, 171, 174, 176, 190, 192, 193
Massacre of the Innocents 163, 164, 193
mastiff 105
maternal imagination (*see also* Duplessis) 131
mathematics 120, 122, 123, 124, 149
matter 11, 105, 130, 134
   inert 124, 134, 136, 200
   material causes 132
McElduff, Siobhán 26, 46, 55
Meadow, Mark A. 109
medicine (disease) 87, 92, 94, 113, 125, 126, 127, 147, 148, 149, 150
   physicians 114, 151
   surgeons 96
Medusa 34, 35, 38
memory 138, 162, 176
   knowledge of past 186
Mercurius Aulicus 75, 79, 80, 81
Mercurius Britanicus 79, 80, 81
mermaids, sirens 50, 51
metamorphosis (change of state, transformation, in writing) 2, 6, 19, 20, 23, 25, 63, 72, 75, 80, 81, 84, 91, 92, 94, 95, 96, 99, 106, 116, 120, 122, 123, 124, 130, 131, 132, 137, 143, 144, 149, 155, 156, 158, 159, 170, 172, 178, 179, 180, 181, 190, 191, 193, 195, 199, 204, 207
   disavowed 138
   trans-period studies of metamorphosis 4–6, 61
mice 90, 101
microcosm, correspondences 126, 198, 235
microscope 127, 198
midwives 96
Milton, John 3, 9, 83, 85, 157
   Maske Presented at Ludlow Castle 83
Minerva 2, 24, 31, 34
minotaur 16
Minyas' daughters 24
mirror 171
misrule 73
modernity 204, 205, 206
monsters, monstrosity 4, 25, 31, 32, 38, 40, 55, 56, 86, 87, 88, 89, 91, 93, 96, 99, 103, 106, 107, 110, 115, 117, 118, 122, 123, 127, 128, 129, 130, 134, 135, 159
   monstrous births 99, 131
Montaigne, Michel de 93, 130, 197
   on animal reason 197, 205
moon 2, 15, 16

morality 50, 167
More, Henry 91, 199
 animal souls immortal 199
Morpheus 30
Morrill, John 76
Mowat, Barbara 120
Mucedorus 188

Narcissus 83
Nashe, Thomas 29
natural philosophy 51, 64, 96, 102, 134, 136, 201
nature, natural world 3, 11, 13, 23, 52, 53, 87, 90, 92, 95, 96, 102, 103, 105, 106, 110, 112, 115, 118, 122, 124, 125, 127, 135, 136, 138, 140, 145, 148, 156, 157, 161, 190, 202
 Descartes and 199
 histories of nature / natural history 111, 127, 178, 198
 law of 184
 nature and art, relationship, *see* art
 terms on which investigated 204
Nebuchadnezzer 7, 138
Nedham, Marchmont 79, 82
Newgate, Newgate prison 29, 30, 34, 35, 36, 37, 38, 39, 41, 42
news 59, 65, 73, 74, 76, 78, 79
Nicolson, Marjorie Hope 199
nightingale 20
Normand, Lawrence 158
North, Thomas 164, 166, 167, 171
nurture 165, 168, 172, 173, 178, 180, 189, 195
 Christian/human 169, 170, 171, 176
 inhuman 177

Oakley-Brown, Liz 46, 55
Oates, Caroline 155
Odysseus 191
Odyssey, Homer 11, 192
oral culture, orality (oral-literate, oral-written, verbal) 3, 12, 13, 27, 42, 46, 137, 139, 155, 157, 158, 159, 160, 167
orang-utang 127
ordination 75
Orgel, Stephen 183
Orpheus (and Eurydice) 6, 25, 56, 57
orthodoxy 8, 10, 138, 156, 159
Ovid, *Metamorphoses* 2, 3–4, 5, 8, 9, 14, 15, 17, 18, 22, 24, 26, 28, 29, 34, 37, 38, 45, 46, 47, 48, 49, 50, 54, 68, 88, 95, 106, 123, 133, 137, 204, 214
 decoration 3, 6, 145, 152, 153, 154, 155, 158, 167
 emotion 213
 Golding, Arthur 6, 7, 9–10, 11, 15, 17, 22, 24, 26, 32, 46, 47, 48, 50, 51, 52, 53, 101, 137, 153
ox 138

Pafford, J. H. 188
pagans 48, 52
pamphlets, pamphleteers 28, 29, 39, 40, 44, 87, 88, 186, 194
parable 52
Paracelsus 132
Paré, Ambroise 88, 89, 91, 92, 93, 94, 95, 96, 99, 127, 128, 129, 130, 220
Park, Katherine 87
Parker, Patricia 23
Parker, Robert
 parish 184, 193, 194
parody 63, 64, 66, 69, 70, 73, 82
partlet 65
pastoral 186, 188, 190
Peacham, Henry 113, 115
 Compleat Gentleman 167
peacocks 56, 119
Peck, John 70
Peck, Sarah 70
pelican 115
Pendry, E. D. 36
petrification 94, 95, 111
phantoms (ghosts, hauntings; *see also* supernatural) 25, 49, 54
 ghost-penis 165, 166
Phoebus (*see also* Apollo) 28, 29, 30
phoenix 123
Philomel (*see also* nightingale) 21
philosophers, philosophy 179, 196, 198, 204
 history of 205
physiology 3, 13, 130, 132, 148
pig 78, 94, 128
plague 66
Plato, Platonism 199
Platt case 78
 Platt, John 76
 Platt, Susan/Susanna 76
Platter, Thomas 113, 115, 135
Pliny 106
plunder 163
Plutarch 90, 164, 167, 180, 194
Pluto 34, 37
poison 94, 102, 158, 194
politics, political 20, 139, 143, 146, 149, 151, 155, 156, 157, 160, 165, 166, 167, 190
Popham, Sir John 30
popular (popular culture, populist) 12, 20, 28, 42, 54, 55, 56, 77, 80, 81, 98, 124, 131, 154, 202
 analysis of the popular (*see also* Davis; Gramsci) 56
porpoise (*see also* Tyson) 125
possession 151
Pouget, Raimbaud de 138
poverty 77

pre-Christian 171
print 12, 15, 26, 29, 31, 44, 80, 87, 155, 158, 160, 167, 188, 195
    print event 80
prison, prisoners, prison literature, imprisonment (*see also* Hutton; Newgate) 30, 35, 37, 40, 41, 42, 44, 149, 184
prodigal 44
profligacy 32
protestantism 59, 69, 74, 138, 160
Proteus 10, 11, 105, 106, 221
Prowse, John 69, 70
psyche 139, 148, 149, 150, 151
psychology 42, 159
Puck (*see also* Shakespeare, *A Midsummer Night's Dream*)
puritan 68, 72, 76
Pyramus and Thisbe (*see also* Shakespeare, *A Midsummer Night's Dream*) 15, 22
Pythagoras 10, 48, 199

Quiccheberg, Samuel 109

rat 35, 38, 134
Ray, John 98, 111, 112, 125, 134, 135, 199, 204
    animal pain 200
    animal reason 200
    animal soul 199, 200
    relationship to Descartes 202
    speech 200
reading, readers, audiences 7, 11, 12, 14, 20, 24, 25, 26, 27, 32, 37, 38, 45, 47, 48, 50, 51, 53, 54, 55, 70, 78, 82, 91, 92, 99, 101, 123, 131, 140, 148, 155, 156, 158, 162, 165, 166, 170, 193, 194, 195, 200, 203
    circulation 96, 112, 113, 152, 155, 156, 187, 195
    simple 7, 9, 15, 26, 49, 53, 159
reason 8, 15, 62, 126, 139, 146, 173, 175, 180, 189, 195, 196, 197
reception 4, 15, 25, 26, 27, 28, 38, 47, 55, 56, 92
    Reception Studies 46, 54, 55, 56
Redi, Francesco 112, 125
Reformation 2, 7, 13, 34, 53, 57, 59, 60, 64, 71, 73, 74, 80, 81, 83, 85, 104, 141, 143, 154, 171
resurrection, re-animation 8, 120, 212
revision (of texts / stories/images / media) 163, 164, 181, 185
rhinoceros 114, 115
riddle 136
roach 83
Roberts, Gareth 158
Robin Goodfellow 159, 212
Roger, G. A. J. 180
role-play 40
romance 18, 88, 188, 190

Rome 165, 166
Romulus and Remus 6–7, 152, 162, 164, 165, 166, 167, 169, 171, 179, 190, 194
Rousseau, Jean-Jacques 161, 162, 192, 193, 204
Rowlands, Samuel 40
    The Discovery of a London Monster 40
Royal Society 112, 124, 125
Rueff, Jacob 204
    The Expert Midwife 96

sacraments 59, 61, 65, 76, 82
Salisbury, Joyce 4, 155
Sancroft, William 198
Sandys, George 14, 47, 51, 52, 53, 153
satyr (*see also* Shakespeare, *The Tempest*) 173, 174, 188
Savage, Catherin 68
Scaliger, Julius Caesar 104
scandal 164, 166, 167, 169, 170, 184, 185, 186, 187, 190, 191, 199
Schott Syme, Holgar 183
science 87, 124, 129, 134, 225
    scientific revolution 125, 202
Scot, Reginald, *Discoverie of Witchcraft* 9, 17, 147
sea-mouse 115
secrets, concealed knowledge 39, 164
Seneca 23
    Agamemnon 23
    Hercules 23
    Hippolytus 17, 19, 20, 27, 32
    Medea 9, 19, 20, 23
senses (*see also* smell) 157, 172, 176, 178, 190, 200
serpents (*see also* basilisk) 90, 91, 92, 99, 102, 104, 123, 164, 194
servants 7, 194
sex, sexuality 166, 167, 187, 189, 191
    guilt 183, 186
    rivalry 189
Seznec, Jean 3, 55
shadow 150
Shakespeare, William 28, 47, 135, 167
    Hamlet 118, 196, 197, 198, 203
    A Midsummer Night's Dream 15, 16, 17, 19, 21, 22, 23, 25, 26, 27, 32, 44, 45, 46, 48, 51, 54, 57: and 1590s 29, 44
    The Tempest 4, 53, 86, 87, 88, 99, 110, 115, 116, 117, 118, 119, 120, 121, 122, 123, 130, 134, 135, 223
    The Winter's Tale 183, 184, 185, 186, 188, 189, 190, 191, 192, 193, 194, 195: as analytical theatre 183, 184, 185, 186, 188, 190, 193, 195; and ceremony 188; renovation of patriarchy, conditional 189; saltiers 188; shipwreck 188

shape-changing 1, 2, 9, 24, 32, 34, 35, 44, 48, 50, 53, 144, 145, 156
   forced 40
shapes, shaping 123, 125, 128, 146, 148, 170, 171, 172, 178
Sharpe, James 158
sheep 72, 131, 151, 186
Sidney, Sir Philip 139, 140, 159, 160
silk-worm 127
sin 21, 50
Sisyphus 37
skins 150, 154, 170, 173
Skippon, Philip 98, 111
smell 172, 173, 174, 175, 176
Soane, Sir Hans 204, 206
social history 65, 80, 81
social science 204
society (*also* social order/disorder/change) 28, 29, 45, 65, 66, 73, 76, 78, 118, 135, 138, 139, 146, 148, 149, 151, 164, 166, 187
   centre and margins, national and local 66, 69
   change, metamorphosis as a response to 44, 45, 65, 139
   civic 143, 149, 151, 153, 156, 170
   discipline 66, 70, 72, 75, 81, 85
   economy 66, 77
   familial base 166
   family and 135
   return to 180
   revolt, riots 41, 66, 76
   social and cultural spheres 195
sociology 72
Soper, Kate 157
soul 7–8, 9, 10, 24, 50, 84, 146, 156, 179, 197, 198, 199
   sensitive 181, 199, 200
sources (*see also* reception) 27, 28, 54, 55
Spenser, Edmund 3, 13
spider 50
Sprat, Thomas 124, 127
stones 88, 92, 93, 94, 95, 96, 99, 102, 103, 115, 123, 133
storytelling 180, 184, 185, 186, 187, 188, 195, 211
   excessive elements 195
Stroud, Sir William 66
Stubbe Peeter 4, 6, 141, 143, 144, 146, 147, 149, 155, 156
   Stubbe Peeter 152, 154, 156, 157
substitution 2, 4, 6, 16, 37, 60, 64, 65, 66, 81, 82, 83, 84, 163
supernatural 37, 41, 42, 53, 72, 90, 102, 107, 110, 118, 123, 129, 134, 140, 144, 148, 158, 165, 185, 187, 191
symbol 42, 81, 82, 83

tales 139, 140, 159, 167, 179, 187, 195
Tantalus 37
taste 173
taxonomy 87, 122, 123
   both and 124
   impossible/undecided/ambiguous 123
theatre 88, 115, 117, 119, 123, 134, 155
theurgy 223
thief-takers 40
things 125, 131, 134, 137, 200
Thomas, Keith 72, 73
thought (*see also* Bryskett; Derrida; Descartes; epoch)
   change/continuity 125
thunderbolt 114, 115, 117
tiger 194
Titan 28, 29, 30
Tityus 37
Topsell, Edward 13, 89, 99, 101, 102, 103, 104, 126, 139, 140, 153, 154, 166, 191, 226
   Historie of Foure-Footed Beasts 13, 14, 153
   Historie of Serpents 101, 110
tortoise 101, 105
Tower of London 139
Tradescants 113
translation, Englishing (*see also* vernacular) 4, 9, 14, 15, 26, 27, 46, 47, 53, 54, 55, 89, 90, 135, 153, 195, 201
transubstantiation 7, 8
treason 75
Trevelyan (Trivillian), Leonard 69
Troy 164
truth, truth claims 110, 111, 117, 123, 162, 164, 172, 184, 185, 186, 190, 193, 195, 204
   scepticism 112, 116, 123
Tyler, Tom 83
tyranny 154, 160, 163, 164, 185
Tyson, Edward 125, 126, 127, 128, 130, 135, 198, 202

Ulysses 6, 18, 26, 50, 51, 141
unicorn 112, 114, 123
urinating, urine 59, 77, 78

vagabond 138, 139
Valentine and Orson 162, 164, 167, 170, 171, 178, 179, 188, 192
   The Hystory of the two Valyaunt Brethren 167
   Valentine and Orson: The Two Sonnes of the Emperour of Greece 168
Vaughan, Alden T. and Virginia Mason 117
verisimilitude 121
vernacular (*see also* translation) 3, 7, 9, 10, 12, 46, 47, 49, 51, 52, 53, 54, 57, 82, 88, 89, 106, 124, 125, 134, 140, 195, 202, 203

vernacular debate 158
vernacular knowledge 56, 99, 112, 127, 128, 131, 139
Verstegan, Richard 145, 156
Virgil 36, 45, 55
  Aeneid 55, 56
  Eclogues 55, 56
virtue 197
vision 122
vitalism (also living, animism and related concepts) 89, 90, 91, 92, 93, 94, 96, 120, 122, 124, 126, 132, 133, 134, 136, 197, 199, 203

Wales, Tim 40
Walker, John 150
Walker-Bynum, Caroline 2, 4–6, 21, 44, 60, 154
wall painting 104
Wallington, Nehemiah 63, 64
Walton, Izaak 83, 85
wandering 25
Warner, Marina 3–6, 9, 82
wasps (hornets) 91
Webster, John 148, 152
  Duchess of Malfi 148, 149, 150, 151, 152, 153, 154, 155, 156, 157, 167
Webster, John (writer on witchcraft) 158
Weeks, Sophie 105
werewolf 13, 84, 137, 138, 141, 143, 145, 146, 147, 149, 152, 154, 155, 156, 157, 158, 159, 160, 206
White, Hayden 141
Whitmore, Michael 170, 185

wild, wildness 139, 143, 146, 152, 156, 157, 161, 162, 164, 165, 166, 168, 169, 170, 171, 173, 174, 175, 177, 179, 184, 187, 188, 189, 190, 191, 195
  and family/state 189
Wild Boy of Aveyron 162
wild children 13, 63, 162, 164, 169, 171, 172, 173, 174, 175, 177, 178, 179, 180, 183, 190, 191, 192, 193, 195, 204
  significance changed at Enlightenment 204, 206
wild men 18, 117, 169, 170, 176
Willughby, Francis 112
wit 51
witchcraft, witch 8, 41, 69, 70
  Pendle 85
wolf, wolves 137, 138, 139, 140, 141, 143, 144, 145, 146, 147, 149, 150, 155, 156, 159, 186, 190, 191, 206
  nurturer of gods 192
  present 226
  relationship with rulers 154
  she-wolves and prostitutes 'lupa' 166
wonder 107, 112, 115, 119, 126, 165, 202, 232
wonders (marvels, prodigies; *see also* marvellous) 41, 86, 88, 89, 90, 92, 96, 99, 106, 114, 116, 119, 122, 129, 131, 134, 135, 151, 162, 168, 177
Wood, Andy 159
Woods, Gillian 232
Wormhill, Derbyshire 158
worms 101, 103, 149
Wright, Louis B. 167

Zetterburg, J. Peter 120
zootomy 126, 127, 128